mBA

International
Public
Relations

INTERNATIONAL PUBLIC RELATIONS

How to Establish Your Company's Product, Service, and Image in Foreign Markets

Joyce Wouters

amacom

American Management Association

Library of Congress Cataloging-in-Publication Data

Wouters, Joyce.
    International public relations: how to establish your company's
product, service, and image in foreign markets / Joyce Wouters.
        p.   cm.
    Includes index.
    ISBN 0-8144-5994-3
    1. Export marketing—United States—Management.   2. International
business enterprises—United States—Management. 3. Corporations,
American.   I. Title.
HF1416.5.W68   1991   90-56413
659.2'89—dc20   CIP

Printing number

10 9 8 7 6 5 4 3 2 1

TO
TIM
who pulled me into the "real" world

Contents

Acknowledgments

Thanks to New York University's School of Continuing Education classes in International Public Relations, who were outstanding in their interest in the subject and their contributions: Karen Abarnel, Dana Aronson, Cilla Benko, Susan Bodlak, Monserrat Domingo, Erin Flynn, Elisabeth Gabrynowicz, Jacqueline Lundie, Pelin Meral, Kathleen M. Reilly, Sarah A. Reilly, Anne-Marie Sawyer, Elizabeth Santelli, Helena Schmidt, Nicole Schneuwly, Carolyn Seaman, Sandra Tansky, Karen Toh Goon Chuan, David H. Quintas-Parquet, and Vicki Weisman.

There were many others who helped, and I particularly appreciate the assistance and input of Leslie Maddin, Len Serwat, and Bernard Boullet of Spencer Stuart, Jim Lindheim of Burson-Marsteller, Peter Absolem and Don McCormick of the American Management Association, Jim Blow, Minister Counselor for Commercial Affairs of the U.S. Embassy in London, and William Martin of the Commission of the European Communities in Belgium.

The support, patience, and encouragement of friends and family who put up with my long periods of isolation are deeply appreciated. You know who you are.

International
Public
Relations

Introduction

Never before have overseas markets played such an important role in American business. Long secure in the market they knew best—the one that has had the most money to spend—American businesspeople today are taking another look. The domestic market has changed. The dollar doesn't buy as much as it did, and more businesses than ever are competing for shares of the market.

Foreign companies introduce products in the United States daily that compete with established products or offer something new altogether. They open plants, buy property, and develop their presence and their profits here. Americans have been slow to accomplish as much in other countries.

The Current Position of U.S. Business Abroad

Some 80 percent of U.S. industry now faces international competition, according to Robert Frederick, chairman of the U.S. National Foreign Trade Council.[1] And Daniel Sharp, president of the American Assembly, observes, "In the global marketplace, as at home, we must remember that we are in the same boat. Protectionist actions in one nation risk being answered by protectionist actions in other nations." Further, "Failure to meet the challenge of global competition will threaten our prosperity as well as our world leadership."[2]

There is no doubt that the United States is up against stiff and increasingly sophisticated competition overseas. Indications are that we

1. As reported in Nancy J. Adler and Dafna N. Israeli, *Women in Management Worldwide* (New York: M. E. Sharpe, Inc. 1988), p. 226.
2. Daniel A. Sharp, "America Is Running Out of Time," *The New York Times* (February 7, 1988), p. 6.

are losing ground. Intensifying the challenge is the prospect of a unified European Economic Community with no internal tariffs or trade barriers by 1992 or soon after, a strong and still expanding Japanese presence, the possibility of an Asian common market, and the troubled but developing Chinese and Latin American markets.

Resources and Ambition: Putting the United States Ahead

Although a lot of information is available on certain aspects of doing business abroad, such as trade, export, and barriers to trade, very little has been written to help businesses with initial information they need and steps they should take in opening offices or introducing products in overseas markets. While every market is different, certain common principles can be applied to minimize risk and to maximize the potential for success.

A sample of 137 established American exporters, most of whom were key decision makers and had at least five years' experience in exporting, reveals some interesting preferences about the kind of foreign market information they consider important to the success of their businesses:

1. The nature of politics and its effect on trade
2. Economic accomplishment and its effect on life-styles
3. Market potential
4. Macroeconomic accomplishment and potential
5. Export restrictions (tariff, nontariff, and transportation barriers)
6. Legal perspective[3]

The most important information, the exporters asserted, were items 3, 4, and 5: the market potential—level of demand for their products or services; macroeconomic accomplishment and potential—level of competition in the target market(s); and export restrictions—regulations regarding imports.[4] These criteria apply equally to a company importing products into a nation and to one exporting to it from another country.

Before the decision for entry is made, surely the political climate, standard of living (and therefore availability of profits), market potential, and promise for the future are vital components in the whole picture of doing business abroad. Basic legal and regulatory information is, of course,

3. Van R. Wood and Jerry Goolsby. "Foreign Market Information Preferences of Established U.S. Exporters," *International Marketing Review* (United Kingdom), Vol. 4, No. 4 (Winter 1987), pp. 43–52.
4. Ibid.

part of the package that any good public relations practitioner, researching new markets, would check into.

Assuming that the exporters' judgment is correct—that indeed these factors are the most important for success abroad—public relations and marketing are clearly associated with the first two. We will see, however, that greater attention needs to be put on certain areas not mentioned by the exporters—especially when actually moving into an overseas area.

Numerous corporate divisions may claim they are best suited to the ground-breaking work required for new market entry. Finance, business development, marketing, operations—even legal—may each consider themselves the one vital component in making the decision to enter a new market. They are all correct, in that a red flag in any of these areas should in turn signal caution and raise the question of whether the project should proceed at all. But the public relations division is ideally suited to the initial role of research, goal setting, planning, organizing, and network development, as well as the drawing together of all the diverse strings that can make or break the venture.

The Broadening Definition of Public Relations

What used to be an adjunct activity, somewhere between marketing and advertising, is now being recognized not only as communications in the broadest sense but as an integral and vital part of the managerial planning function. Public relations is ideally suited to the diplomatic digging for information that is indispensable to the process of entering a new market successfully and for establishing from the start the most hospitable environment possible. Public relations is adept at seeing the broad view and at the strategic planning that is so needed. It has the people skills that can make such a difference, and should be the unit that first assesses the environment, recommends plans that synergize with other corporate divisions, and finally spearheads entry with a well-developed, comprehensive program.

Public relations is not just communications; it implies a linkage between policy and action. It contains the idea that people count—an idea that has gained strength as it has become clear that robots, electronic systems, and technology cannot replace human judgment and that all these instruments serve basically to meet human needs. Public relations must be behind the basic strategy for production as well as marketing.

Once the company and/or product is established in the marketplace, public relations retains an essential maintenance, coordination, and trouble-shooting role. However welcome a foreign corporation may be abroad, the host country always views it with some degree of trepidation. The very fact of its foreignness causes some anxiety; if it offers a large number of new jobs, there is a fear that the local community may become dependent upon it. If it offers few jobs, the question arises as to the benefit of having it there.

No company can thrive for long in a hostile atmosphere. Since too often the first steps taken create a negative rather than a positive attitude, the section of the company that specializes in awareness of the human environment, effective communications, and understanding of political and community structures must study the possibilities and advise whether or not the organization should enter a particular market. If the light is green, public relations should continue on the job, backed by marketing and specific study by market research, to make first entry into the marketplace.

International public relations is not a new field. As far back as 1962, Philip Lesly included a section on it in his *Public Relations Handbook.*[5] More recently, others have written on the subject, but generally they have failed to recognize the very basic and urgent contributions public relations professionalism can contribute to the success of any business venture abroad. Only recently has its value in recommending corporate policy and determining strategy been appreciated. Yet public relations, in both its broadest and in its most explicitly defined sense, is essential in the overseas initiative.

The Scope and Purpose of the Book

International Public Relations offers an overview of markets abroad and information on challenges and opportunities inherent in moving overseas. It gives specific guidelines to follow in thoroughly investigating a new market from the public relations, marketing, and strategic analysis points of view in order to decide whether or not the company should proceed and how, or if not, why not. It moves from formulating realistic goals to introducing the item or company into the marketplace and gives straightforward advice on how to get it right the first time. It provides information that is useful to all organizations, with references to specific industries, such as high-tech, medical, entertainment, financial services, and investor relations.

Recognizing that the reader may be a public relations professional in an agency, may handle public relations in a corporate environment, may be a consultant to a corporation or head of a public relations/ marketing concern, or be an interested member of corporate management, I have written from the standpoint of corporate public relations.

5. Prentice-Hall, Inc., Englewood Cliffs, N.J., 1962.

The reader should be able to apply the information to his or her own situation.

Actual case histories are included to dramatize the lessons that have been learned. Companies that have tried and succeeded, and others that have tried and failed, lend valuable insights to techniques that work and why. The book does emphasize retail and consumer business, although most of the basic ground rules are applicable to any industry.

International Public Relations gives the reader a better concept of what to look for when researching and entering an overseas market. It should inspire an increased sensitivity to the social and cultural differences that affect the company's reputation as well as its sales. It should impart some specific ideas of what a company must contend with in certain foreign markets, and an appreciation of the importance of public relations as the front runner for any new venture or significant retrenchment. It also suggests some reasons for and solutions as to why U.S. businesses are lagging in export trade.

International Public Relations is essential reading for the international business executive/consultant/marketing or public relations professional. It is concerned primarily with the "Triad"—Japan, Western Europe, and the United States and Canada—in which some 650 million potential customers reside. In this area, tastes, aspirations, and lifestyles are becoming increasingly similar despite the Eastern, unique individuality of the Japanese. In the triad, 90 percent of all the world's high-tech manufactured goods are both produced and consumed. The level of communications and the communications facilities are generally similar. The same computer terminals, copiers, facsimile machines, and telexes prevail. They all "speak" in the same two or three languages.

Clearly overseas opportunities are not limited to France, Germany, Spain, the United Kingdom, Italy, and other European countries. Recognizing the growth in markets of Hong Kong, Singapore, South Korea, and Taiwan, and the ASEAN nations of the Brunei, Thailand, Singapore, Malaysia, and the Philippines, the book looks into doing business there as well and draws examples from various countries.

Eastern Europe's potential for the future is widely recognized, and therefore some basic current facts on it are included in the Appendixes. Development of that area will take time. Similarly, and also for reasons of space, Africa, South America, Scandinavia, the U.S.S.R., and some other areas are touched on only briefly or are excluded from coverage in this book.

International Public Relations investigates the changes anticipated in the European Economic Community (EC) as of 1992, and discusses other developments on the international business scene. It aims to serve as a guide to the public relations and marketing professional or manager in any company, small or large, that seeks to enter these markets or has been previously unsuccessful.

"The key to the problem of how to truly become global can be summarized in one word: attitude. Until you have the attitude that you are truly an international company, not just a U.S. company also doing business abroad, you cannot achieve your goals," says Paul Oreffice, chairman of the board of Dow Chemical Company.[6] Erasing the parochial thinking so prevalent in American companies and guiding corporate management to view the entire globe as its prospective market are the primary goals of this book.

We need to recognize the substantial opportunities available to us in other nations, and know how to skillfully enter and establish our businesses in those areas. Pointing out pitfalls and underscoring areas essential to successful entry that are frequently ignored are this book's additional goals.

6. Preston Townley, "Globesmanship," *Across the Board*, Vol. 27, Nos. 1 and 2 (January/February 1990), pp. 24–34.

1

Defining the
Corporate Strategy

The initial but indispensible steps to be taken prior to entering a new market, developing a business abroad, or introducing a product in a foreign market are often skipped. Perhaps they are overlooked because they are so basic. The biggest and apparently most sophisticated companies are sometimes the worst offenders.

The decision to establish a post in an overseas market may have been made for a variety of reasons, but usually financial opportunity weighs heavily and possibly exclusively in the final decision. Sometimes the plan fits into an overall strategy of expansion or diversification. In that case, the purposes and goals may already be clearly outlined. The company and you, the public relations or marketing professional, need to know what you want to gain from this market.

Once you are clear on what you want to achieve, you can define the purpose and strategies of public relations in the context of the overall corporate goals. It may seem obvious that corporate goals need to be established and accepted before the goals of individual divisions can be put in place, but companies often expect public relations to go out and make the company famous while the "worker bees" stay at home, tend to business, and eventually come up with corporate goals that may or may not be consistent with public image and communications efforts.

Even when goals are in place, changes may have to be made. As new facts come to light, your goals and possibly even the corporation's goals may have to be adjusted. Certainly a yearly review is mandatory.

Establishing Goals: The Key to Success

In the long run, of course, goals keep the corporation on track and give it direction, drive, and muscle. In the short range, even at this e stage, awareness of an ultimate purpose is valuable. In digging for solid information on which to build a basis for entry strategy, marketing plans, personnel recommendations, and so on, a clearly defined purpose gives perspective to the research and grounds on which to base judgments.

More finely honed and definitive goals can be developed when there is greater awareness of situational realities abroad and specific tailoring to the industry and the product is needed. However, establishing basic goals at this time can help prevent misunderstandings among management personnel later and can aid final decision making.

Keep your goals realistic, and build substantial flexibility into the plan. You may be adapting an international stance; you may be entering markets that have many basic similarities, but what applies in one may be wrong in another.

World-champion global marketing strategy might be illustrated by the Sony Walkman, first introduced in 1979 and now as widely recognized as the sun at noon. The Walkman illustrates how to capitalize on potential customer similarities and desires by organizing to spearhead the development of markets worldwide. The Walkman caught on first not in the place of its birth, Japan, but in California. Once it caught on in a marketplace that appreciated its unique characteristics, customers in other markets became susceptible to its lure.

Multinational marketing so successful with Sony's Walkman becomes more meaningful today not only because technology has made both communications and transportation more simple and direct, bringing markets closer, but because the overall quality of life has appreciated. The differences in markets still exist: Unilever, for instance, molds the positioning and advertising for its Cup-a-Soup country by country. Swiss chocolate makers don't push 100 percent Swiss chocolate in the United States; they use an American formula. Danish meat merchants sell British-style bacon in Britain, and Fanta orange drink tastes tart in Italy but sweet in Germany.[1]

Corporate Strategy for the Market Abroad

Organizations that have formulated their corporate purposes and goals will also have established a format and generally accepted terminology for them. In this case, outlining the priorities for the new market should be a relatively smooth operation. If your company does not already have goals established and written, this is the time to push for them.

For companies endeavoring to establish or strengthen an international outlook, certain characteristics will assume greater importance as

1. Preston Townley, "Globesmanship," *Across the Board*, Vol. 27, Nos. 1 and 2 (January/February 1990), pp. 24–34.

they appear in the strategic outline. Top management requires a shared vision, a cosmopolitan view of the globe, and a dissatisfaction with the status quo. Since the rest of the world is predominantly long-term–oriented compared with the United States and because any substantive change takes time, management must be able to focus on the long-term horizon and at the same time be flexible. Global marketing is a journey, not a destination. If necessary, draft your own plan, applying strategies that are in line with what you perceive the company's structure, strengths, and objectives to be and submit them as the first step in establishing fully accepted, corporatewide goals.

In many companies, goals are tied to personnel appraisal reports and bonus recommendations, which in the best cases help make such appraisals more objective and less susceptible to personal prejudices. The following language and format for setting out goals is typical:

Mission:	A long-term purpose, which, when set, is the guiding principle for years to come.
Critical Issues:	Major issues the organization needs to deal with to ensure its survival and profitability.
Strategy:	Techniques and plans that will be put into place to satisfy the critical issues; these may change as the environment changes, but they will change slowly.
Objectives:	The means that will be implemented to fulfill the strategies.
Programs:	Actual specific programs created to meet the objectives. The programs may change yearly as the goals are reviewed, or even as frequently as weekly or monthly as opportunities arise.

Once the corporate goals are in place, goals for the new market venture must be established. A similar procedure should be followed. Those goals may not be much different from the corporation's plan as a whole, but information gained from rudimentary research should be considered when they are being formulated. They may be modified as research progresses. Then each section, as it becomes involved in the venture, must delineate its prospective role, what it plans to achieve, and how it will pursue those purposes.

Keep in mind that the best strategic plans are not those that are brilliantly formulated, but those that are successfully implemented. Implementation often requires creation of a new mindset at all levels of the organization. All companies, no matter how big or small, have problems implementing strategies. Some more experienced companies have begun to anticipate where potential problem areas may arise, and try to plan around them, sometimes averting them completely. If this is not possible, they seek to mitigate the effects or manage the problems better. Contingency planning has become an integral aspect of strategic management procedures.

Once the mission is established, flexibility needs to be built into the strategies you establish.

Developing Public Relations Strategies

Since public relations is spearheading the planning, research, and entry strategy, it should be the next group to formulate its goals. These plans will naturally be derived in accordance with normal public relations responsibilities and will also be fine-tuned later specifically to the marketplace.

Certainly any professional would agree with the following minimal purposes as reviewed in an industry publication.[2] A strong public relations program should:

- Be economical,
- Extend the advertising of the company,
- Add to company credibility,
- Evaluate interest,
- Generate sales leads, and
- Build an image

not necessarily in that order.

Among the many ways to achieve these basic goals are: publishing newsworthy articles in the periodicals that most closely relate to your audience, which will usually include both public and trade press; contacting market research firms, informing them about your products, and keeping them updated; participating in trade shows and developing your own special events; and keeping your own employees informed. Properly handled, employees can provide strong and favorable public relations for your company. We discuss these and other techniques later in the book.

Needless to say, formulated goals for public relations or any other corporate department must always be consistent with and supportive of the overall purposes of the corporation. Public relations goals should synergize the efforts of the company's profit centers to ultimately increase the market share and profit picture. They should attempt to es-

2. "Managing in the 1990s," a publication from Management Centre Europe, Brussels, Belgium.

tablish an environment within the community that is conducive to better business.

The public relations department at a large U.S. financial services company established goals for its entry effort into Japan (see Figure 1-1). The company, whose major divisions comprised charge card services, travel services, and travelers' checks, had to consider several target mar-

(text continues on page 16)

Figure 1-1. A company's goals for entering the Japanese market.

Mission:
 To aid all company activities by producing a flow of information between the company and government, business, media, and the public and by improving the overall image of the company in Japan.

Critical Issues:
 1. How can we establish the company as a leader in the financial and travel-related services industries and be viewed as a good corporate citizen?
 2. How can we obtain positive and favorable publicity from all public media and private programs?
 3. How can we support the promotion of the company's products and services in Japan?
 4. How can we improve communications among employees?

 Critical Issue #1: How can we establish the company as a leader in the financial and travel-related services industries and be viewed as a good corporate citizen?

 Strategy A: Develop close and ongoing business and personal relationships with leaders in government, business, press, and public relations.

 Objective: Ensure that 85 percent of established key contact list for business council members have been contacted by the designated senior officers of the company.

 Programs:
 1. Compile key contact list.
 2. Set up a series of small General Manager's Dinners to include top corporate and government representatives for informational discussions.
 3. Arrange speeches for president.
 4. Produce and distribute annual report.

(continues)

Figure 1-1. (*continued*)

---

5. Organize sending of year-end and New Year's cards.
6. Develop and implement worldwide marketing program.

Strategy B: Actively support specific community activities and charities that are representative of the company's image.

Objective: Work with corporate foundation and support five or more community, nonprofit, or charitable activities.

Programs:

1. Participate in the Prince Takamatsu Trophy Scholarship.
2. Actively support Refugees International.
3. Support *Japan Times* Charity Relay Race.
4. Contribute to College Women's Print Show.
5. Contribute to and enthusiastically sponsor international schools.
6. Support programs sponsored by Japan Performing Arts Foundation.
7. Participate in Primary School Financial Education Program.
8. Develop awareness of Fulbright Foundation programs and cooperate when advisable.
9. Participate in American Product Fair.
10. Support World Dance Festival.

Strategy C: Produce special events that command high public and media visibility and have strong appeal to particular market segments.

Objective: Organize and sponsor two major corporate events, one of which is the technology seminar.

Programs:

1. Sponsor and produce a technology seminar bringing in international experts and securing industry participation.

2. Use the coming visit of notable corporate directors to attract attention of
opinion leaders and press.
3. Organize a half-day tour of local corporate operational facilities to acquaint key leaders with the company's
operations.
4. Develop specific corporate foundation
programs.
5. Introduce Japan's second cause-related marketing program.

Critical Issue #2: How can we obtain positive and favorable
publicity from all public media and private programs?

Strategy: Continually create, write, and disseminate accurate, newsworthy information by mail and personal contact to key government, industry, and press
people with the aim of achieving forty printed items
for a total of $1,664,000 in publicity value.

Objective: Establish systematic and productive
communications and maintain up-to-date personal contacts with Japanese and English media.

Programs:
1. Plan and organize a tour of at least
one company facility outside of Japan to acquaint key press people with
the company's global identity.
2. Develop and update an information
library on the company's businesses
for easy access and utilization.
3. Build and create a bank of informa-
tion/stories that would create interest
among the press for good writeups.
4. Issue timely releases on company
events.
5. Entertain press in order to cultivate
relationships.
6. Computerize public relations' press
lists, invitation lists, and other data.
7. Arrange three major interviews or
speaking sessions for the general
manager and twenty-five minor ones.
(continues)

Figure 1-1. (*continued*)

---

8. Set up specialized interviews for other company executives.
9. Create and maintain a supply of appreciation giveaways.
10. Establish a contingency plan of programs should additional funds become available.

Critical Issue #3: How can we support the promotion of the company's products and services in Japan?

Strategy: Bring the company's products and services to the attention of target markets through publicity and public exposure generated by product promotional events.

Objective: Implement public relations planned promotional events.

Programs:
1. Support travel reader participation program.
2. Cooperate with marketing for mention in industry book.
3. Cooperate with marketing to aid success of golf club promotion.
4. Cooperate with marketing to aid resort promotion.
5. Develop travel video plan with travel's cooperation.
6. Sponsor a best cook contest with marketing cooperation.
7. Work with travel on vacation club.
8. Organize year-end gifts for press and special customers.
9. Develop corporate foundation programs.

Critical Issue #4: How can we improve communications among employees?

Strategy: Build an information exchange process network that accumulates and disseminates information within the company to employees inside and outside the local area.

Objective A: Arrange all formal local office meetings and other subsidiary meetings as requested.

Programs:
1. Arrange annual business meeting.
2. Set up employee information meeting once or twice a year.
3. Use visits of top U.S. management to solidify employees' company feeling.

Objective B: Produce excellent employee newsletters.

Programs:
1. Develop and implement such materials as the *Five Principles* brochure.
2. Produce new company newsletter to include information on operations and automation, and disseminate information among subsidiary operations and to headquarters.
3. Work with marketing and sales for special letter going to field salespeople.
4. Provide newsletter to subsidiary retail offices.

Objective C: Identify communication needs.

Programs:
1. Issue and analyze returns on employee survey.
2. Meet with management group to assess needs.

Objective D: Send twenty news items to four offices on a particular basis.

Programs:
1. Structure and implement a daily monitoring program on selected news media to be distributed the following day to Japan management and other offices.
2. Redefine, structure, and implement comprehensive timely clipping service from broad base of media.

Figure 1-2. Chosen strategy.

FRAMEWORK

- Identify critical success factors
- Specify critical linkages and pathways
- List potential problem areas

SYNTHESIS

- Timing
- Measurement criteria
- Project management

- Develop a detailed action plan

- Monitor progress

- Revise strategy

- Comprehensive list: tasks/activities
- Accountabilities/ responsibilities
- Resources
- Feedback
- Reporting systems
- Environment scanning
- Modify
- Abandon

Source: Adapted from Godfrey Devlin, "How to Implement a Winning Strategy," *European Management Journal* (published by Basil Blackwell for the European School of Management), Vol. 7, No. 3 (September 1989), p. 378.

kets. Successful introduction of their products meant establishing recognition and credibility with the public, trade organizations, service groups (such as hotels, airlines, and restaurants), government representatives, the community, and the media. The goals and strategies outlined in Figure 1-1 reflect this broad thrust.

This strategy is clearly defined and very specific, but needs the financial plan necessary for implementation. In many cases it will be necessary to outline objectives in a more general way initially, proceed with research, and then delineate specific goals.

Understanding what the company wants to achieve in its overseas market precedes substantive research. After a thorough assessment, the company may make changes to decide on the best strategies and programs to move it nearer to its goals. This analysis and procedure vitally affect the energy and singleness of purpose with which entry is effected. Research, which certainly must be considered in final planning, comes next.

Establishing the goals and objectives is a major first step in the comprehensive process. The next step is assigning responsibilities to the people who will implement strategy, building time spread sheets, re-checking and detailing budget allocations, and defining procedural details and information needs.

Strategy needs to be rechecked at regular intervals as the program develops. Project results, which should, if possible, have been defined ahead of time, should be quantified and recorded.

Godfrey Devlin, senior consultant for SRI International Europe, U.K., gives the structure shown in Figure 1-2 for the implementation process of strategic plans.

Devlin explains that there needs to be a *champion* who is responsible for the strategy and its implementation. The champion should have good communications with management, should view the task as important and challenging, should have the necessary skills to carry it forward, and should have real decision-making power. There should also be a project manager (such as the public relations executive), and progress needs to be monitored regularly. In addition, flexibility is important to ensure that adjustments can be made as new information or unexpected problems come to light.

2

Researching Your Market

Broad-based research is essential to intelligent planning and implementation. Unfortunately, many companies tend to skim over this preparatory step, concentrating on statistical information and downplaying the wider picture.

You need some vital statistics on your subject to give you a background canvas against which to paint in a clearer idea of your target market. 'Your initial research should cover certain basics to form part of your report to management. With this information, you can take the first steps in determining which government officials and business leaders are likely to be helpful to your effort. Specific, in-depth digging for information then needs to follow the broad research.

Initial research can be covered by the basic resources widely available in books, newspapers, magazines, directories, and almanacs. It should yield a good background on the history and geography of the country, the political organization and system of government, current official government positions including names as well as titles, principal products (especially exports), level of technology and communications, general standard of living, and intrinsic characteristics of the country. A sample information sheet is depicted in Figure 2-1.

A good library can supply all of the above. Start by checking your destination country in *Political Handbook of the World*, edited by Arthur Banks, and *Statesman's Yearbook*, as well as a good geography book and an encyclopedia.

Most libraries also have computer databanks by which you can pull up copies of articles covering business in your target area or in your particular industry. Various systems and databanks are used. One I have found to be particularly helpful for business and subject research of articles from a wide variety of periodicals not readily available on newsstands or in general libraries is "ABI INFORM," which can be found in some university data centers.

Figure 2-1. Country information fact sheet (blank).

Country's formal name:

Geographical location:

Size:

Population:

Education:

Religion (Is it state supported?):

    *Minority groups:

Major industries:

Exports:

Imports:

    *Major corporations:
    *Major American multinationals:

Gross national product:

Average income/standard of living:

Form of government:

Political environment (stability, influences, historic ties):

    *Top government titles and people holding them:
    *Names of ministries (if different from above):
    *Social environment (civil rights, welfare):
    *Major social problems:
    *Defense:

Business environment (free enterprise, government influence):

    *Regulatory environment (industry):
    *Legal environment (industry):
    *Press:
    *Press agencies:
    *Broadcast media:

Transportation and communications:

    *General tax structure:
    *Other:

    Published information may be old. One way of updating it is to visit the commercial officer of the destination country's embassy, who can give current names of foreign government officials and their titles as well as other background information that may be subject to change. Some embassies offer resource materials for people interested in the country, and while they may contain some bias, they can be helpful. Periodicals originating in the country but published privately rather than by the government give you a special keyhole look into the country and often are published in English. Universities, language schools, and corporations based in the country are often good sources of such material, and occasionally libraries and consular and press offices will have copies.

Then pick up the phone and call the U.S. Chamber of Commerce, the Department of Commerce, and the Department of State in Washington, D.C. (Information on these is in Appendix I.) In addition to the target country's consular or ambassadorial offices, newspaper advertising or editorial offices for the country's major newspapers can also be helpful. You can get their names from the library or from the Overseas Press Organization.

An overseas phone call to the commercial officer of the U.S. Embassy in the destination country may be worth the investment for answers to specific questions, information on how embassy staff can help, and an introduction for your later essential visit to the country. Don't forget to request specific publications relative to your market and your industry.

In England, for example, the commercial section of the U.S. Embassy produces annually a "Best Prospects Plan" to make American businesspeople aware of potential market opportunities. For a minimal fee of $125 you can avail yourself of Agent Distributors Services (ADS). The embassy will identify prospective local representatives according to industry, review the 500 most likely, and refer you to the most promising, whom they have interviewed—usually about fifteen candidates. Of those, about half will still have a serious interest in working with you after you provide them with product information, specifications, prices, and your marketing goals, according to James L. Blow, Minister Counselor for Commercial Affairs, U.S. Embassy, London. Of course, you make the final choice.

The embassy can also help you find "Bird Dogs"—helpful, informal people with their noses to the ground who can provide you with market information, hints on what the competition is doing, and the generally helpful scattered pieces of knowledge you miss by not being there yourself. To some extent the embassy commercial staff can also do this.

The advertising offices of newspapers can often supply you with valuable general information including facts on population, literacy, advertising, and demographics, and they are generally eager to help, especially if they think their help may result in an ad being placed eventually, which it might. This information usually can be supplemented by up-to-date facts from the editorial department.

If product export is your primary interest at this time, visit the International Trade Administration (ITA) office near you (see Appendix

I). A division of the U.S. Commerce Department, it has forty-eight district offices and nineteen branch offices, as well as 175 U.S. officers overseas to channel information on exporting and overseas markets. The Trade Opportunity Program is the arm for information from overseas. The ITA also has country desks for every nation with an officer who deals specifically with trade opportunities with U.S. companies. Trade development officers can provide information for exports of a particular industry, plan international marketing programs, and work with you on negotiations aimed at eliminating trade barriers. The Trade Information and Analysis office conducts economic and econometric analyses. It also puts together trade, finance, and investment data.

The International Planning and Analysis Center (IPAC), also part of the Commerce Department, has put together a correspondent network of foreign companies that can help with export information and services.

Another resource may be trade associations in your industry. Some industries cross national boundaries very effectively to disseminate information on regional markets, new product development, people, regulations, and so on.

In an era of ongoing change, political risk is another area of evaluation that now demands more serious consideration than it may have previously. At one time, a country's political stability seemed reasonably evident—some areas were high-risk and others low-risk. From the uprising in Tiananmen Square to the breakdown of the Berlin Wall, from the once predictable to the changing, apparently rudderless ship of state in Japan, from the bursting forth of Eastern Europe to the volcanic Middle East, judgments on country risk are more difficult. Political risk analysts are the people to consult on this. No economy operates freely from its politics, and no political assessment can be done without an evaluation of economics: Witness Iraq's mid-1990 invasion of Kuwait and the carrying home of coffers of approximately $4 billion, roughly doubling the size of Iraq's assets. Political instability does not necessarily bode ill for your investment. It may not even affect it. It is important, however, to make a judgment. Banks and consulting firms conduct this kind of analysis. Among those that do are: Business International Corp., based in New York City; Council of International Business Risk Management, Business Environment Risk, in Washington, D.C.; and R. J. Rundt and Associates in Montclair, New Jersey.

Consider also the value of political risk insurance. Providers in the public sector include Overseas Private Investment Corp. (OPIC), a federal agency, and World Bank's Multilateral Investment Guarantee Agency, both in Washington, D.C.[1]

1. Kate Bertrand, "Politics Pushes to the Marketing Foreground," *Business Marketing* (March 1990), pp. 51–55.

Collecting adequate information is vital to your final result. It is an area where public relations skills and the standard of professionalism can be especially valuable.

Uncovering Potential and Problems

Occasionally you will encounter resistance in your company to using available information that delves into areas other than basic facts and figures. The importance of understanding the cultural patterns and outlook of people in the target market, for instance, tends to be glossed over and even considered a waste of time. This amounts to a denial of the uniqueness of the foreign entity and stems from either arrogance or carelessness. It is your job to try to overcome barriers such as this and achieve a recognition of differences—a chore that may demand a variety of different approaches.

Sometimes there is a lively ego that assumes that a company well known in the United States will not only be known but accepted in a foreign market. Often there is an assumption that the people who are sent to establish, develop, or turn around a company presence or a product line, who are skillful in their own environments, will be just as skillful in the new environment. While success is often a good predictor of success, both the company and the managers concerned need more than a good track record in their hometown to conquer this sort of new challenge.

Other executives think they are more knowledgeable than they are. Some think anyone can pick up what he or she needs to know about social customs by watching the behavior of others. It is important to recognize that there are cultural differences and that you and your company are the ones that will need to do the adjusting. The society, the culture, even the spending habits of people will adjust to you only in the most minimal way, if at all.

Companies have successfully sold products that seemed alien to a particular culture, but that is the exception to the rule or a failure by those watching to recognize change and foresee trends developing. So gather as much information as you can in order to raise your opportunities to understand areas of possible conflict and prepare for them.

The target country market may be more or less sophisticated than those your company currently operates in, but certain basic steps are no less necessary. Knowing one foreign market outside your own does not always prepare you for another, different foreign market, any more than New York City prepares you for Beijing, but it can sensitize you and give you working tools.

Your initial research should cover the areas listed in Figure 2-1.

Those with asterisks are less imperative and can be researched somewhat later.

Several of the major accounting firms, Price Waterhouse being one of them, publish booklets describing the tax situation and background information on virtually every developed country. These are available at many libraries or can be requested from the firm itself.

Basic background information provides a good start for any research on a prospective market leading to decision making and should be the backbone for later information that is tailored to the particular industry you represent. The fact sheets, filled out similarly to those in Figure 2-2, will provide a useful overview of the country under consideration (see Appendix III).

As your research intensifies and becomes more targeted, it should include a minimum of at least one visit to the target country for on-the-spot information gathering. Before that occurs, phone calls and personal interviews should take place with commercial counselors from the country, academicians (every university has business as well as cultural information on major countries), industrial representatives, and businesspeople to build on the information gathered from the basic sources. As mentioned earlier, talk to experts at the Department of State and the Department of Commerce. Get to know who plays what role in your business scenario:

- What politicians may be involved in your industry and your community?
- Who are the other corporate leaders?
- Who are the best suppliers?
- Who will be buying your product?
- Where will you pull your employees from?
- Who do you need, and who do you need to know, to do business?
- What publications and television or radio programs are important to your industry and your product?

Once your research is complete enough to give you a well-informed idea of the national environment of the country, its problems and potential for your business, communicate your opinions to management by means of an audio (and visual, if you can manage it) presentation with a written, more detailed backup to be distributed when you finish. Recommend how you believe the company should proceed, and why. Your recommendation should be as specific as possible and backed by statistical and other information. Parts of the outline for this book can be utilized to form the basis for your presentation. By the time you get to the end of the book, you should have the information you need

(*text continues on page* 26)

Figure 2-2. Country information fact sheet (filled in).

COUNTRY'S FORMAL NAME: Republic of France.

GEOGRAPHICAL LOCATION: Western Europe; bounded on the north by the English channel, Belgium, and Luxembourg; on the east by Germany; on the south by the Mediterranean Sea and Spain, and on the west by the Atlantic Ocean. Corsica and several other territories are also part of France. Over 1,875 kilometers of coastline.

SIZE: 213,000 square miles in Europe, second in size only to the U.S.S.R.

POPULATION: 55.7 million (as of January 1987); lowest rate of density in Europe; 20 percent of the population is in Paris.

EDUCATION: By district: primary school until age 11, four years of first cycle *enseignement secondaire,* then second cycle at age 15 for three years leading to baccalaureate or two years leading to *brevet d'études professionnelles* (commercial, administrative, industrial options). Following the baccalaureate come two-, three-, or five-year university courses. Public and private schools coexist.

RELIGION (IS IT STATE SUPPORTED?): Primarily Christian, 90 percent of those Roman Catholic.

MINORITY GROUPS: 160,000 political refugees from Eastern Europe, Asia, Latin America, and Africa.

MAJOR INDUSTRIES: Europe's leading agricultural nation; occupied about 7 percent of population in 1985; steel, motor vehicles, aircraft, mechanical and electrical goods, textiles, chemicals and food processing, aerospace, telecommunications, tourism.

EXPORTS: Cereals, sugar, dairy products, wine, livestock.

IMPORTS: Energy (mostly oil).

GROSS NATIONAL PRODUCT: $9,540 per person (1985).

FORM OF GOVERNMENT: Republic. President and prime minister, with a bicameral Parliament: Senate with 319 members and National Assembly with 577. Senators are elected for nine-year terms by an electoral college from the National Assembly; the assembly is elected by universal suffrage for five-year terms. President is elected directly by popular vote; he or she appoints ministers, including the prime minister.

POLITICAL ENVIRONMENT (STABILITY, INFLUENCES, HISTORIC TIES): Generally very stable. France still has four overseas departments: French Guiana, Guadeloupe, Martinique, Réunion; two collective territorials: Mayotte, St. Pierre, and Mignelon; and four overseas territories: French Polynesia, French Southern and Antarctic territories, New Caledonia, Wallis, and Futura Islands.

SOCIAL ENVIRONMENT (CIVIL RIGHTS, WELFARE): Social security compulsory for all wage earners and self-employed. Contributions from both employers and employees provide: sick care, unemployment, maternity, disability, family allowances. Socialized medicine. There is a minimum wage.

DEFENSE: Compulsory service for twelve to eighteen months; active armed forces number about 547,000 plus 390,000 reserves. 1987 defense budget was FF178,000.

BUSINESS ENVIRONMENT (FREE ENTERPRISE, GOVERNMENT INFLUENCE): After strong trends toward socialization, in 1986 a five-year program was introduced to privatize sixty-five state-operated enterprises.

PRESS: Free, but some restrictions such as on official secrets, libel, false information, and on children's literature. Almost 3,000 newspapers and periodicals are published, including eleven daily newspapers with national circulation (total circulation 2.7 million) and eighty provincial dailies (total circulation 7.5 million). Some provincial papers pool advertising. There are two major news magazines. Papers are independently owned and nonpolitical except for the Communist party organ, *l'Humanité*. Major respected metropolitan papers are: *Le Monde* (363,663), *Le Figaro* (443,006), *France-Soir*, *Le Parisien Liberé*, and *International Herald Tribune* (in English, 168,908).

PRESS AGENCIES: Agence France-Presse, Agence Parisienne de Presse, Agence République d'Information (politics, domestic and foreign), and press services. Associated Press and other foreign agencies have bureaus in Paris.

BROADCAST MEDIA: About 58 million radios and 25 million television sets. The Communications Commission supervises all French broadcasting.

TRANSPORTATION AND COMMUNICATIONS: Nationalized and generally excellent, with high-tech, computer/telephone work stations available to every home provided by the government, an excellent train and bus system, the world's fastest long-distance trains (TGV), and a fine, extensive subway system in Paris.

OTHER: Soccer, bicycling, and rugby are the most popular sports, with tennis enjoying a boom, and swimming, golf, fishing, boating, sailing, camping, mountain climbing, and various winter sports also popular. Extensive literary, artistic, and musical productions are available, both traditional and modern.

to fill in the contents for the presentation itself, which might follow this format:

I. *Corporate mission.* How does your company see itself and what is it trying to accomplish overall?

II. *Corporate strategy.* Why is the company considering entry into (this) overseas market?

III. *Fact sheet for the country.* An overview of what it is and where it is.

A. *Technology and communications.* Including a general view of how communications and publicity can be handled.

B. *Description of the media.* Also how it is organized, including a mention of major target press and general facts on broadcast media.

C. *Mention of your target audiences.* Plus other means of reaching them, such as:

1. Trade fairs
2. Direct mail
3. Billboards and displays
4. Special programs

D. *Government contacts.* Describe both position and who fills it, and why the contact should be made.

E. *Local community considerations.* If relevant at this point.

IV. *Credibility.* Why it is important and how you will start developing it.

V. *Availability of public relations agencies.* Also how to make the best use of them, and of free-lancers.

VI. *Language and cultural differences.* How to develop sensitivity to them and accommodate them.

VII. *Internal public relations.* Its importance to the venture as a whole and how to carry it out.

VIII. *Concerns of foreign governments and communities.* Toward American multinationals and others entering their markets.

IX. *Common problems faced by U.S. companies abroad.* Structure and techniques that make for success.

X. *Standardization in public relations.* How it may apply to your company.

XI. *Recommendation.* Whether there are any serious barriers to entering this country; summary of the potential and problems you anticipate; mention of likely goals for public relations.

Present several options in the event that your own recommendation is not management's optimal choice.

Once a positive decision is made to enter an overseas market, you can put your growing knowledge about it to further use. Knowing that executives may be transferred to the country to run the operations, or at the very least will be traveling there on a regular basis, set up a series of preparatory sessions to educate them about the country and give them an idea of what to expect. Even those officers who will not be visiting the country should be briefed in order to raise the level of understanding and support for the operation.

If at all possible, your initial sessions should be followed by additional acculturation with a consulting firm that specializes in such training. For married personnel, the individual's family should also attend these sessions. Language study should be arranged for both the individual and the family before departure as well as after arrival at the new location.

Preparations on the other side also need to be made. Staff at the new location doubtless are quite apprehensive about the new people due to arrive. Much can be done to create a positive situation and hospitable atmosphere. Credibility starts right at the beginning and judgments are often made disastrously quickly. Rule number one, then, is do what you say you are going to do. Don't say it if you can't do it.

Nearly as important, say what you are going to do before you do it. This is a good general rule in any environment. People like to be prepared and a sudden action without forewarning will surprise and often upset them. In a strange environment, talking about what you plan to do is even more important. The response you get may change your mind about doing it.

Finally, communicate carefully and fully, and recheck that you have been understood correctly. People often agree even when they don't really understand the message. Even if you speak the local language, a difference in customs, habits, and purposes can easily lead to misunderstandings.

Technology and Communications Abroad

Every major industrialized nation has modern technological communication facilities available. Some work better than others. It is important to quickly get a handle on what is available for different types of communications, as well as general costs involved. Basic means are telephone, facsimile, telex, cable, and computer transmissions, although some of these may be unavailable in remote areas.

Electronic data interchange (EDI) is being used increasingly, especially for international transactions that often involve a greater number of people, documents, and data. It also facilitates information transmission around the clock with reduced risk of loss, since the sender can deposit information in the recipient's computer despite the time at the destination site. It will then be available, often in a confidential manner, when the recipient pulls it up and at the start of the workday.

Television is available in the major cities of most industrialized countries, made more useful with the help of satellite transmission. While this is not cost effective for the communications requirements of most companies, some have the facilities to utilize it.

Video press releases are becoming increasingly commonplace, either through satellite time or video by delivery. VCRs (VHR) can be put to practical use, often in conjunction with overnight mail service (DHL, Federal Express, or others). Check on the speed and reliability of the local postal system and the services it offers.

It will come as no surprise that Japan has highly sophisticated communications transmission equipment and has used facsimile transmission on a daily basis, internally as well as externally, much longer than the United States. Because of the inefficient postal service in Italy, facsimile transmission is also in wide use there.

Although the Japanese language makes computer usage in Japan cumbersome in some ways, one of the more miraculous communications devices, in use by Japanese newspaper and news agencies abroad, is a dual-language computer. A story input in Romaji (the Anglicized spelling of Japanese) is converted to Japanese *kanji* (calligraphy) by computer process, transmitted directly from the U.S. press office, set in type, and made ready for publication in Japan. Another device is a pocket-sized "slate" on which a reporter can write by hand in *kanji* and then, by plugging into the master system, send the printout to the editorial offices.

In Taiwan, fax machines must be licensed by the government and are therefore less widely disseminated and used much less frequently. In times of political uncertainty, transmission may be curtailed or terminated.

Hong Kong also rates high in technological sophistication, as does Singapore. Other Asian countries are catching up.

Korea and the Philippines are not far behind, although availability and maintenance may sometimes be a problem. Malaysia and Thailand trail behind somewhat, with Indonesia further behind that. In Laos, Cambodia, Burma, and China, sophisticated technological equipment, other than the telephone, is not generally available. Perhaps surprisingly, Vietnam has telephone, cable, facsimile, and telex facilities available to business travelers there. Unfortunately, the systems frequently don't work.

Although the telephone is still the communications instrument in widest use in Europe, fax machines are increasingly popular. Few offices are without them. Their use helps reduce misinformation and speeds up communications, which by mail is sometimes slow in some countries. Despite the general American assumption that everyone in Europe speaks several languages and communications across borders is easy, many people are more proficient at reading a second or third language than speaking or hearing it. The messages they send may be misleading or imprecise; strong accents may limit full comprehension. Messages in black and white stand a better chance of being understood. Communications is rated by many Europeans, in fact, as the number one barrier to unity.

In addition, fax messages that are lost can quickly be identified and sent again. One sacrifice may be privacy. Unlike in the United States, the problem of junk mail coming through fax machines generates few complaints.

Facsimile transmission may be particularly convenient to you in your overseas office. Besides being virtually immediate, it has the advantage of being convenient and explicit. You can send during your own office hours and have it picked up as soon as the recipient's office opens the next day, and vice versa. Messages that may become confused or forgotten by telephone are confirmed in writing—a special boon when there is a language difference and translated material must be transmitted. Illustrations that support and graphically clarify the text can also be used.

In the financial industry, rapid information transmission is vital. Various marketplaces utilize various systems. In the United States, for instance, QUOTRON is a popular information/price system within investment houses and securities and commodities exchanges. Another, QUICK, is a Japanese-developed system available in Japan, the United States, and elsewhere.

Attracting considerable attention in Europe is PIPE, the information system being developed by the Federation of Stock Exchanges in the European Community. The system will transmit prices and market and company news. The federation's long-term goal is to make PIPE a Europewide trading system that would support a pan-European market. Driving development of the system is the Europewide listing of several hundred blue-chip stocks and the goal to start trading these Eurolist stocks in 1991. This would allow specified stocks—the blue chips—to trade on all the exchanges in the European community and in some other European countries.

It is helpful for public relations professionals, especially those in financial services, to be knowledgeable about information systems available and in development. At this writing, it is uncertain how extensive PIPE will become and how successful rival systems will be, but near future developments will be significant for the industry in the United States and abroad.

Telephones—Traditional High-Tech Instruments

Virtually every country has a telephone system, but even in some European countries it is slow and frustrating. Discussing phone systems may seem simplistic—after all, all telephones function basically the same way. However, the differences in available operator information, coin or card usage, coin denomination, distance and time length on public phones, and so on, can be daunting. In visiting a foreign country, it is often such simple things that cause the most frustration.

If you, in France, sit waiting for the call from New York that never comes, it may not occur to you, especially in view of France's sophisticated telephone technology, that the lines are overloaded and the New York caller can't get through. Or picture yourself in Japan, escorting the company president to the next appointment. You see that traffic will make you late, and you signal the driver to pull up at the next public phone—public telephones are readily visible there. You're faced with a bank of phones—all different colors. Which to use? you ask yourself, while the president sits watching and waiting in the car. Such basic knowledge as which public telephone to use can help put you at ease and enable you to perform better.

British Telecom recently updated its whole system to the annoyance of many traditionalists who hated to see the famous red phone booths disappear. Although the overall system is quite good, it is not uncommon to call one number and get a totally different one. Operators are polite, but if you don't have specifics as to locations (town, at least) of the party you wish to reach, directory service can't give you the number. In a country as small as Britain, the system could be expected to be more comprehensive.

Similarly, overseas information is virtually impossible to get from within the country. (I tried, over a period of days and at various times, the numbers 150, 152, 153, and 155—all recommended by operators for overseas information. None worked. Also, 100, the number to dial if you have trouble, worked only once over many tries.) Local information is 142 and it does work. London is divided into districts (with 071 as the prefix for the general central area of London and 081 for the city's fringe), which you need to know as well as the number itself. The nationwide emergency number is 999.

The basic calling unit is 10 pence, but it is better to start with 20 or more. (In France the basic call unit is 10 centimes; in Japan 10 yen.

Additional money brings additional time in each case.) If you wish to call outside the country from Britain, the international access code is 010, followed by the country code (United States is 1), the area code (301 for Maryland, for instance), and the number. Your number for calling the United States would be: 010-1-301-XXX-XXXX.

France is known to have a highly sophisticated, well-run, but somewhat expensive telephone system. Germany's is also highly rated. In France Minitel, the computer-linked phone system, is available to every household. Information on residences and businesses is readily available by punching into the computer console. The user can locate virtually any individual or business even without knowing the correct spelling of the name by pulling up a listing of all similar names. You can search by region, address, names, type of business. Similarly, you can send messages via screen as well as phone to virtually anywhere in the country and outside it to foreign subscribers.

The downside to this wonderful system is cost and apparent limited capacity of the lines. The initial equipment, provided free by the government-run phone company, is available to each household, but the usage cost is high, which has caused many to stick with the old system. It can also be inconvenient. Calls from the United States to France, for instance, frequently terminate before connection, forcing the American caller to try again at another time.

Japan's system is simple but sophisticated. Even for foreigners, it is easy to use if the destination number is easily available. Public phones come in a variety of different colors: red, pink, green, and yellow. All can be used for domestic calls. Red, which are the most commonly seen, are usually good only for local calls because they generally accept only the basic coin unit, Y10. Pink and yellow phones usually accept both Y10 and Y100 coins (although some red ones do, too) for longer-distance calling and extended time; the more coins you put in the longer you get to talk.

Green phones can be used with calling cards and some can be used for direct-dial overseas calls. Public phones are found everywhere in this country—often just outside or just inside coffee shops, newstands, restaurants, and subway stations. Shopkeepers are generous about giving change.

France, Britain, and Japan are among the countries that have telephone cards for use in public phones. They can be bought in shops and stores all over the main cities in a variety of denominations and are extremely convenient if you are a visitor or spend a lot of time outside the office. When you buy the card, it is an outright cash purchase. The card you get contains a number of calling units based on the amount the card is worth. The units translate into number of calls based on time and distance. On most phones in Europe, and on the card in

Japan, there is an indication of the amount you are using when you make your call and the number of units left to use. Microchips in the European cards are the secret.

The situation with telephones in Eastern Europe varies considerably from country to country. Hungary and Czechoslovakia are probably closest to Western standards. The service and technology are the best in the region. Romania and East Germany suffer the most serious lag. Generally speaking, the telephone systems are antiquated and the instruments themselves are scarce. Quick communications by phone cannot be taken for granted anywhere in Eastern Europe. The situation is not simplified by the fact that English is not generally understood, although the attitude toward visitors is friendly. Printed media are popular; newspapers and magazines proliferate.

Another part of communications and technology is transportation, which applies to the basic job of getting around in a new environment. It helps to know the basic systems, the approximate distances and directions, and so on.

In Eastern Europe the transportation situation is much the same as with telephones. Taxis are available but slow in Czechoslovakia and Hungary. Rental cars, the Hungarian State Railways system, buses, and streetcars (in Budapest) make transportation relatively easy as well as cheap. The Prague *metro* is similarly convenient, clean, and cheap. In Poland's main cities, taxis are readily available, as are trains. In Romania, transportation is difficult. Taxis and rental cars are antiquated. Sources for further information on these countries can be found in Appendix IV.

Even sitting in your New York or Chicago office, you may need to know the geography of foreign cities, approximate distances, and the meaning of postal codes. If you are setting up appointments for yourself or another corporate executive, for instance, you will want to plan appointments in the same geographical area close to each other. You'll want some idea of traffic congestion and frequency, safety, and availability of buses, taxis, and subways. Maps, guidebooks, and other publications directed at tourists can be helpful in giving you a feel for the city. You may need to suggest restaurants or come up with recommendations for an evening's entertainment.

In London, *Nicholson Guides* or *A-Z Guides* have detailed maps of the cities, and *Time Out* and *City Limits* have weekly listings of various activities and programs. In Tokyo, there's the *Tokyo Journal*, *Weekender*, and *Tour Companion*. All are in English and the two latter ones are freely available in hotel lobbies and the airport. They give information on places and events; maps and other information are generally available for free at the information desks of major hotels. English language subway maps are available for free at major subway stations and tourist offices.

Even though you are visiting abroad on business, don't be shy about visiting the tourist information center found in nearly every major city—usually in or near major train stations and airports. It can help you feel much more at home during your first visit or two, provide maps and the kind of information mentioned above, as well as give you an idea of currently popular cultural events. This type of background is often helpful as you get to know the local people you will be meeting.

Familiarity with available office equipment is crucial for your communication with the home office as well as the conduct of daily business. For your initial trips abroad, it is good to know that most first-class hotels have typists, fax machines, desks, and sometimes library resources available, often free, for visiting businesspeople. For professional communicators, whether you're on an initial fact-finding trip or based abroad for the long haul, it's also important to determine at an early date the most efficient vehicles for communicating with the press.

Identifying the Publics You Need to Reach

While each company has its own audience depending upon its product or service, there are certain publics in an overseas market that virtually any company must bear in mind. These are:

1. The government
2. The press
3. Industry and business groups
4. The public
5. The local community, especially if you have manufacturing facilities
6. Customers, labor unions, and other groups special to your company

You also need to remember your employees. The government ministry or particular group that deals with businesses in your industry should be of most immediate interest. Although you may believe that you will never need to seek regulatory changes or favors from government groups, it is a good insurance policy to know who in the government would be concerned with your business and then to at least become acquainted with them. If you have trouble determining the foreign government agency under which your own business would fall, call and ask. Our state department can also be helpful with this.

Learn the scope of authority of the ministries or departments you will be dealing with and make sure the information you have is accurate, down to the proper spelling of names. If you have concerns about regulations, trade policies, and such, this is where you clarify the areas of responsibility and identify persons in authority.

As you get to know representatives of the foreign government, however, keep in mind that you are stepping on dangerous ground if you try to influence policy directly. That is for your own government to do. Your purpose is to keep your contacts informed of your needs and problems, and the positive aspects of doing business in their country.

You should also be aware of representatives in the U.S. government who could make a difference to you. If your company is large enough to have a lobbying activity in Washington, that's a good place to start. Any company entering a foreign market should, as a matter of courtesy if for no other reason, identify the ambassador and commercial attaché and contact them. It may also be helpful to know the information officer.

Here are some of the resource materials that may be helpful to you initially:

Statesmen's Yearbook (St. Martin's Press, Inc.)
Political Handbook of the World, Arthur Banks, Ed. (CSA Publishers)
Encyclopedia
The World Almanac
European Marketing Data and Statistics (Euromonitor Publications Ltd.)
The European Directory of Marketing and Information Services (Euromonitor
    Publications Ltd.)
Directory of Market Research Reports and Studies (NSA Directories)
Directory of Foreign Press in the United States, Foreign Press Centers (USIA)

In addition, there are the international trade periodicals, available in many library and trade organizations, and finally, of course, your personal network.

Rare is the company that has no need of press contact. Even if the public press is of no interest to you, almost surely trade press will be of concern. In any case, know the basic facts about the public press: Who are the major players? Who owns them? What market do they cater to (liberal, conservative, pro- or antigovernment, upscale or down market)?

If the public press is one of your primary targets, learn in addition who owns the various media, what the tie-ups are between print and broadcast media, who the major publishers and editors are, and finally what reporters generally cover your "beat." If the trade press is of major importance to you, collect similar information about them.

Industry leaders and organizations in your industry abroad may already be familiar to you because a worldwide network exists in some industries. If that is the case, you may have already met some major players and be ahead of the game. If not, find out who they are. Publications may be the easiest answer, both in terms of printed information and conversations with reporters, who generally are keyed into the best people to know. On the government side, both the United States and your target country have agencies that also can be of help.

Your buyers may be the public, segments of the public, or a completely different group. How you approach them in a foreign market-place is a matter of your own education. Certainly the routes you use in the United States will be helpful in the new market, as long as they are appropriately tailored to the new environment. Even if your buyers are wholesalers, you generally need to be at least somewhat concerned with how the public views you.

Your relationships with the local community can have a serious impact, pro or con, on how you are viewed by the public over the longer period. Make friends with local community leaders. It can make a difference should you want to expand your business or need assistance on labor or other local problems.

If you already deal with labor unions, you know how important they can be. In foreign areas they can be more or less so. In Japan, for instance, if you have a relationship of mutual trust and respect with your employees, labor unions are not likely to be a problem, even if all your workers belong to the union.

In Japan, many unions are company unions. Relationships between management and workers have been so developed over recent years that the labor-management connection is not viewed as adversarial or competitive as it still is traditionally in the United States (and even more so in Great Britain). Even in Japan, however, or perhaps especially there, your success in labor relations depends upon your developing your own relationship between your workers and yourself.

In France, on the other hand, labor unions are strong. Workers cannot be disciplined or discharged easily. The unions, and the government as well, keep a close eye out. The same is true in Belgium and many other European countries. If you ignore the rules or try to go outside them, you will probably find your business in deep trouble.

Virtually all companies will have other specific groups connected to their industry that are important to their growth and well-being. In many cases, the publics that are important to your company may become clear as you work out your goals and the strategies you are to implement to reach them. Become clear at an early stage about who your audience is, and why.

3

Credibility: Your Most Important Resource

Nowhere is credibility more important than in the new markets you are entering. Companies that are young or less than giant-sized very often are totally unfamiliar names to the new marketplace you are entering. No reputation precedes them; but that can be an asset as much as it is a liability. Such companies have the opportunity to start from scratch—to determine how they want to be known and what kind of image they want to sculpt. They can make a great deal of progress in a short time if they determine in advance what their strategy will be.

Larger, older companies will probably find that their reputation precedes them. It is often not what they thought it would be and even less frequently what they want it to be. Even though it has negative aspects, however, size implies power that is usually appreciated. They can build on that.

Credibility, especially for the smaller companies, starts with simple things: timeliness, promising only what you can deliver, showing sincere intent. This does not rule out hard bargaining or a tough stance when appropriate, but it does mean no trickery, no deceit, no extravagant advertising, and putting a tight rein on opportunism.

It is unfortunate that Americans have developed a reputation abroad for being impulsive and changeable, among other traits. In Japan, the closing of Drexel Burnham Lambert in early 1990 left an embarrassing shadow in a country where few companies of substantial size ever close their doors and those that do follow a pattern of procedure that is predetermined and considered honorable. The company had its top Japanese manager reassuring its customers during the week prior to closing. When the end came, it was abrupt, leaving everyone, apparently even the manager, unprepared.

The Japanese Ministry of Finance insisted that the company remain open another six months to allow customers to file claims and to conclude the business in an orderly manner. The company was also compelled to give all employees at least one month's notice and to make good on pensions and other benefits it had guaranteed. The government itself stepped in and helped place many of the employees in other jobs. A top Drexel bond salesperson, Ann Natori, was quoted as observing, "Americans are so unreliable." She was not alone in her sentiment. A spokesperson from the Ministry of Finance commented, "The impact on their reputations (American executives) was not negligible."[1]

The manner of the closing has long-term effects on other businesses that want to open in Japan, and even on products that by association are judged unreliable. American companies in Japan customarily pay their employees two to five times as much as their Japanese competitors do. The Japanese argue that American companies offer less job security. That argument becomes more credible in the light of such events as the Drexel closing.

Several months before the Drexel closing, McGraw-Hill closed its World News arm. In Japan, treatment was similar to Drexel's. There was no prior notice. The staff heard the news of the closing only when it moved over the newswires. They called their bureau chief, who happened to be out of town at the time. Their call was the first the bureau chief heard of the closing. He had to fly to the head office in New York at his own expense to fight for reasonable compensation for himself and his staff.

Before that, *Reader's Digest* ran into trouble when it closed its Japanese office. The company suffered continued bad press when employees fought back by going to court for compensation and fair treatment.

Eight years after American Express closed its travel office in Okinawa, demonstrators were still agitating for compensation. Since some compensation, which was generally considered insufficient, had been paid, the company was less fearful of bad publicity and unusually willing to risk negative publicity.

In Japan, unlike the United States, according to tradition there is a spirit of cooperation between management and employees. This lends sympathy and support over the long term to the employees' side of the argument and makes such situations as those mentioned rare and very public when they do occur. The complainants receive considerable sympathy from public, press, and courts. Needless to say, since it happens virtually exclusively with foreign-owned companies, it dirties the overall image of such companies.

Try to fire employees in France or Belgium, and you'll find similar resistance. In some companies, the resistance may not be there, but the

1. James Sterngold, "Slow Death for Drexel in Japan," *The New York Times* (April 22, 1990).

reputation of the American company is tarnished nonetheless. Knowing how you can handle layoffs or closings is one of the responsibilities of the foreign businessperson in a new marketplace. It makes a difference not only to your own company and your employees but to associates who helped you when you opened and to companies that try to follow.

The values that are honored in the local society should be researched and adhered to as much as possible. "Taking the high road" usually pays off—even if the society you are dealing in appears to be tolerant of unorthodox business practices. Keep in mind that your assumptions may be inaccurate, that you are a neophyte trying to beat old-timers at their own game, that you have your own standards and regulations to honor, and that making a wrong move early on that involves such basics as value standards could cost you heavily in the long run. Your purpose at this time is to gain the respect of the people you will be doing business with.

Developing Relationships With Influential People

In setting up in a foreign country, most companies need to become acquainted with:

- The U.S. ambassador to that country
- The highest career official below the rank of ambassador
- The U.S. commercial attaché in the embassy
- An important official in the foreign government ministry or legislature that relates to your business
- The head(s) of the primary industrial trade organization for your business
- Major public media and the reporters that specialize in your type of business
- Trade press and those who run it
- Customers
- Leaders and organizations in the local community

These major contacts will allow you to introduce yourself, your company, and your product and get from them any information that will help you in developing your business and in dealing with legal and regulatory restrictions. A good impression is essential not only because it helps you gather the information you need, but because the support you develop or fail to develop could turn out to be crucial to the success of your business.

Do not overlook the importance of U.S. official agencies abroad, thinking that because you have done your basic homework and will be dealing with the local population, you therefore do not need the assistance of American officials. Once you begin business operations in your new area, potential customers and business contacts will find it natural to use the resources of the American Embassy's commercial attaché and other officials for information on your company. Your credibility could be at stake if you have failed to take the appropriate steps to familiarize these officials with you and your business to enable them to talk about you knowledgeably and favorably.

Once you get your networking program under way, begin assembling a key contact list and include the following information:

Name
Title
Company
Address
Importance to your company
Referrals to or from the above person
Meetings and what was discussed
Person's personal background
Comments and observations

There is no information more elementary or more important than a person's name, particularly to a reporter or public relations professional. Pronounce it right, spell it right, and get it in the right order—not always an easy task when you work internationally.

In Japan, Saito Hajime's family name is Saito. You address him as Saito-san or Mr. Saito unless he asks you to call him Hajime. Mrs. Saito is also Saito-san. Using the English honorific may be the safest way if you are unclear about his (or her) status relative to yourself. Halfway across the world, in Hungary, the surname also comes first.

In China, surnames also come before given names. The first given name indicates generation: Lo Mei Ling is of the Lo family and all her siblings are named Mei. Ling is her personal name. In Korea, the name that is used with "Mr." is determined by whether he is a first or second son.

In Spanish-speaking countries, many names combine the father's and the mother's names. Juan Rodriguez Carvalhos would be Mr. Rodriguez because Rodriguez is his father's name. In Brazil, where Portuguese is spoken, the custom is reversed. He would be Juan Carvalhos Rodriguez.

Keeping track of the many new contacts you make will lessen the chances of forgetting someone should the occasion arise to issue invitations to a gathering. The simplest and most direct way of becoming acquainted with people once you have identified them, if you have no mutual acquaintances, is to indicate interest in making a courtesy call. You should start doing this from the United States before you move abroad. Plan at least one trip to the target country before the company moves with the basic intent of contacting the right people to initiate a relationship. Write in advance, introducing yourself and your company, and send relevant materials. Follow up with phone calls to set up a meeting.

Planning a Pilot Trip

Prior to visiting your target area, you should have done as much homework as possible to prepare yourself. The following checklist can help.

1. *Compile a fact sheet on the country.* (See Appendixes III and IV for samples.)
2. *Make a list by name and title of government leaders* under whose jurisdication your industry may fall.
3. *List U.S. representatives abroad.* The ambassador, chargé d'affaires, commercial attaché, and others you should contact for courtesy or assistance.
4. *List media you plan to target* as well as major general media (whether or not you consider them of immediate importance to your strategy).
5. *List industry groups* such as the U.S. Chamber of Commerce as well as local organizations that may be useful as information providers and/or as speaking forums for your company's representatives.
6. *Send a letter* to each of the above outlining the reason for your trip, what you hope to accomplish, and who your company is—briefly. Request an appointment within a specific time frame to tell the reason—also briefly.
7. *Telephone a week or ten days after mailing* to set a definite appointment, referring to the letter when you do so.
8. *Confirm the appointment by facsimile (or letter).* If you have not yet succeeded in setting a definite appointment, repeat your request by facsimile, referring to your letter and phone call, and offering two or three definite times from which you wish the prospect to choose.

     Always give an indication of the amount of time you'll need (2:30 to 3:00, for instance), and stick to it. Never send a facsimile for your first contact with an individual. If time constraints preclude your making the first contact by mail, call and explain by phone, and then confirm your conversation by fax.

     If language becomes a problem, you will sometimes get

a call back by an English speaker if you leave your name, company, and number. Expecting that to happen, however, is an imposition. Try to determine, when you are compiling the list, who does speak the same language(s) you speak and who a good substitute may be if you have no languages in common.

   If friends or associates have given you names to contact, be sure to use them. Try to get the friend to call or write and let the contact know you will be getting in touch soon.

9. *A map of the city you are to visit can be helpful* in setting up appointments. Try to arrange those in the same area within a common time frame. It will also help you to judge travel time.

10. *Start a file* on whom you'll visit, their addresses, phone numbers, and intended topics of conversation. Make notes following the meeting.

11. *Know the information* you wish to collect on your trip and keep track of it as you compile it.

12. *Apply for passport, visa, and shots* as needed. Double check what the travel agent tells you.

13. *Carry sufficient cash.* Both travelers checks and credit cards can be a problem for small purchases and local transportation and telephones. Usually, the conversion rate is better in the destination country.

14. *Recheck time differences and schedules.*

15. *Purchase appropriate gifts as needed.* A good information source is *Do and Taboos Around the World,* compiled by the Parker Pen Company and published by The Benjamin Company, Inc., New York, 1985.

16. *Be sure to carry a sufficient supply of business cards* and give them out when you meet new people abroad. You may want to have them printed in the local language on the reverse side.

17. *After your appointments, send thank-you letters.*

Make a Few Trips

Ideally, you should make several trips, starting with when you can reveal your sincere intention to open business abroad to the actual public announcement that you are going to do so. You will find this easier to do the earlier you start. Do not wait until after you are established at your destination.

   Friends and business associates can be counted on to introduce you to helpful people they know in the area you are targeting. Usually their contacts will be more on the commercial than the government side, and clearly these are contacts that can be helpful.

   The first people to approach should be those who head the list.

The best start is to have a mutual friend make the first contact and introduce you. Failing that, initiate the contact yourself. This can be done by introductory letter and a follow-up telephone call from the United States indicating that you will be making a trip to the country, telling why you are visiting, and requesting an appointment. Generally, even a small company will be welcomed with considerable interest.

Once the contact has been established, it can be strengthened through business and social activities within the country. This is one of the reasons to put together a good strategic program that includes special events.

As you go about the delicate business of developing contacts, keep in mind that different rules may apply in these new business settings than those you are used to. Introductions are a vital necessity in some places. However, the fact that you are a foreigner may work in your favor.

Once you've managed to arrange a meeting, be aware that in many countries business will not take place until a personal relationship has been established. This is true throughout Asia, but especially in Japan. It's also true in Rio de Janeiro, where a *simpatico* relationship needs to be established, and in most of Africa. Even in Europe, where the constraints are more relaxed, business goes faster and more easily once a personal relationship is established.

All of this takes time, of course, and time is something you don't have much of. Although to the businessperson time is money, time is also money well spent. In parts of Indonesia, *rubber time* is a familiar expression that suggests the belief that time is what you make it. It's not a system that governs your actions, but a convenience you use to your advantage. You stretch it or compress it as you wish. Business may be put aside to allow for something more pressing—a celebration, for instance. Waiting is a creative, friendly activity, not a frustration. The attitude in Thailand is similar, as is the case in many developing countries.

The *mañana* of Latin America is the same concept under a different label. Eventually, business will get done.

Management-Employee Relationships

The quickest, surest way to build credibility as well as to break it down is through your own employees. Labor unions aside, if your work force is restive and resentful, they will talk about it at home and to their friends. The word will be out: Your company officials are insensitive, demanding, quixotic, or whatever. Conversely, a good report will make the company a desirable place to work and with a ripple effect enhance the company's reputation and credibility.

American managers in the local areas should be aware that their actions may have more serious consequences in the foreign arena than the same actions might have at home. This applies not only to the company but to the individual as well. Usually, however much authority the head office invests in management abroad, it is watching the operation closely. There is a lot of money invested and your operation may be the flagship for others to come.

Nowadays in the United States it is generally conceded on both sides that no loyalty is expected, and none given. Many managers exercise dictatorlike authority and vent personal frustrations quite readily, depending on the insecurity of their employees and a relatively tight job market that keeps employees working hard. Their subordinates sometimes complain and sometimes quit. Similarly, bosses who find they have a personality clash with a subordinate have few qualms about forcing the employee off the team. Dismissals are common, for no real reason, when new top management comes in and wants its own people. The result is that existing employees are often out. Also, many companies put their human resources budget into new recruiting efforts rather than retention or retraining for employees whose jobs are becoming obsolete.

In some cases it's almost expected that employees will not like or respect their bosses. When things get too uncomfortable, they move on. Rarely does top management blame its own managers for a high level of turnover. It's thought to be in the nature of things; managers don't have to be popular to be good, it is thought.

The attitude is different in many countries. Often, bosses are at least expected to be kind and benevolent if not paternal and even nurturing. Predictably, foreign bosses may be judged even more severely than those who are homegrown. After all, they are an unknown quantity and bring with them strange customs. It takes a special talent for an expatriate manager to build up the needed respect.

American companies' record of reversing their management strategy repeatedly in regard to management abroad underlines this difficulty. Often American managers just haven't made the grade and are recalled, to be replaced by a local national. After time, the local national is often replaced for other reasons. Needless to say, this does not make the public relations job easier. American managers need to be aware that whether they intend it or not, an image is being created—of indecisiveness, changeability, and uncertainty. It will take more than a few dollars in the public relations coffer to overcome the effects.

An international financial services company in Japan is one company that had trouble with its management. The general manager, sent to Japan because of his successful track record in other places, was so insensitive to his Japanese staff that some fourteen members of middle management wrote letters of complaint to the chairman of the board.

Their action was particularly surprising given the high level of loyalty to the organization, dedication to the job, and cooperative spirit characteristic of Japanese employees. The offending manager was replaced.

Basic traits of character and familiarity with the values of the society will take an American manager a long way in a foreign environment. Advance awareness of customs and attitudes is invaluable. Even such apparently simple work aspects as hours can be disconcerting. In Japan, employees work long hours, and continue "working" after hours in pubs and restaurants. This is genuinely regarded as an aspect of the job as well as an indication of group spirit. The foreign manager that repeatedly opts out is seldom well regarded.

Within the office environment, the atmosphere may seem very laid back to some Americans. Personal calls are few, but casual, and personal conversation is common and is seldom frowned upon. It is viewed as a valuable means to developing familiarity, loyalty, and common commitment to the company. The company is a surrogate family.

In Thailand, the relaxed pace can drive ambitious Americans to distraction. Although there is a slow but perceptible birth of economic ambition in that company, it is still not unusual for workers to disappear for days after they've been paid to enjoy the fruits of their labor.

To add to the confusion Americans face, the traditional Thai day is divided into six-hour segments rather than the two twelve-hour periods most of the world is accustomed to. You may find your employees eating at what seems odd times or arranging work hours creatively.

In Austria, there has been no change in the length of the work week since 1975, while in Belgium it has shrunk to 37.5 hours with no drop in pay. Finns have it even better—the work week is 32 hours. The trend to fewer work hours seems to pervade European industry, despite the emphasis on improving international competitiveness. To take up the slack, considerable investment is being made in new machinery toward raising individual productivity, and available machinery is used for a longer period of time. New schedules such as flextime, part-time work, and work at home, aided by new telecommunications technology, are being brought in to allow more flexibility and to make more effective use of the machinery.

Holidays and vacation days beg for attention, too. Every company has a national day, and usually it's observed quite seriously. Celebrations for the New Year are also common around the globe—but New Year's Day in China is weeks away from New Year's Day in Spain. Get a list early and see what the official holidays are and which others are optional at your discretion. Look into the attitude toward vacations— whether everyone takes off in August, as is the custom in France, or largely ignores vacation time, which is often the case in Japan.

Another cultural attitude that affects relationships in the workplace is the concept of *face* that is so often associated with the East. It is an observation that still prevails, not only in Asia, but in the Middle East as well. The idea is double-sided. It implies a publicly humble stance that reassures the group that one member is not trying to put himself above the others. It also implies a public respect for others—not causing another individual embarrassment or discomfort.

In cultures that respect *face*, age is usually honored as well. Age symbolizes authority, which commands respect. Although older people in a company may have senior titles and therefore, you think, warrant deference, it may not be the title that commands respect. Older, lower-level employees will be listened to and deferred to despite their rank. Similarly, if you, a high-level executive, are very young, you may sometimes feel overlooked. Those who are older are considered to be wiser and closer to God. At times it will be wise for you to defer to them.

Understanding such differences and acting from knowledge can make a major difference in the effectiveness of a manager. It also affects how internal public relations programs are conducted. Whether an American manager understands local traditions and trends often determines how well he or she is respected. It is not true that a smart person can learn all he or she needs to know by watching others. By the time you learn what you need to know, it may be too late!

4

Identifying the Right Media for Your Industry

Y ou should be familiar with the major press in your overseas locality and the trade press that pertains to your industry. It does not necessarily follow that those same newspapers, magazines, and broadcast media that are the most popular are the most important for you to use to get your message across. Often the opposite is true: Quality national papers, which are more likely to be appropriate for carrying the message you want to convey, frequently have substantially lower circulation than do the more sensational but less business-oriented publications.

While high-circulation dailies are important for information about the local environment and topics for small talk, they are unlikely to be appropriate targets under ordinary circumstances. That may change if a crisis develops in your industry or your company. Such newspapers are quick to pick up controversial or scandalous news, and for your own protection you should have a basic acquaintance with the publications and their reporters. Similarly, if you have dramatic news that you want to impart quickly and on a broad basis, these publications may be interested in carrying it.

Major quality publications are the place to start, however. Research and list the major daily press and then the specialized media in which you have an interest and that are likely to have an interest in you. Find out the circulation, type of news coverage, audience, the top editorial people, reporters for your area, and identifying characteristics, such as whether they lean left or right, are respected or not, and how they may have treated your company or your competitors in the past. Find out their addresses and telephone and facsimile numbers. Learn what kind of stories they are likely to be most interested in. Every publication has its own area of interest and own target readership. You will also want to know about deadlines.

Much basic information of this kind can be found in a number of publications mentioned in Appendix II. You may have to supplement the information found there with phone calls. Similarly, you will want to double-check on the names listed in the book if you intend to address any mail to them; reporters change beats and publications periodically, and all directories are somewhat outdated by the time they are published.

Doing Your Research

As you investigate print and other media abroad, keep in mind that the nature of what is acceptable is sometimes more important than style. The countries on which we focus our attention in this book all enjoy press freedom. Others that are mentioned, or that you choose to investigate, may not.

The U.S.S.R. has been known for years as possibly the most legally restrictive in terms of what could be said and what could not. News in the dailies had to pass through bureaucratic approvals before publication and frequently was no more than propaganda. The signs of change are dramatic and give every indication of continuing. In mid-1990 the Soviet parliament approved a press law that promises to "limit censorship, guarantee the rights of journalists, and allow citizens to publish more newspapers."[1] However, the parliament also approved a law imposing penalties for insulting the president in public. If such an offense occurs in the press, the maximum penalty is six years. Also likely to be adapted is an ethics code that would affect not only the 87,000 union members but free-lance journalists as well. Violating a variety of admirable standards, such as truthfulness or objectivity, could cause you to lose union membership or your job. Nevertheless, that such attention is given to the legal and ethical rights accorded to both writers and readers is remarkable in terms of this country's history.

While the U.S.S.R. may be remarkable for its traditional restrictiveness, it is not unique. Criticizing the president is illegal in Iraq, among other countries. Even in the United Kingdom, while criticism as such is not illegal, respectful tradition protects the royal family from gratuitous attacks and revelations about their private lives.

Most countries have strict laws against revealing government secrets. In Japan, there is no such law and nothing that would label someone a traitor who put national security at risk. Perhaps there is an unspoken assumption that no Japanese would betray his or her country—and also that no noncitizen would be privy to government secrets.

1. Marcel Dufresne, "A Soviet Press Code," *Washington Journalism Review* (July/August 1990), p. 28.

Similarly, libel laws vary greatly from place to place. In the United States, the victim has to prove malicious intent. In other places, protection may be stricter or looser, but public relations professionals should be aware of the guidelines.

Go to the Source

As is the practice in the United States, most publications are happy to give you information on the kinds of stories they prefer to run, and may even supply you with a list of editorial themes for the coming year. This is helpful whether you want to submit stories you yourself write, interest reporters in covering particular aspects of your business, or arrange interviews on specific subjects. Advertising departments usually carry this information.

Then look at whom it would be best for you to know: the executive editor, the managing editor, editorial writer, news writer, columnist, national editor, international editor, beat reporter, specialist in your field? Often it helps to know more than one, but what you're looking for is a sympathetic, or at least impartial and interested, channel for any information you may want to impart.

Keep in mind that reporters often change beats, become editors, or move to other publications. A contact made now may be even more useful next year, or of no use at all. Don't expect reporters you know well to introduce you to editors or the other way around. The size of the publication, internal relationships, and their level of interest in you all determine how far into the organization one contact will lead you.

Take the same steps with magazines and trade publications. Find out what niche each one targets. Feature stories and interviews often should be targeted to magazines, whose editors and writers tend to change more slowly than do those of daily newspapers.

You can start on this before you ever leave the United States by getting in touch with the publications' correspondents in this country. One resource to help you do this is the *Directory of Foreign Press in the U.S.*, which lists correspondents in the United States for publications abroad. It is published yearly in January by the U.S. Information Agency.

The largest concentration of international media personnel in the world is in the United States, based in Washington, D.C., New York, and other major cities around the country. Contact the U.S. Information Agency, based in Washington, which operates Foreign Press Centers in New York and Washington and acts as a clearinghouse and resource for foreign journalists in the United States. The agency produces comprehensive directories of journalists who are available for minimal fees on request. The correspondents are unfailingly helpful in putting you in contact with the right people in their home country, but when you have a story, be sure to share it with them first.

By calling U.S.-based foreign correspondents, you can ask to be guided to reporters abroad who speak English if you are dealing with a country whose language you do not understand. Most major, quality publications deal easily with this situation, especially if you have news that is of interest to them. If you are calling on a general information basis for future use, keep in touch with the local reporter. As a matter of courtesy, if you later have some real news, give it to the U.S. correspondent first. Remember that while you are pitching information for your own benefit, reporters are looking for news. If you can provide it, they will print it.

In order to get acquainted and talk comfortably about matters of mutual interest, it is entirely proper in most places to take an editor or reporter out to lunch. When you have some real news to impart—and the opening of your company in an area may be of real interest—you might want to stop in at newspaper offices for a visit. It will be easier if you've called first to introduce yourself and to set up an appointment. Other media people are a wonderful source of information as well. Exchange of information is what they're good at.

It takes time to develop relationships, and you need to also make short-term decisions to serve your publicity needs. Explore the most effective way to get coverage. Should you send out press releases? Invite reporters to a press conference? Invite them in for interviews? Invite them for breakfast or tea? Usually, they are quite willing to let you know the most effective means. They are looking for news, and if you have it, they want it.

Foreign Correspondents on Both Sides Can Help

Although your ultimate goal is most likely the local press, it is often helpful to get to know American foreign correspondents abroad as well. In some areas, this may be easier at first than developing relationships with foreign press, given the common language and cultural identity. Reports filed by American foreign correspondents abroad may show up in U.S. papers or local press printed in English. Occasionally, they may be translated into the local language for indigenous press or picked up for further investigation.

The primary value of coverage in English language press is that it seems to impress head office executives. Intellectually, they realize the value of local press coverage but since they can seldom read it, it doesn't seem as valuable. For some companies in some countries, coverage in the local English language press will be influential in their target market. This tends to be more true in emerging nations, but English press in Japan sometimes exerts a certain influence.

Other references for media abroad are *Bacon's International Pub-*

licity Checker, and *Gale International Directory of Publications*, edited by Kay Gill and Darren L. Smith (see Appendix I).

Publicity can be placed in overseas publications from the United States but it is more difficult to get it into print. Sources that can be useful in distributing your press release overseas are the local offices of the overseas press you are targeting, wire services (see Appendix II for some of the international wire services), chambers of commerce (contact the foreign trade department, U.S. Chamber of Commerce, Washington, D.C., for more information), Trade Development Commissions overseas (Consul General of foreign governments in New York and other large cities), U.S. embassies abroad (talk to the Department of State, Washington, D.C., or you might mail releases to the commercial attaché of the U.S. embassy in your target country if you've already been in contact with that individual).

You may do better to run your story on PR Newswire, Reuters, AP, UPI, or any of the foreign wire services, if you have that capability and your story has substantial news value. You can also, of course, mail or fax information to specific press abroad. With the proliferation of facsimile machines, checking the overseas press lists for fax numbers and sending it that way is likely to be the most efficient choice.

For relaying specific information that deals with dangerous and defective consumer products, if that is of concern in your industry, you can contact the International Organization of Consumer Unions. This clearinghouse for such information operates a two-way communications channel to correspondent organizations in about thirty countries who then relay the information to appropriate spokespeople, such as media and legislators. This body has had official nongovernmental status in the United Nations since 1981.

Valid Editorial/Advertising Compromises

If you are light on news of sufficient value to be picked up by the media, but eager to deliver some message quickly, most countries have some version of the advertorial or paid coverage that appears to be editorial copy rather than advertising. You can use this purchased space to educate your audience about your product or company, to introduce your top executive, or whatever you choose. The price you pay will not be low. Advertorials are usually most effective in crisis situations where you have a viewpoint to express that editors deem inappropriate for news—or feature—coverage. Advertorials are sometimes useful in other situations, but keep in mind that editors are usually good judges of what their readers will read, and that most readers seldom read a full story anyway.

Regular advertising is also always available and can be more attention-getting. It may be important to good, effective promotion of your company and its products.

Keep in mind that the interests of the press and the interaction between the press and business may vary considerably from one country to another. In the United States the relationship is quite relaxed; the press is accessible and many companies have public relations people or certain executives who respond to inquiries from the press. The same is not quite true in Britain and Japan, for instance. In France, corporate executives do not easily respond to press inquiries unless they are acquainted with the reporter and often are reluctant even then. You as a corporate representative may also find the press themselves less than eager to hear your story. Introductions always help.

How the Press Is Organized and How to Approach It

In the United States, the press is organized very much like any corporation, although there are usually two distinct functional areas. At the top of the chart are the publishers. Then on the editorial side come editors in various degrees of seniority. Below them are reporters. Interspersed are researchers, rewriters, headline writers, photographers, and so on. Business operations, which includes advertising and subscription sales, is a separate area except in the smallest of publications. The editorial hierarchy is less formal than in most corporations in that reporters often have a large amount of discretion in the stories they cover. Virtually every editor has at one time been a reporter and has probably also taken a turn in research, writing headlines, and other areas. In the end, it is the editor, and in very special cases the publisher, who decides what hits the printed page.

Newspapers get their information from abroad through various sources: wire services, reporters at their own bureaus, traveling reporters sent on assignment, stringers, and free-lance writers. They may also pick up stories from other publications and rewrite or additionally research and write stories on the same subject. Stringers and free-lancers may submit virtually the same story in various forms to several publications, and often write for local press as well.

In a country like Japan, the general level of remuneration is higher than in the United States. A foreign correspondent can command a higher rate for either writing or editing work (in English) for a local publisher abroad than for a U.S.-based publication. The writer may rely heavily on outside work for Japanese English-language media, if the principal American employing paper allows it, and often even if it doesn't. Supplementing their income as correspondents, many reporters will write under other names for local publications. Stringers will certainly put their time first where it brings in the most money—on Japanese publications—devoting attention to pieces written for home-country publications in order to build their professional reputations. It is quite common for them to write a story for the principal publication, and then vary it for submission to other publications, often using another byline when they do so.

Journalists fully employed by one publication may be forbidden from submitting stories to other publications, although many do so anyway under *noms de plume*. However, the structure of the news-gathering business in other countries may be different and may affect your ability to get coverage on your own news.

In Europe, each country has its own, highly influential business press. Reaching one publication does not mean reaching the others. Make sure the medium you choose is appropriate to your message and covers all the audiences you wish to connect with.

It is difficult to generalize on the influence of print media versus electronic media, or print media in Europe versus print media in the United States, because there are many variables according to country and industry. It is safe to say that print media are still powerful in both Europe and Asia. In 1990, before unification, what was then West Germany alone had 120 daily newspapers plus magazines, which are read avidly. Japanese commuters use their three-to-four-hour-a-day train rides to catch up on their reading (and sleeping). Countries with a high proliferation of television seem to continue to maintain a high rate of reading—perhaps in line with a high literacy rate. In Europe, Italy may be an exception. Although daily newspapers and other periodicals are widely and fervently read, television seems to be the primary medium of the masses.

It is safe to assume that with the unification of Europe will come pan-European networks for communications. There are already numerous pan-European business magazines, but their influence is minimal compared with the influence of country-specific magazines. No doubt this will change.

New Markets for Pan-European Newspapers

There are also several pan-European newspapers that report, operate, and are delivered across the continent. All use English as their medium, and although they reach an important managerial audience, it is still a small audience.

New newspaper networks are being created: Major newspapers from Britain, Spain, Italy, and France are joining in consortia to exchange news and stories, similar to the activities of existing wire services. However, communicators generally expect it to be a long time before pan-European publications gain any real prominence or a major share of the market. In addition to language differences are the strong nationalistic interests and loyalties that help local publications hold their readership.

The national business press in Europe is increasing at a rate hovering between 5 and 20 percent annually. The number of current business publications (38) throughout the EC is increasing, as are the 15,000 trade press. Tie-ups for fuller information exchange are under way in these areas.[2] As information crosses borders, the demand for wider information does so too. Readers expect more from what were once local publications, and corporations are thinking more inclusively.

Maintaining quality in terms of accuracy, consistency, and—from the corporate viewpoint—positive reporting can become more of a challenge. Facts may be repeated without rechecking, raising the spectre of temptation to report unconfirmed information. By the same token, however, misinformation discovered can be quickly corrected.

The Press Changes as Markets Change

As technology invites reporting across wider borders, the style of reporting is likely to become more uniform; the press may become increasingly impartial in regard to what it prints as the quantity of available information soars. As far as business reporting, size of organization will certainly be an important determining factor as to whether its news gets reported. The challenge will be for the marketer to have the information provided put to use, which is basically no different from the challenge now faced.

In Japan, a press release sent to an editor stands little chance of being used unless the recipient is familiar with the sender. Reporters belong to news groups that cover certain beats. In fact, there are about forty press clubs for various industries, government ministries, financial and economic associations, sports, entertainment, and other groups. Each club consists of reporters from various national media who follow that specialty closely.

Press releases and press conferences are best arranged through the club that is responsible for the particular industry. The club will distribute the releases and arrange the press conference. It is also a useful source for arranging interviews. Getting the cooperation of the clubs almost guarantees dissemination of your news and at least some print coverage. The degree of influence depends upon the industry and the club, but the rotating chairpersons are influential.

While you can contact reporters directly, and often they are very interested in a story or interview, you can contact editors directly when you have a big story. Most of what gets space will have come from the

2. James B. Lindheim, "1992: Meeting the Communication Challenge," *IABC Communication World* (July/August 1989), pp. 35–39.

beat reporters. Find out where the news groups for your industry are located, who is in charge, and how to approach them.

Economic and financial news, for instance, invariably reaches its destination if it is properly distributed at the Keidanren (federation of economic organizations), where reporters from various news media have mailboxes and often wait to receive news of events or to meet prominent people. Press conferences are also held there as well as speeches of note. Sports reporters, entertainment reporters, and others all have their own groups in various places, as mentioned.

Know the Press Organizations

There are also general press clubs for local and foreign reporters. Both groups of reporters can join both clubs, and very often nonjournalists can also join in some capacity. If you can afford the time, this is one good way to get to know those in the news field. The general clubs, the Foreign Correspondents' Club of Japan and the Nippon Press Center, also arrange press conferences, speakers, distribution of releases, and so on. Foreign correspondents' clubs exist in most major cities, but Tokyo's is still one of the best.

Press conferences are an acceptable means of relaying information in virtually every country that boasts a free press. There are many differences in style, however, and adhering as closely as possible to what is appropriate in each country is advisable. The jazzed-up, decorated shows that some companies sponsor as press conferences in the United States are inappropriate in some other countries, where a business activity is expected to be far more dignified. Germany is one example of this. Dark business suits, white shirts and ties are *de rigueur*. An organized, briskly paced, but formal presentation is in order.

In some countries, the expenses journalists incur to attend news conferences are paid by the organization holding the press conference. This may even be the case if they come to a corporate office to do an interview. In Japan, it is not uncommon to reimburse a reporter for his transportation if he agrees to come to lunch.

In other places, the press has editorial charges for certain types of news such as personnel changes—much like our classified ads. The Middle East is one place where this is practiced.[3]

You must also familiarize yourself with the format of releases. Don't assume that an English press release translated into Swedish or Japanese will be fine for that country. Don't even assume that press releases, even if they contain interesting news, will be used at all. In Britain, the more highly reputed the paper the more traditional its practices are. Such

3. Robert S. Leaf, "International Public Relations," *Lesly's Public Relations Handbook*, ed. Philip Lesly (Englewood Cliffs, N.J.: Prentice-Hall, 1983), p. 380.

papers don't accept press releases; all texts are written by the reporters themselves. Papers of a more common denominator will, however, often use information sent in releases. France is another country where press releases are more often shunned than used. Similarly, paid editorials are not accepted in the United Kingdom.

Different Countries, Different Styles

Not every country uses the American inverted triangle format in writing a press release. Readers not familiar with the press practices in the United States may not be aware that news beat stories here are always written with the important news up front with increasing quantities of color and less real information as the story progresses. It is designed so that the report can be shortened quickly by cutting off succeeding paragraphs starting from the bottom. This, far less important now than in the days of hot type and lithography, facilitates speedy makeup in order to get the paper to the presses with minimal time between news gathering and distribution. Modern computerized methods have modified this style only slightly.

Feature stories, on the other hand, are written to be produced in full in any format the writer thinks is most appropriate. Interviews generally come under this general category. Makeup is done with more lead time than with news. The Gunning Fog Index, that now-famous measure of the simplicity and (hopefully) clarity of one's English, can be as helpful in writing for press overseas as here, helping you keep your language straightforward and understandable.

In Japan, news was written in a style more closely akin to the polite, formal kind used in letters and literature until the Americans came along. They worked valiantly to teach the Japanese to write in the "professional" style American reporters and readers were accustomed to. It didn't entirely stick. Press releases written in Japanese today often take a more story-telling type of approach than do English releases. Releases sent out by American writers, even when translated into Japanese before they are sent, often require more rewriting time than editors are able to spend.

Sometimes the question is raised about the validity of print press coverage when broadcast media have proliferated so broadly in all developed markets. While the nature of publications has undergone some change, print is a medium that requires attention from its readers and in nearly all cases enjoys a pass-on factor of two, three, or even more readers beyond the original.

In addition, news and feature stories are almost universally acknowledged to enjoy more credibility than do advertising or commercials. In advertising, three to five "hits" (separate exposures) are considered necessary to reach the target audience in print media. Furthermore, print has a secondary and tertiary readership, which raises the value of a single exposure. In television, where people turn on their sets and then wander to another room, talk, or change channels when a commercial is shown, the required number of "hits" is higher. On radio, it reaches about twenty before the target audience is covered.

Nevertheless, radio may be a very valid medium for your particular audience and geographic area. If your audience is made up of people who live in small apartments, especially if television has not proliferated, if they are commuters who drive to work or teenagers who listen to Walkmans regularly, think about radio. If you can construct a message that's effective with short sound bytes, even better. In parts of Africa, for instance, radio is clearly the best medium and sometimes the only one available.

In some countries—India, for one, is notable—nothing is more influential than the cinema. Messages dispersed either in the movies or at the theaters reach a large, diverse audience. Consider all the possibilities when you construct your plan.

Television and Other Broadcast Media

In looking at broadcast media, there are also certain basics you should determine: Which are public and which are private stations? What is the proliferation of radio versus television and which markets do they serve? What are the prime times during the day and during the week? What is the geographical coverage? Demographic? Which types of programs are most popular?

Many countries have much more restrictive guidelines for radio and television advertising as far as content than does the United States. Sometimes the rules are not spelled out but are known and adhered to by unspoken agreement. That does not make them less restrictive. Find out what is acceptable and what is not. Taste is another question. What appeals in the United States is probably not going to be what appeals in another country, even if it is culturally and legally acceptable.

Japanese television programs, for instance, are every bit as gory and violent as those in the United States. Sex is just as much of a commodity. The style, however, is different. The gore on Japanese television is usually in an incredible context—monsters from outer space or historical soap operas portraying an era long gone. Sex is not sold on television the way it is on cable television in New York and other areas, but it is equally suggestive, if less explicit.

Japanese television departs from the American approach in other ways as well. When the emperor died in 1989, there was never a photo of him lying dead. Although his temperature, blood pressure, and heartbeat were reported by the Imperial Household Agency, that's all that was reported during his illness and all that was demanded.

In the now infamous government "Recruit Scandal" there was never a scoop, despite the fact that the scandal was uncovered during a reporter's investigation of a local bribery case. Investigative reporting became mainstream in this scandal and forced the government to take action.

Kazuo Hiramoto, veteran reporter and newscaster for Japan's TBS (TV), considers good character to be the primary requisite for a good journalist. "To be a good journalist," he says, "we must first be a good, respectable human being."[4] Japanese audiences have a good deal of interest in foreign news, largely because they know more about foreign countries, according to Dan Rather.[5]

The style of advertising, too, is very different as many Americans now realize. Several years ago, American advertising professionals saw Japanese commercials and considered them unsophisticated and naive because they seemed never to sell. In fact, they were selling ideas and reputations rather than products. To the Japanese eye, American ads seemed simplistic and boring. In Japan, many viewers enjoy the commercials more than they do the programs. They are creative, often humorous or fantastic, and seldom show even a product name. The idea is to create a mood and link that good feeling with a company to enhance the credible image of the company. Ads appeal to the senses, or to the viewer's poetic nature; they create an aura for the imagination to take hold.

Many American companies have tried to adapt some of the Japanese aspects of advertising, and many Japanese companies have begun introducing their style of advertising into the United States. In some instances, the switch in style has been effective. In others, it has not. The use of American entertainment and sports superstars to sell products on Japanese television has been a major, and apparently effective, fad. The use of Japanese-style commercials on American television has been less captivating.

There are differences in the advertising styles of most countries that can alert you to subtleties you may not have noticed. Even in Europe television commercials vary considerably by nation. Britain tends to rely on witticisms; Germany seems more announcement-oriented and bunches its commercials together; the French, by contrast, seem more flamboyant.

Hard, Recent News Required for Television

Television overseas is generally not a sympathetic medium for corporate information of anything less than major proportions because of regula-

4. At New York University's Washington Square Tisch School of the Arts Symposium: "Japan and American Television News," September 26, 1989.
5. Ibid.

tions in so many countries and tight competition for coverage in other places. Nevertheless, a foreign executive of a prominent company is often a welcome interviewee even in major international cities, especially if there is some important news or information to impart. Of course, the size of the audience and the quantity and quality of broadcast competition both play a part in programming. In less-developed countries, interviews or discussions about your industry or company are usually even more of a possibility because of its probable uniqueness and because the audience believes it may learn something.

If you can sell the program, language needs to be no more than an inconvenience even if your corporate executive does not speak the local language. Pretaping the interview and dubbing or overdubbing the sound into the appropriate language is common. Using interpreters, even simultaneous interpreters, is cumbersome and should be done only when the message is strong and no better format is available. Similarly with subtitles. The exposure may be better than none at all, but it is awkward. The demand is great for a strong message to overcome the inconvenience to the listener.

Television is booming in Europe. The 1988 level of 50 channels in Europe programming about 180,000 hours per year will have doubled by 1992, with some 100 channels programming about 500,000 hours per year.[6]

Satellites are also gaining ground. About 30 million people are connected to satellites directly or by cable—a signal for the future. Programming is likely to increasingly cross borders. Britain, for instance, gets programming from Europe as well as the United States. Switzerland picks up programs in Italian, French, English, and German, among others. The opportunities for mass communications are astounding. While no one seems to be talking about it, the opportunities for simultaneous translation through alternative broadcast channels seem almost inevitable.

The type of programming popular in different countries is interesting. The French seem to love discussions, usually with just two or three people and all kinds of subjects, especially philosophical ones. In Italy, family shows and game shows are popular; Britain loves drama, selected American TV programming, and news, and so on. Everyone likes entertainment, but the type of entertainment that is popular varies. So does the time allocated to commercial use. In Britain it is virtually nil, at least on BBC. In Belgium, no television commercial time is scheduled. In Germany, only about twenty minutes of advertising are allowed on daily television.

In Austria, there are only two channels, both government owned, although there are three additional cable channels and other program-

6. Lindheim, op. cit., pp. 35–39.

ming can be captured from Switzerland and other parts of Europe by viewers who have parabolic antennae. Although commercial advertising is expensive, television is the most cost efficient means of reaching your target market, if it is a broad-based public market. Even in Austria, the marketing language is English, which makes life easier for Americans who wish to initiate business there. Advertising comes from the United States, which is regarded as the marketing/advertising innovator. One factor that makes television commercials viable to many advertisers is that there is only one major newspaper. Image advertising in print media, therefore, is done through magazines.

As James Lindheim points out,[7] the rapid flow of information around Europe means that the senders must conceptualize an international audience when they send a message. Corporate executives who speak to the media must be trained to think in terms of a pan-European audience.

Other Communications Media

The news agencies you will be involved with are likely to be either the well-known American wire services, particular industry-oriented services such as Blumberg's or Dow Jones in financial services, or the Britain-based Reuters. It may be helpful to know that there are six global news agencies. Only two are major commercial, transnational companies: Reuters and Associated Press (AP). The other four are state-owned globals: Agence France Presse (AFP), TASS, Novosti (APN), and Hsin Hua (New China News Agency). However, there are a great many news agencies of all sizes that handle various kinds of news. Once you find which serves your needs best in disseminating your particular information to your specific audience or in providing you with up-to-date news spots, you may want to subscribe to at least one. Reuters has a very wide reach around the globe and is making major headway in financial markets by tying up with various exchanges to create information systems such as SITUS and GLOBEX. While intended for use by investment banks, securities and commodities exchanges, and others in the financial industry rather than the public, these services almost inevitably will at some time include not only trade statistics, but general market information and news that can affect trades. The Associated Press is known for its many bureaus around the world and its rapid, reliable reporting. Agence France Presse is, of course, based in France and also has correspondents in major cities. AFP is particularly interested in political news. TASS and APN are Russian. The restrictions that have for years accompanied their reportage have loosened somewhat, but the

7. Ibid.

influence of these two outside of the Eastern Bloc does not approach that of AP or AFP. Similarly, Hsin Hua is a major information source in both Chinas and a source for Western publications on news inside China.

Paid advertising is often an important supplement to your publicity and other public relations efforts. Virtually every country has numerous opportunities for you to get exposure at a price. Sometimes that price is rather moderate.

Direct mail, billboards, and point-of-sale (POS) efforts may be worthwhile. Direct mail has a high per-exposure cost but is often best for reaching a carefully targeted, specific market.

One expert in this field has specific recommendations for tackling international direct mail. James Thornton, managing director of Mailing Lists (Asia) Ltd., claims that the best approach is to use multinational rather than local lists because the most responsive lists are multinational. He gives the following tips:

1. Test your domestic control package (with minor modifications). Use an English-language package. Use the local language when you mail to local language lists.
2. Test small and large countries; smaller countries usually produce a better response.
3. Be cautious in countries with foreign exchange restrictions. Avoid controlled circulation lists and stick to a multinational list of previous responders to a foreign currency offer.
4. Avoid mailing at certain times of the year. These periods include before, during, and after the Chinese New Year in Asia and Ramadan in the Muslim countries.
5. Seek out those categories of lists that work best. These include name selections from large U.S. and U.K. lists. For the most profit, target small selections from larger lists and focus on smaller countries.
6. Some lists should be avoided. Beware of compiled lists. Research shows that 50 percent of individuals have never responded and will never respond to a direct mail offer.
7. Always offer a credit card payment option.
8. Shop around for the best postal rates.
9. Use a lightweight package.
10. Test, test, test.
11. Analyze response, not only by list but by country within list.
12. Provide written instructions to printers and lettershops. A study found that there were 127 steps on the critical path of managing a single direct mailing—127 opportunities to mess up. Spell it out in detail—and in writing.[8]

8. James Thornton, "How to Plan a Multinational Mailing," *Folio* (August 1990), pp. 125–126.

Figure 4-1. Summary checklist for contacting international media.

▪ Construct a basic list of major daily press in target country.

    —Get specific information: address, contact number, names, circulation.

    —Find out deadlines, type of stories they want, what they'll accept from you.

▪ Research magazines and trade press in a similar way.
▪ Follow up with news services that reach your target media.
▪ Ask similar questions for television.
▪ Investigate other publicity media.

a. Radio
b. Direct mail/marketing communications
c. Billboard
d. Advertising, brochures, point-of-sale pieces, etc.

▪ Determine if your company or client views any particular medium as a "must."
▪ List target media and pertinent information.
▪ Contact U.S.-based correspondents of target foreign media; give information outline and ask for contacts abroad.
▪ Contact referred reporters abroad if at all possible.
▪ Determine who arranges translations for foreign media.
▪ Determine who approves press release copy.
▪ Determine who must approve final translated copy.
▪ Arrange to track coverage through press clipping services.

Ads in buses, taxis, and subways can be very effective, depending upon the city, the culture, and the type of product you are promoting. Radio commercials are almost always substantially lower in price than television commercials and may reach your audience directly. As mentioned earlier, experts advise that it takes twenty radio "hits" or separate exposures to ensure reaching your audience, as against three to five in print advertising.

Whichever choice you make, be sure that your advertising is coordinated with your public relations efforts and either is used to establish initial awareness that public relations efforts will continue and enforce, or to support the publicity already under way. Make sure both public relations and advertising are carefully coordinated with your overall strategy to make the most of every campaign. Use the summary procedure list shown in Figure 4-1 as a guide.

This can be accomplished in almost any industry in a number of ways. Once the company has decided what it intends to accomplish in its market and together with public relations has outlined the strengths the company can bring to the marketplace, the public relations department needs to consult with advertising to formulate a campaign theme. Once this is decided, the campaign can be launched on the heels of appropriate public relations fanfare—publicity teasers followed by a press conference announcing the theme, timed to coincide with the first appearance of the ads. Thereafter, news announcements, interviews, and special events can be keyed into the theme as well as marketing communications, brochures, and so on.

Smaller companies and those with very limited budgets may want to handle promotion with the emphasis on public relations, supported by advertising and marketing. In this case, the real accomplishments of the company—those that are of public interest—are showcased. Breakthroughs in scientific fields, humanitarian programs, and new product introductions are some of the themes that are strong enough to be used to drive a campaign. The advertising, which needs to be sufficiently creative to utilize and spotlight such themes, is low-key and minimal budget. Marketing communications as well as sales efforts become nearly effortless tie-ins.

Other efforts your company makes, newsletters and annual reports from the overseas area, for instance, can add to your overall success only if they fit into the overall strategy. Be sure that they do.

This chapter has described the media that you must familiarize yourself with to operate effectively in a new market. Whether you start your research from home base or find yourself quickly out in the field, the basic steps you take to pull together a publicity plan are similar. Again, the summary procedure list shown in Figure 4-1 will be of help to you.

5

When Special Projects Are Appropriate

While there is a wide variety in types of special events, the reasons for them are few: to develop corporate news where no other exists; to promote a new product that may otherwise be overshadowed when it is introduced; to introduce or entertain people important to the company; to establish good community relations; and to express thanks.

If you're new to an area, a special event is a good way to develop further the contacts you've initially made through courtesy calls. Since it is likely to include many guests who already know each other, it can probably attract some people you'd like to know but have not been able to call on.

In some cultures, an invitation to dinner or a party after one introduction may be construed as too forward or aggressive. That barrier can be lowered by tying the invitation in with an occasion of mutual interest or a specific event. In addition, the comfort level for invitees can be raised by making it evident that the occasion is large enough for the invitees to assume that they will already know some of the other guests. Certainly, getting a few well-known local citizens to agree to come will help attract others to the event. In almost any culture, people feel reluctant to attend an event unless they can be reasonably sure that they will know somebody there.

The event can be simply a party, small or large, basic or elaborate. To be effective, it should have some underlying excuse such as the celebration of a holiday, introduction of a new product, or visit of a notable person.

Celebration of an American national event such as the Fourth of July or Thanksgiving Day may be met with interest by your foreign guests. Celebration of a local or national holiday of the host country is also a possibility if you have enough reliable advice about local customs to be sure that what you do is in no way offensive. Many holidays are tied to traditional or family celebrations, and business-related invitations may not be welcome.

Special events usually, but not always, imply an opportunity for accompanying publicity. Consider carefully the pros and cons of using the event for publicity. Early in the game, you are likely to look exploitive, depending upon who attends the party and what the purpose is. Don't be afraid to give up some quick press coverage for long-term relationships. Particularly if distinguished people are on the guest list, be sure that photographs will not compromise or embarrass them. Also keep in mind that many of your guests may welcome publicity and may even resent your being the focus of media attention.

Special programs can and should take a variety of forms. Whatever is consistent with the products and image of the company that can be construed to further its purposes, and fits into the local culture and mores should be considered for possible promotions.

Tailoring Programs to the Culture

Any reasonable person knows that if you're operating in a strict Muslim country you don't introduce a couple of lambada dancers for entertainment. Few choices will be as straightforward as that, however.

When Lane, Crawford, the English department store chain, wanted to promote its jewelry in Hong Kong some years ago, it was up against an entrenched market of small Chinese jewelry shops throughout the colony. On the plus side were its already prestigious name and the fact that jewelry in general was already worn and coveted by wealthy Chinese women as well as the many tourists who visited the colony.

On the minus side was the fact that its primary target market consisted of Chinese people, who tended to frequent Chinese shops. The secondary market was made up of tourists, most of whom were Americans who had never heard of Lane, Crawford. Another drawback was that Lane, Crawford was primarily a department store; jewelry was still a small part of its business, and its prices were higher and not subject to bargaining, as they were in Chinese-owned shops.

The store had to figure out a way to make a splash and attract both public and press attention. The attention that was created had to stimulate excitement and at the same time preserve the dignity of fine gemstones, top-quality Mikimoto pearls, and other jewelry. It had to have a unique character that would cause wealthy Chinese women to sit up and take notice.

Further, the campaign had to extend for a considerable time in some form to gradually create enough name value so that in the future, the reputation of the store and the quality and dependable value of its jewelry would be known by tourists even before they arrived. Added to that, of course, were the familiar budget constraints of a company seeking to make its name in a new product line.

Our resulting public relations campaign was designed around the prestige and personal enhancement of the customers. We hired a top-ranking, well-known Chinese model/actress, put the world-famous tailors of Hong Kong to work with equally famous Mikimoto pearls, and came out with a pearl-covered bathing suit. It was a smash. It reminded people of Hong Kong's moonlit beaches, luxurious pools, and thriving economy.

We innovated exotic scenes and photographic backgrounds that were revolutionary at the time. By setting diamonds, pearls, and other precious jewelry against sun and sand and by staging suggestive night shots, we managed to formulate an attention-getting, memorable campaign that gave welcome front-page coverage to Mei Ling, the model, and thereby helped the budget. The suit and the model were invited to hotel special events, charitable society functions, and low-key promotions staged by us for tourists around the passenger liner tied up in "Fragrant Harbor." The press had a field day—even prestigious papers welcomed a chance to lighten up the news with a glamour shot at some function.

After the campaign had enjoyed a good run, we spurred momentum with a new twist. Using an American singer to display the jewelry, we were able to continue this campaign for many more months. Again with budget in mind, the singer chosen was a beautiful woman whose face was unknown but whose voice was familiar to thousands. She had made her professional name in Hollywood as the behind-the-screen voice of many movie stars who could not sing. She recorded and promoted a song written about Hong Kong for Lane, Crawford.

The records were distributed with appropriate public relations fanfare to the press, disc jockeys, and then to special customers. Air time, free to us because the song caught on, was excellent. While a plan to make the record available for sale in shops eventually fell through, the campaign, which ran well over a year, brought in substantial new business, opened the way for the chain to open several new jewelry boutiques in the colony, and made the store famous for its jewelry line.

The exotic Chinese model was very popular among the Chinese who knew and admired her. Therefore, she was able to retain an aura of glamour and luxury that spilled over to help the store. She was key to successfully promoting the idea of the exotic Orient in the minds of tourists, who found they could fulfill their romantic dreams of Eastern jewels without the risk of negotiating in shops where quality and value were inconsistent.

Conversely, the American singer, although less dynamic as a personality, was still attractive to Chinese women who were taken with the image of a wealthy, successful American. She was equally popular with tourists, who identified with her.

More recently, American Express decided to enter Japan's charge card/travelers checks/travel market. It looked for a high-impact special event to announce its presence and initiate its network of contacts. Having staged successful cause-related marketing events in the United States and elsewhere, it hit on the idea of helping with preparations in Japan for the Olympics that were to be held in California in the summer of 1984.

Since cause-related marketing was a totally new concept in Japan, the public relations campaign started with an attempt to educate the public about what the concept meant. The first step was to identify and meet the significant officials on the Japanese Olympics Committee. Once the committee had a workable and acceptable concept of what the company intended to do, articles were placed explaining how use of the card or travelers checks would benefit the Japanese Olympic team, but it was not until the special event was staged that the campaign finally took off.

Several weeks into the three-month campaign, a major event occurred at a local hotel that housed the largest ballroom in the city. It was a party where a guest-participation mini-Olympics was staged. Various Olympic games that could be adapted to an indoor environment such as throwing events, golf shots, and basketball, were set up with suitable decorations and fanfare. A former Olympian and team members for the forthcoming games were honored guests.

This event drew strong opposition from Japanese staff members and advisors. It had never been done before, they claimed. Also, it was felt that the guests, mainly conservative and rather old, senior businesspeople would consider it beneath both their dignity and their physical stamina to actively participate in such a party. Nevertheless, the event was staged and the acceptance rate was above that anticipated. What took place during the evening, however, was a real eye-opener.

The games were played with full participation and enthusiasm. Normally if an invitation said 6 P.M.–8 P.M. people would be out the door promptly by 8 P.M. These guests refused to leave. The party was talked about for weeks and became a permanent memory associated with the company. Needless to say, it achieved two goals: It effectively paved the way for further development of relationships with the important guests who came, and it spurred participation in the Olympic cause-related marketing program.

The momentum started by the party was maintained with continuing news about funds that were being raised, the progress of the Japanese Olympic team in its training and final selection, and ads featuring Olympic contenders.

Deciding to hold the party was a calculated risk, but a rather minor one once it had been determined that there was no serious cultural barrier. Opposition stemmed mostly from a familiar Japanese reluctance to take on a project that was not already tried and true. Nevertheless, staging a special event abroad should not be something in which much risk is involved. The long-term effects can be serious.

Techniques that can be used in special promotions vary from country to country. A promotion that has been effective in one place may not be possible, or may need to be varied, in another. For instance, in the United Kingdom, Ireland, Denmark, Sweden, Holland, Italy, and Spain, free mail-in offers such as coupons are allowed. The same promotion in Norway or Germany may not be. Mail-in sweepstakes are regarded differently, depending on the country. Belgium, Denmark, Italy, Norway, and Sweden will not allow them, but they are fine in France, Germany, and Holland.

Denmark, Finland, Sweden, and Germany have the most stringent sales promotion regulations in Europe. For example, Germany doesn't allow free premiums on products, a standard practice elsewhere.

Travel clocks, an innocuous gift or giveaway in the United States or Japan, would be a disaster in China, where a clock suggests your life ticking away. To help its clients, one agency, International Marketing & Promotions, a unit of D'Arcy Masius Benton & Bowles, has published a European Promotional Legislative Guide.

Trade Fairs and Alternate Vehicles for Exposure

Trade fairs are predictable events that can be very useful to your company in terms of visibility and contacts. Virtually every industry, even those in the service sector, stages some sort of trade fair, and such fairs are held in some form in most countries. Whether it is appropriate for your company to participate in one is a management decision, but you need to be aware of where and when they are and the rules and requirements for participation.

At the very least, a trade show is an effective way to study the competition. Many European trade shows are attended by top-level managers.* They serve as corporate summit meetings that provide an instant immersion experience into European corporate culture. Trade fairs are a particularly popular vehicle for exposure in Germany. At a trade fair there, visitors are cautioned to wear conservative clothing and

---

*This is often not the case in the U.S., where trade shows are visited by marketing and technical people and booths are manned by lower-level executives and salespeople. U.S. shows are frequently informal, with a convention-like atmosphere. Shows abroad tend to be more formally structured and dignified, although much depends upon the industry, the country, and the particular show or fair.

to keep manners formal. Exhibitors spend as much time as possible with visitors, conducting negotiations and making sales. As much as 70 percent of yearly sales are made by some multinational companies at these fairs.

Seminars and lectures can also be useful depending upon your circumstances. They are a good way to get industry members together, to build the general level of knowledge, and to establish yourself as an active participant if not a leader in the local community. They are also an excellent means of expanding your network of contacts.

6

Using Foreign Agencies and Consultants

Public relations has not necessarily developed in other countries to the same extent that it has in the United States. Sometimes public relations activities are carried out under different names such as publicity or marketing, and often the emphasis, approach, and style vary considerably from "accepted" public relations practice in the United States. Often the name given to public relations people reflects the underlying concept. In France, we are called *attachés de presse*—which signifies the "flack" concept that public relations professionals in France are finally managing to move away from. In Canada, public relations people are called "relationists"—which again signals a general concept of responsibility. These concepts can make a difference to you in your staffing and training requirements.

Most countries where public relations is a recognized commercial field also have public relations agencies, but where the field is still relatively unsophisticated, they are sometimes owned by foreign entities, often American or English companies. In other places, public relations is offered as an adjunct service by advertising agencies; marketing consultants also offer a kind of public relations service at times.

Locally owned agencies may have a different focus. Sometimes they will perform the services you need better than you can; sometimes, not as well. You need to find out what services are available and what particular agencies can do well. The International Public Relations Association (headquartered in Geneva; see Appendix I) can be a source of information on agencies abroad. For Europe, Chester Burger's *Euro-Directory* is excellent (see Appendix I). Local consultancy associations in some countries such as France and England will provide lists of their members (see Appendix I for some of these organizations).

An American agency in another country, for instance, may be very good on worldwide connections and creativity but of less value in supplying influential personal contacts or negotiating for space in the press. When shopping for an agency, don't overlook the possible clout an advertising agency with a public relations arm may exert with the press or the possibility that the influence of one side of the business is less powerful than the other.

In Japan, Dentsu is an old, respected, gigantic ad agency that bills about $7 billion annually worldwide. No surprise that its influence with the Japanese press is strong! If influential executives in that company give the word, Dentsu can apply its considerable clout to make sure a public relations story will be seen. However, it will not be done lightly, or for a small company, or for free. Substantial obligation or *giri* will be incurred on your part, and somewhere along the line that marker will be called in.

Not incidentally, public relations agencies that are under the wing of advertising agencies often are not quite as good at what they do; they are sometimes regarded as poor sisters to the larger agency with fewer resources and less skillful staff. Generally speaking, you should look for the following services, eliminating those you don't need:

- Introductions to government officials
- Media contacts, press conferences
- Writing, translating, designing
- Strategic planning
- TV monitoring and taping
- Press monitoring and clipping
- Reports and analysis
- Publications: annual reports and house organs
- Program development
- Creative ideas/advisory services
- Whatever else your particular business needs

The availability or level of expertise in some agencies over others may reflect the sophistication of public relations in that country as well as the agency itself and the nation's economy and culture. In Austria, which recently has seen rapid development because of the privatization of some firms, its ambition to join the European Commission, and the growth of its stock market, public relations concentrates on press relations and press conferences.

With growth in financial and investor relations expected in Austria, it is also reasonable to assume the public relations agencies, now mostly small shops, will grow and new ones will come in. The three important ones are now seen as Publico, Pubrel, and Press Buro P.R. The latter, with access to Hungary, Czechoslovakia, and Yugoslavia, is capitalizing on the role Vienna plays as a gateway to the East and the West. Burson-

Marsteller is one American company that has opened an office there. In Sweden, Young and Rubicam acquired Hall & Cederquist to form the largest agency in Sweden.

In France, public relations is still in the development stage, although new agencies appear to be springing up daily. The push for 1992 and a trend toward privatization and merger and acquisition activity have led French companies to look more to communications and therefore to public relations agencies and consultants. Francom, Information et Enterprise, Bellescize & Associates (Shandwick), Actis (Ogilvy-Mather P.R.), Burson-Marsteller, and Delaitte & Associates (part of the GCI Group—formerly GreyCom P.R.) are considered the market leaders.[1]

French industry tends to look to agencies that specialize in a particular type of public relations. Given the resistance of newspapers to accept press releases or PR-arranged interviews, it's not surprising that public relations is developing strongly in advising and organizing and in financial and commercial communications.

In Japan, agencies are invariably excellent at implementing programs, arranging parties and the details associated with them, meeting deadlines, and delivering top-quality work, especially in such areas as printing. On the other hand, they tend to be weak on goal setting, creative planning, comprehensive programs for market entry, and selling ideas. American companies are good on the creative side; they more readily understand problems peculiar to American companies in Japan and therefore can be relied upon for problem solving and advice but not as much for media space achievement and introductions to senior people. They do not have the heavy advertising commitments that many Japanese companies have to offset their solicitations for publicity coverage.

The European Commission, one of the largest but certainly not the only international organization based in Brussels, has been the source of income for many public relations firms there. The role of public relations is expanding in Belgium as elsewhere in Europe, although Belgian companies still favor local public relations operations over international ones. As elsewhere, financial public relations is on the rise. Corporate advertising and internal communications have shown importance, perhaps because of the strong M&A activity. Special events (not surprising in light of the number of conventions, seminars, and other meetings held in Brussels), strategic planning, media relations, and social issues management are among the hot topics. Public affairs is another strong specialty, unsurprisingly.

In the Soviet Union, one agency, Sovero, fulfills the functions of both a public relations and an advertising agency. There are no branches of American or European agencies. All aspects of foreign trade are still

---

1. From Chester Burger's *EuroDirectory* (1990).

heavily controlled and regulated by the state, which means that any foreign company that wants to conduct business within the U.S.S.R. must utilize the state-owned and -operated Sovero. From New York, it can be contacted through Amtorg, the Soviet Foreign Trade office. In Moscow, it can be contacted directly.

Sovero's promotional brochure says that it lists "some 60,000 Soviet enterprises in its data base . . . broken down into specific industries, trades and sectors. . . ." By telling it whom you want to reach, Sovero says, it will see that thousands of Soviet organizations receive detailed information about your product. Sovero will arrange symposia, covering every aspect of the arrangement. It will also place your ads in any of "200 trade journals and dozens of trade papers," put together comprehensive advertising campaigns, including broadcast media, and handle direct mail as well as general public relations. In the People's Republic of China, Shanghai Advertising Corporation represents a market of over a billion people. Advertising there is straightforward and unsophisticated. Since virtually all companies are state-owned, public relations is still in the developing stages, along with the economy itself.

The Regrouping of Public Relations Agencies

The growing popularity of internationalism and the advent of a unified European Economic Community are two factors that have inspired hookups of public relations agencies in Europe and elsewhere. International groupings are formed in any of five ways: (1) a cluster of wholly owned subsidiaries, (2) a joint venture, (3) operation of a network through a jointly owned holding company, (4) a voluntary association, and (5) ad hoc arrangements. The pattern is for the lead agency to acquire a client and then to direct the efforts of the other agencies on behalf of the client.

Abroad as at home, smaller agencies are often more appropriate for smaller companies. The fees are more modest and the client is more important than it would be to a larger agency, which translates into your being able to demand more service. On the other hand, their resources may be more limited.

There are four mega-agencies operating in Europe: Saatchi & Saatchi, Burson-Marsteller Inc., Shandwick Inc., and Hill & Knowlton Inc., but they control less than one percent of the total market. Other groups, such as Dewe Rogerson, Edelman, Chester Burger, Pinnacle Group, P.R. Exchange, Worldcom Group, MSL Worldwide, and Leipziger & Partner are consolidating into various types of larger organizations. They use different approaches. Leipziger & Partner, Germany's largest independent public relations firm, forms joint ventures or takes minor equity positions in other companies.

In 1989 Burson-Marsteller acquired Conti Public Relations and now claims to be market leader in Germany. ABC (Dusseldorf, Eurocom) and Leipziger & Partners were previously the top two. Other big ones are Kommunikation & Marketing (Shandwick), Kohtes & Klewes, and Trimedia.

German public relations seems to draw specialist lines on a geographical basis: Bonn is big in public affairs, Frankfurt in tourism and financial public relations, Munich in high-tech, and Hamburg in consumer public relations.[2] As with other European countries, financial public relations is on the rise, especially in investor relations. The Frankfurt-based firm of Charles Barker has a twenty-year reputation in this specialty.

The Worldcom Group is a network of about sixty agencies that service other members' clients on a charge-back arrangement. Burson-Marsteller opens its own offices and staffs them principally with local people. Shandwick, a Britain-based giant, acquires smaller agencies and brings them under its umbrella.

Each arrangement has its advantages and its downside. Opening wholly owned offices is probably the best way to maintain consistency and control while capitalizing on awareness of the agency's name; acquiring local agencies and allowing them to continue to operate largely on their own is expensive and hard to control, but it takes advantage of the local agency's reputation and know-how in its native area; taking equity positions allows operations to continue with virtually no interruption, but loyalty and cultural compatibility are risks. The international network approach sounds good, but there is almost no product control and little name recognition to sell to prospective home-country clients.

Agencies Adjust to Serve Global Corporations

General consensus seems to be that the global path is necessary for survival. As major corporations go, so go the agencies. This does not bode well for small agencies, which find it difficult to bring resources to bear on their activities so that they can compete with the giants. On the other side of the debate, however, are the small, localized agencies that specialize and therefore find themselves employed by the larger agencies to work for the agencies' clients, rather than directly by the client companies themselves.

Large agencies do seem to be getting bigger, whether through acquisition, franchises, group-formation agreement, or other arrangements. As corporations become more global, coordination of their information dissemination becomes more critical. Integration of pro-

---

2. Ibid., p. 185.

motional programs becomes more urgent, both in terms of cost-effectiveness and impact.

For example, an inexperienced company, planning to release news to the press at 1 P.M. New York time—just soon enough for most major daily reporters to write and file their stories before deadline and in time for publication in the next morning's editions—receives a call from Switzerland. A reporter there has heard about the pending news. She argues that if she gets the details of the news immediately, which is 4 P.M. her time, she can still make her deadline. Even though it is only 10 A.M. in New York, corporate officials decide that no harm will be done by recognizing her time zone and releasing the information at what they feel is a proper, even a late, time for the particular reporter. The result is that she files her story based on the news. An hour or two later the news comes across the wires and the American reporters are angry and chagrined that the story was released earlier than promised and that someone else got the jump on them.

Of course, the longer the reach of the public relations agency's arm, the more difficult it is to coordinate service and quality control. Nevertheless, keeping up with clients who move overseas means moving with them, or at the very least finding some satisfactory means of satisfying their international needs.

Billing is handled in a variety of ways in different countries, although in some places there are customary ways to do it. In Japan, billing procedures are similar to those in the United States. The agency may be on retainer, it may bill on a project basis, it may bill on a per hour basis, or it may use any combination of these depending upon the agreement. However, it is common to bill for a large array of extras, which may come as a surprise to an American, who expects them to be included.

Free-lancers, either individuals or associations of individuals, may be a viable answer to your manpower problems. As with agencies, the billing arrangements may be any of the above, but prompt payment is particularly important.

Getting the Most Out of Your Free-Lancers

In considering either agencies or free-lancers, it is a good idea to gather recommendations, interview several, and if possible give them initial small projects to handle. Make sure the reporting line is clear. Put whatever agreement you come to in writing to minimize future misunderstanding. Last, treat them at least as well as you treat your own employees. They, too, are your public relations representatives.

As with your employees, it is important to know what various factors may motivate them to greater effort. Cultural differences often make a difference in priorities and effective motivators. In Japan, for instance, recognition for a job well done is as strong a motivating factor as anywhere else, but recognizing the group effort rather than singling out an individual is far preferable. If commendation of one person is in order, it is usually best to do it privately, just as we in the United States recognize that criticism should be done privately. Financial reward can create a difficult situation. To the surprise of many American managers, the rewarded person may choose to sacrifice the money rather than run the risk of sacrificing the goodwill of his or her fellows by earning more than they do. Although attitudes may be changing, they change slowly. The support and inclusion in the group is of great importance to Japanese workers. Further, salaries are not an individual's private business as they are in the United States; everyone knows what everyone else earns.

Intending to reward an employee and motivate him further, an American expatriate manager of Grace & Co., once raised the pay of one of his Japanese office workers only to find that the employee, rather than thanking him, seemed discomfited and declined the raise. After considerable embarrassment, the Japanese *sarimen* (salaryman) explained that raising his pay above others in the office would undermine the camaraderie they enjoyed and set him apart. This thinking is not as foreign as it may sound; Americans saw much the same attitude in the movie *The Long-Distance Runner*. The central character intentionally lost a race that would have brought much glory because doing so would have severed his friendship with his fellows.

In Hong Kong, an American manager learned that her ambitious employees had a very different idea of what good managing and motivating meant. When one was given an opportunity to fill in for his supervisor, he was less than eager. The reason? "You Americans are always trying to get people to do your jobs," he said. "I have no desire to do my boss's job."[3] Like many self-motivated employees, his intention was to master every aspect of the job he was doing, rather than trying to do someone else's.

In another case, when a Western supervisor "managed by walking around," overworked Chinese secretaries thought their efficiency was in question. When it was announced that help was being hired to lessen their load, those that worked hardest planned to quit. Proud of their ability to handle the workload, they interpreted the move by management as lack of faith in their ability to get the job done.[4]

American mentality says that since the agency is working for the company, the company, as client, gives the orders and is allowed to

3. Anne B. Forrest, "The Continental Divide; Coping With Cultural Gaps," *IABC Communication World* (June 1988), p. 20.
4. Ibid., p. 21.

make demands on the agency. Sometimes the demands may seem excessive, but the client is boss. This approach is not appropriate everywhere. In some places the agency is seen as the benefactor because it is giving the company needed help and assistance. The company is in the inferior position and needs to court the agency.

This situation may be cultural in nature or merely economic. It is similar to the situation when certain goods are so hard to obtain that the buyer must seek out the seller rather than the seller advertising and offering services to draw the customer. This is a situation that exists currently in Russia and many Eastern European nations. Public relations agencies in Tokyo include Tokyu Advertising Agency, Inc., McCann Erickson Hakuhodo, Pacific Press Service, Hill & Knowlton, International Public Relations (IPR), Burson Marsteller, and many others.

Outline Requirements Ahead of Time

What you can expect from agencies and free-lancers varies as much according to the level of public relations sophistication and cultural attitudes as it does according to the individual or agency. Language, even when experts are at work on it, can be a stumbling block. Even the most fluent of translators can encounter difficulty in achieving the right nuance; they often will disagree with each other even when both are equally qualified. Suffice it to say the people you hire may not always be the most competent in their field. Great care needs to be taken.

Whenever you produce an important message, translate a document, or even when you exchange major information verbally, review it and retranslate it. If the original is English and it has been translated into Malay, retranslate it again into English before sending it out. Check not only for correct words, grammar, and facts, but for the nuances and implications, which may have been misunderstood and/or misinterpreted from the original. The same rule applies, of course, if the original language is Swahili, which has been translated into English. Have it checked again after retranslating it into Swahili.

The annual report for the subsidiary office in Japan of a major American multinational was written first in English to ensure that not only the facts but implications of the report accurately reflected the outlook of management. The material was translated into Japanese by a team of six professioinal translators as it was compiled and written in English. Upon completion, it was again rechecked several times. Nevertheless, after printing, one paragraph in the Japanese language version so aroused the ire of the head of the subsidiary that he had all 60,000 copies destroyed before distribution, the offending paragraph retranslated, and the entire edition run again. After publication he had had his secretary retranslate the entire Japanese language edition into English. He felt that his secretary would understand the text in a way similar to other "average" Japanese and that the implications of that one paragraph had given her an incorrect idea of some of the company's activities. From then on, all materials were retranslated. One moral of this story may be to have a different agency do the retranslation if at all possible. Words are the first cross-cultural barrier; even translation does not always solve the problem that words may present because the background of cultural understanding may be different. Even when English is the common language in both countries, the meaning of words can differ. It's also a common failing to assume that because the language is the same, the culture is too. Very often, there are significant differences.

The physical form of words on a printed page can cause problems. In headlines, marketing communications, and advertising, be wary. In some languages, upper and lower case letters have different meanings.

Translation and interpretation are highly specialized skills. Literacy and fluency in a second language is no guarantee of translation or interpretion capability. Every language has nuances that escape the non-professional and can seriously distort the meaning of what has been said. The best translators have successful track records and come through personal recommendations and professional sources. Public relations agencies customarily have a roster of capable translators that they employ. Nearly every country has translation agencies (whose reputations should of course be checked out before they are used). Free-lancers are fine, but should come with excellent credentials.

Interpreters, and even translators, should understand the basics of your business. Few professionals who work in the political area can be expected to do a fine job of interpreting in the financial sector, for instance. The skills are distinct and specialized. Perhaps translators can be likened to writers, who in virtually every case need editors to bring out their best. You'll also find that translators need editors. Their ability to establish accurate meaning in another language does not mean that they can write well.

Although the editing requirement is more or less stringent depending upon the languages involved and to some extent the skill of the translator, material to be printed in Japanese, for instance, almost invariably demands a Japanese translator. The reason is that written Japanese is so complicated as to require nearly lifelong and continued exposure to it to get it correct to a sufficient standard for publication. A Japanese translator may be able to write sufficiently well to do a good job in English because the written language is comparatively simple, but he or she may still have trouble with colloquial expressions if the piece is informal.

The skill of a translator can be checked only by having several of his or her translated articles retranslated into the original language and then rechecked independently. If an interpreter is needed, go through a similar process verbally. Although most interpreters can translate, their rate of pay is often higher. Most translators do not do interpreting.

Summary of Steps Toward New Market Entry

If a formula had to be developed to ensure the most positive impact in tackling overseas ventures, it might be found in the following Strategic Six Steps. Boiled down, your public relations activities in preparing for entry and your initial approach into a foreign culture can be summed up this way:

Strategic Six Steps

1. *Research* the cultural, political, ethical, and social climates as well as the business environment thoroughly.
2. *Reveal* potential problems and endeavor to turn unpromising differences to an advantage.
3. *Recognize* who your friends are and the importance of favorable initial personal contacts; they can affect your business for a long time to come.
4. *Rehearse* the introduction of your headquarters management executives to the local area.
5. *Reliability* is essential; it leads to credibility and the reputation you need for long-term success.
6. *Recommend* entry strategy to your management, well integrated with corporate goals and marketing strategy.

To these, a seventh step may be added, especially for communicators and translators:

7. *Review and reaffirm.*

7

Recruiting and Hiring

Recruiting is often a problem for American companies abroad, especially if the company is not large and well-known, with an established reputation. Unless the population is underemployed, recruiting good people can be a problem.

As a newcomer, the foreign company is often regarded with suspicion. Prospective employees have no prior reference as to how the company will treat its employees, whether it will understand local and community concerns, or even if the new company will grow and prosper, providing long-term employment.

Job changing is far more common and frequent in the United States than in virtually any other country. The tendency of American companies to lay off workers with little or no notice and little compensation is not a common practice elsewhere, nor has it gone unnoticed. Despite these obstacles, there are certain steps you, the foreign company representative, can take to make your recruiting practices go more smoothly.

Sources for Potential Candidates

Personal recommendations from people you have become friendly with through your networking efforts are invaluable as you staff your upper ranks. These connections will continue to be valuable well into the future and should be strengthened with time. By creating a strong bond with your employees at every level, management or staff, you enhance the reputation of the company and increase the interest of employees in bringing in qualified associates.

Personal Recommendation Implies Responsibility

In most countries, hiring employees recommended by mutual friends carries a strong implicit obligation on both sides to act fairly and honestly to avoid embarrassing the mutual friend. In Japan, the employer and employee have an obligation not only to each other but have incurred a debt to the mutual friend that introduced them. Such a recommendation, because of the inherent obligations, is not given lightly. The bond that usually develops between employer and employee becomes strong and contributes to the stability of the overall work environment.

In France, the United Kingdom, and many other countries, the level of authority an employee can aspire to is predetermined by the school he (or she) has attended, which in many cases is also predetermined by who the parents are. Potential employees recommended by current employees are therefore likely to be of the same class, with similar promotion potential.

Class is not the dirty word in every country that it is in the United States. Because most societies are less flexible than our own in terms of hiring and promoting, the judgment of business associates, other employees, and clients needs to be considered as well as the ability of the individual in question. At the same time, American managers need to be careful about their own prejudices and refuse to allow their perception of local custom to justify prejudicial decisions in hiring and promotion beyond those that are absolutely necessary in the local environment. In today's world, where nearly every country pursues human rights as a matter of ideal, if not practical application, American managers can often afford to set a higher standard than local managers are able to, both because they are foreign to the environment and because Americans have a reputation abroad for actively pursuing equal opportunity. However, foreign managers need to talk tactfully and step softly.

Recruiters exist in virtually every developed country. While this may seem to be the easiest means for staffing up, recruiters are often expensive and may or may not have the best contacts. Those whom you are most likely to feel comfortable with and expect to understand your needs best are often "outsiders" to your particular overseas locale, because recruiting is still a new business in many countries. Many American-based recruiting firms staff their overseas offices with professional, influential, local nationals. This can give you the best of both worlds: recruiters who are skillful at understanding what you want and can deal knowledgeably with high-level prospects with top international credentials.

Government Officials Can Be Helpful

By making yourself known to government officials in overseas areas, you can avail yourself of their knowledge and assistance. Your preparatory work will have indicated the employable human resources in your new location. Guidance on employment practices, restrictions, labor rules, unions, pensions and retirement, insurance, and benefits are available from government offices and from expatriate Americans and their organizations, such as the Chamber of Commerce. Very often the American Chamber of Commerce will have a system set up to assist managers abroad, such as a monthly newsletter, that briefly lists qualified prospective employees whose résumés are available on request.

Recruiting Recent Graduates Is Common

Universities are another source of promising employees, just as they are in the United States. You may have to actively recruit by visiting campuses to organize student interviews; or student or campus officials may initiate contacts with you.

As your image development and corporate awareness efforts take effect, one evidence of your success should be greater ease in attracting and hiring new employees. One of your objectives is likely to be to generate a greater interest in local citizens to work for your company as the company grows. As you learn local customs and human resources practices, find out the traditional and most common way to recruit. Then judge whether it would be beneficial for you.

Japanese companies stage impressive recruiting drives to attract the college students who graduate in March. The school year there runs from April to March with about a five-week vacation from the end of July through August and one month from mid-December to mid-January.

Major companies hire only current graduates. Because lifetime employment, at least for men, is the rule in major companies, the power of the companies' future work force and leadership depends upon the effectiveness of their efforts at this time. Although the large companies put as much effort into the recruiting process as do the smaller ones, they have fewer worries about filling their quotas—they are swamped with interview requests.

The dream of nearly every graduate is to work for a Mitsubishi or a Sumitomo. American companies, if they are highly reputable and have a history of treating their employees well, will attract some of the Sumitomo, Mitsubishi, and other major corporate rejects. These will be well-educated, motivated people. The American company will have a highly educated, well-connected, future managerial work force. However, where small Japanese companies find it difficult to recruit from top-levels schools, most American companies find it even harder. For a few students, and a very few, the international aspect of working for an American company will be attractive, but not if they get an offer from a major Japanese multinational. Qualified women, however, may choose the American company because of what they perceive as superior opportunities for advancement.

Job hunters in Japan look for corporate growth and stability, a compatible corporate culture, good pay and benefits, and the industry, which is not much different from what they look for in other countries. Year after year, the most popular companies with new recruits are among the top fifty corporations.

While Japanese recruiting practices by major corporations are very rigid, even French, British, and other European countries hire their managerial ranks in nearly as rigid a pattern. Fast trackers come from certain schools after having passed prior "cream separator" milestones set up by the educational system itself.

Southeast Asia may be among the most flexible regions in hiring because of the previous British presence that tended to disrupt previous power structures and because of current economic levels. Foreign companies are already seen as desirable.

The Company Is Part of the Community

The split between business and private life, so common in the United States, is hard to find in Japan, as it also is in many other countries. The corporation is an integral part of the community, and often the influence of the corporation extends even to the family of the wage earner.

Consistent with the group philosophy mentioned above, Japanese identify strongly with the company they work for, mentioning their company before their names when they introduce themselves, for example, "Matsushita no Sato Hideki" or "Matsushita Company's Hideki Sato."

The company in Japan is not considered an impersonal master to which one devotes eight or so hours a day and then retires to one's real life. It is thought of as a living organism that transmits its values from one generation to another via corporate philosophy. The philosophy is generally a set of ideals and moral injunctions stated by the founder and may be written or unwritten. Dentsu, the world's largest advertising company, had its "Ten Spartan Rules" written in 1951 by its president and bases its corporate philosophy on them. At YKK, the world's largest zipper manufacturer, the "endless recycling of goodness" is the principle adhered to.[1]

It is easy to see that American companies, which offer promotion

1. David J. Lu, "The Endless Recycling of Goodness," *Across the Board*, Vol. 25, No. 5 (May 1988), p. 57.

based on merit rather than seniority, which give no assurance of permanent employment, and which offer freedom rather than the familial protection so comforting to most Japanese, would attract mostly Japanese who are outside the usual mold.

Women Can Be a Valuable Resource Pool

Recruiting qualified women is one way American companies can staff up with intelligent, well-educated employees. Many Japanese women, knowing their chances for advancement in most Japanese corporations are still limited, will opt for an American or British corporation, where their language ability will be valued and their potential for promotion is somewhat better.

In the past Japanese women worked for several years and then retired to have a family. Nowadays, most couples have only one or two children and the women are eager to return to work as soon as possible. Devising a schedule that incorporates part-time workers to do full-time jobs or applies flextime will increase the hiring advantage.

The Japanese Equal Employment Opportunity Law of 1985, which became effective in April 1986, prohibits gender discrimination with regard to recruitment, hiring, promotion, training, and job assignment.[2] Although it is not common to see women in senior positions at corporate giants, newcomers to Japan should be cautioned not to impose their own biases and ideas of role modeling on another society.

Women in Japan are highly educated and fulfill a vital role in cultural strength. Their influence in offices is often much wider than it appears to be on the surface. It is certainly strong on the domestic side. Women are also part of the labor supply pattern that has made lifetime employment (for men) possible in so many large companies. Nevertheless, it is true that there are few women in high corporate positions although they often run family businesses and frequently start their own.

In Singapore, women are hired and promoted on a basis of equality. Women are as well educated as men and tend to hold positions of responsibility. Even Japanese companies have been known to hire Singaporean women for responsible positions in that country.

In EC countries there has been a net growth in the working population since the early 1970s, largely as a result of more women entering the work force. Efforts are being made by the European Parliament

2. Linda N. Edwards, "Equal Employment Opportunity in Japan: A View From the West," *Industrial & Labor Relations Review*, Vol. 41, No. 2 (January 1988), pp. 240–250.

to promote change in favor of women, who still often lack training equal to that of men. The parliament is aiming for equality in education and training, equality in hiring and promotion, equality with respect to new technology, sharing responsibilities and developing attitudes, and fuller enforcement of the existing EC law. The Women's Employment and Equality Office and a women's information service have been set up to maintain close contact with other organizations that work on behalf of women.[3]

Outdated prejudices also limit the many American companies that are reluctant to relocate American executive women abroad to staff or head up their ventures in foreign countries.

Many companies ignore half the potential pool of talent for overseas posting by refusing to send women. In a study on the role of North American women as expatriate managers, 686 Canadian and American companies were surveyed. Of 13,338 expatriate managers, 402 (or only 3 percent) were women.[4] Most of these were on current or recent assignment.

Corporate executives are clearly reluctant to post women to overseas assignments. They are concerned about the women's safety, their social lives, their willingness to go, and prejudice on the part of businesspeople overseas. They are worried about what other executives and companies may think of them if they send a woman. They are concerned that a woman may not have sufficient status or enough aggressiveness to make a necessary impression.

Given that many areas of the United States are as threatening to life and limb as many overseas cities, that women have been shown to adjust more easily to restrictive mores that may inhibit their social lives, and that a great many are eager to go abroad, the only rational reason not to send women would seem to be prejudice or fear of it.

Research shows that in virtually all the countries of the world including Asia, American women are not only as well qualified, but as easily accepted in their business roles in the local area as men.[5] This research indicates that a woman from any restrictive culture—even a minimally restricting one—is treated more equally in a foreign culture than in her own, and also more equally than the women indigenous to the culture she enters. Title, background, and support from parent company management are as important to her status and success abroad as they would be to a man. My own experience supports this research. Many women also report that their difference becomes an asset; they find that doors are opened to them that would ordinarily remain closed to many expatriate businessmen.

3. "Women in the E.C.," *Europe*, Issue 278 (July/August 1988), pp. 30–33.
4. Nancy J. Adler and Dafa N. Israeli, *Women in Management Worldwide* (New York: M. E. Sharpe, Inc., 1988), p. 233.
5. Op. cit., pp. 235–247.

Overcoming Cultural Differences

Recruiting and hiring in any foreign country present some of the same problems that hiring foreign-born workers in the United States may present. American employers often try to hire English-speaking workers to make their own lives easier. This is particularly true for office staff; similarly, English-speaking workers may be particularly attracted to American companies. It is easy to overestimate an individual's overall abilities because the grasp of English is exemplary, or fail to appreciate an individual's stronger qualities because of an awkwardness in expressing ideas.

This problem can extend into the work atmosphere and play a part in evaluation. As mentioned in Chapter 6, the ability to understand words does not always indicate a full understanding of the meaning, especially when it is implied or suggested. In addition to missing nuances or failing to appreciate the impact of a statement because of dissimilar cultural environments, people often have difficulty in admitting they do not fully understand; pretending comprehension is a common face-saver.

Cultural differences, such as an emphasis on modesty, may prohibit an individual from accurately recounting his successes, although he has the words to do so. An unperceptive manager may never realize the problem and uncover the real story, yet such lack of awareness can have a snowball effect and create problems with morale and loyalty.

In Thailand, for instance, a public relations agency photographer assigned to shoot a clutch of foreign (American) VIPs arriving at the airport returned with some fine shots. The expatriate manager gave little thought to the pictures until she received a call from an editor at the *Bangkok Post* asking for copies. The paper's photographers had been unable to get any decent shots, and described a bad dream: The lighting had been horrendous, the confusion constant with crowds fighting to see the guests, the airport guards restrictive, and the guests themselves cantankerous and disheveled after a long trip.

The photographer came up with good, printable shots only because he was creative, tactful, and very determined. The manager, but for information from a third party, would have considered it just an average job. Considering the conditions, it was outstanding, but traditional modesty kept the photographer from giving any hint of the difficulty of the job.

Essential Internal Public Relations

If the need for public relations efforts inside the organization is not recognized at the top, no amount of effort on your part will make much difference. Important in any organization, internal public relations is vital to a company operating abroad where the mere presence of outsiders, especially when they are at or near the top of the organization, causes stress. Good relations start with treating employees fairly, creating an atmosphere of inclusion, and making a real effort to keep them informed. The larger the company grows, the more critical is a planned internal campaign to keep employees informed and motivated.

Traditionally, internal public relations is handled through any or all of several means: formal communications such as house organs, newsletters, and video programs; informal means such as "management by walking around"; or conversations, meetings, and special events such as parties, picnics, and combined business and social gatherings. Even necessary regular activities such as sales meetings and management meetings, usually open only to selected groups and not under the umbrella of internal public relations, can be a useful tool to encourage employee participation and overall awareness. Good internal public relations is often expressed in an alertness to cultural differences and divergent ways of thinking. In one case, the vice-president of a U.S. company abroad believed that certain problems could be corrected if there were more openness and communication between hierarchical levels. He visited plants abroad and strongly encouraged shop foremen and middle managers to "pick up the phone and talk to me anytime about what you need, what's going wrong, whatever." The employees nodded in agreement, but the result was less openness and communication. The VP was operating out of an American mentality in a foreign culture. Instead of recognizing that they may have had alternative ways of interacting, he assumed that the American values of democracy and informality could apply. By asking them to ignore established hierarchies, he violated their sense of propriety and dampened their interest in further communications with him.[6]

Another American company in Portugal sent in trainers to work with middle managers who spoke English in the workplace. The trainers used approaches that stressed individual goal setting, simulation games and role playing, small group discussion, and other "active learning" methods. The program was postponed after the trainees complained. The training group had brought with them American biases about teaching. They hadn't realized that their methods were acceptable only in certain restricted settings and that their typically American style clashed with the cultural view of the managers that people learn in respectful silence. Learners were viewed as clearly subordinate to teachers and therefore didn't share duties such as setting learning goals.[7]

6. Cornelius Grove and Constance Franklin, "Using the Right Fork Is Just the Beginning: Intercultural Training in the Global Era," *International Public Relations Review*, Vol. 13, No. 1 (1990), p. 14.
7. Ibid.

Many companies, fearful that open internal communications may cause employees to unify against management, discourage large group activities or participation by the members of one division in the activities of another. In such a company, employees are generally distrustful of management activities and job security is slight. On the contrary, when management is confident enough to encourage interaction among employees, the result is almost invariably positive. When employees are encouraged to understand what other divisions are doing and when they get to know other employees on an informal basis, especially when organizational structure has encouraged this to occur, morale increases and overall communications, including that moving upward from employees to management, increases.

Employees Should Be Represented on Boards of Directors

One type of employee participation that has seen increasing application abroad is worker/union representation on corporate boards of directors. The employees on the board are involved with policymakers on issues such as capital investments, products, and markets. Their effectiveness in representing employee interests depends on the way in which they were selected, their training, and their acceptance by the board.

There can be conflicts of interest, of course. These workers face problems of dual loyalty, role conflict, and demands on either side for confidentiality.

Keep in mind that each of your employees is a representative of the company, positive or negative. Especially as a newcomer, much of your reputation in the foreign environment is based upon what your employees say. However good your product or service, however well funded your external public relations efforts, if your employees are disgruntled and complaining, word will get around. This is particularly important in your recruiting efforts. As previously mentioned, your best candidates come through recommendations of satisfied current employees. Recognizing this, many companies in the United States have programs in place to encourage an internal recruiting effort. The same type of program can be applied overseas.

Internal Relations Vary by Country and by Company

If your operation abroad is large enough, major responsibility for internal public relations may be assumed by the human resources department, although this depends on the company and the culture. In Japan, the relationship between employer and employee is seen as vital to the success of the company. The division that watches over it, general affairs, is often the division in charge of what we call public relations/communications as well.[8]

General affairs is invariably the largest and most influential department in Japanese companies. It oversees the welfare of employees in their personal lives as well as business lives. It facilitates training and education, organizes hobby and language classes, assists employees with domestic problems, aids as matchmaker for marriages, and in general sees no conflict of interest at all in watching out for the welfare of the employee as well as for the company's interests; they are one and the same.

Human resources are seen as vital to the company's survival and success. In a Japanese company's accounting books, personnel is a fixed cost. In view of the prevalent idea of *nenko,* or lifetime employment in major companies, this is understandable,[9] but even in small companies where *nenko* does not exist, the value of the employee is recognized.

The rights and resources of employees are taken very seriously in many other countries as well; European countries are no exception. We will discuss this further in Chapter 11. In terms of your enterprise abroad, your employees are clearly your most important resource. Have you made them assets or enemies?

8. James S. Browman, "Japanese Management: Personnel Policies in the Public Sector," *Public Personnel Management,* Vol. 13, No. 3 (Fall 1984), p. 197.
9. N. Ellen Cooke, Dennis Briscoe, and Robert F. O'Neil, "Fixed vs. Variable Labor Costs: The Nenko Path to Higher Profits," *Personnel,* Vol. 59, No. 1 (January/February 1982), p. 71.

8

Recognizing and Handling Cultural Differences

Picture yourself in Thailand, flattered that one of your staff has invited you to his home. A rather recent arrival to a new land, you are making every effort to be friendly and sociable. You've brought a gift to thank him for his hospitality—a beautifully honed set of steak knives, as you've heard he loves American-style steak.

He shows you into his living room and gestures for you to be seated. You take a seat opposite him, settle back, cross your legs, and begin to talk. Soon his small son wanders in. Amazed at the fair-haired visitor, he shyly comes closer to look you over. You comment on how cute he is, speak to the child, and pat his head to show your approval.

Meanwhile, a maid enters with a tray of drinks. As she approaches, she drops to her knees, scuffles forward, and places drinks on the table before you. Taken by surprise, you manage to stifle a plea for her to get off the floor. She retreats and reappears with what appears to be a large plate of fried chicken and some other finger food, places a few pieces on a plate, which she hands to you, and repeats the process with your host. You nibble on a piece, and then as you reach for another you glance down. Staring up at you is the beady eye of the chicken, whose severed, fried head has been put on the plate of you, the honored guest. You shudder, repress a scream, and put the plate on the table, too upset to eat anything further.

In due time, you thank your host, bid him good-bye, and leave. The next day at work, your host is unmistakably cold. Worse yet, you hear whispers behind your back. What's wrong?

Good Intentions Sometimes Mean Poor Results

Sometimes, good intentions alone are just not enough. Although your host may have recognized your friendly spirit and eager efforts to please, he has his own cultural concepts to deal with, his own prejudices to overcome. Generous as he may try to be—and not everyone is inclined to make even that effort—you committed some serious breaches of etiquette. When you crossed your legs, you may have been totally unaware of the fact that your foot was pointed at him. He noticed. In Thailand, the foot is considered the lowest part of the body in spiritual as well as physical terms. Pointing this low-level, earth-bound instrument at him had an implied significance. He was gravely insulted.

The head is nearest the gods and only to be touched by those closest to a person and of clearly no danger—and then only when necessary, such as in washing the hair. Yet you touched the most sacred part of his son's body—an act for which you might have been killed many years ago and that even now may have serious consequences in some rural areas.

Even the gift was a serious mistake. Surely anyone who gives a knife to another person cannot be motivated by goodwill. A knife is an instrument of attack and violence—something you give to a person you wish dead.

While you managed to stifle a protest, you should have been aware that by keeping her head lower than yours and your host's, the maid was showing respect. Earlier we mentioned class levels in other countries. The maid, while not considered an inferior person, is lower in status. She was serving her employer and his guests and her posture indicated proper respect. Whether or not you ate your food seems irrelevant in light of your other faux pas, but in some countries leaving food on your plate would be considered a gross indication of ingratitude.

The United States is a jumble of many cultures adapted to a new land. We are, and are proud of being, perhaps the most open society in the world. Even many standards of proper behavior that were required a generation ago do not now apply. While Thailand may tend toward the more rigid end of the ladder compared to others, virtually every country has its strictures, some more important than others.

Table Manners Vary in Importance and Style

In China, table manners are definitely flexible. The table is a place to eat, enjoy, talk, and share. It is relaxed and bound by few rules. It does have some, however. A bowl of food cleaned of every morsel says to the hostess that you haven't had enough to eat, while leaving some food suggests that your hostess has been generous in supplying more food than you can possibly consume. Until diets became fashionable in the Unites States, food left on the plate told the hostess that you didn't like it. Now it could merely mean that you're on a diet, or it could still mean you don't like it, in which case the hostess is not expected to take offense. At a Chinese banquet, a bowl of rice is served as the penultimate course. Again, if you eat it, you insult the host by implying that you are still hungry.

In England, dinner has more requirements of those dining. Use the salad fork for salad, the dessert spoon for dessert. The courses come in a certain order. At a formal dinner, you converse with the person on your right during the first half, with the person on your left during the second. You wait for the hostess to take the first bite. If you do not know the difference between a fish knife and a butter knife, you are considered inadequate to be present in proper company. Not much leeway is granted you for being a stranger.

To slurp your soup would immediately relegate you to barbarian status—even if you were from Japan, where the only proper way to eat noodles in broth is to slurp them.

In the United States, the United Kingdom, and most Western countries, strict protocol accompanies use of a napkin; in Japan and other Asian countries, napkins are not used. In France, bread is put on the table rather than a bread-and-butter plate and is usually not buttered. It is broken, not cut, and what is taken is eaten, never left. In the United States, bread requires a bread-and-butter plate, or at the very least the edge of a dinner plate, anywhere but at a picnic.

Children are not taken to good restaurants in France, whereas in China and Japan they are seen everywhere. Smoking and canned music are equally unwelcome in fine French restaurants, despite the prevalence of a smoking public. For a child in France to call an adult by his or her first name is just *ça se fait* ("that is not done"). Adults are *Madame* or *Monsieur* or *Mademoiselle* or whatever the case may be.

The French table is a place of honor. You do not leave it, except for dire emergencies.

In Japan, if you pay a visit to an acquaintance, you will be served refreshments your host or hostess thinks you will enjoy. A guest who is asked if she would like tea, or cola, or juice, or coffee is embarrassed to reply, and in most cases will refuse anything at all. Even when presented with a cup of tea, for instance, you are supposed to refuse three times before accepting. Such formalities tend to try the patience of Americans even when they know the rules.

Both food and drink are popular gifts in Japan, especially when they are gourmet items. Gifts of good whiskey, a melon, or jars of jam are greeted with delight. In the Middle East, such presents would suggest to the recipient that he was too poor to buy his own food.

Social manners are as important as business manners, which are probably the first you will encounter. Some you can learn by attending classes, by talking, reading, and listening. Others you learn only by trial and error.

In Japan, you may enter a business meeting and humbly sit yourself halfway down the table, politely leaving the head of the table for the senior member of the Japanese company you are visiting, only to find that you have usurped his seat and left him the least important one in the room.

You hand him your card in a friendly manner, trusting your casual charm will be as engaging to him as it is to the folks back home, only to find out later that you should have given it to him while you were standing, presenting it with both hands in a dignified manner, and bowing, if possible, while doing so. That you did it your way may or may not harm your negotiations, but it will brand you a barbarian in the same way that not knowing the right fork will in England.

While interaction among businesspeople in Germany is similar to that in the United States, dress is more formal and a subtle recognition of proper social/business status is important to harmonious relations. Promptness, meeting deadlines, and accuracy are more highly valued than in some other societies. France has resisted the American innovation of breakfast meetings, considering them uncivilized. Some inroads have been made, however, and rather than cut into the treasured two-hour-or-more lunch, many French businesspeople are warming to breakfast meetings.

"In-House" Manners Can Be Surprising

In Hong Kong and other Asian areas, employees may be reluctant to "climb the ladder." They often prefer to stay in the job they are doing and become thorough experts at it. Dedication is common, and the concern, offers of assistance, and even "management by walking around" may be miscontrued as distrust, interference, and nagging.

Personal dignity or maintaining "face" is widely honored all over Asia and sometimes takes forms that are bewildering to Americans. At a meeting in Hong Kong where a Chinese employee was reporting on work her group had done that had won recognition in an international design competition, she was applauded at the close of the presentation. The applause was led, however, by American staff. A British staff member later observed that the applause was inappropriate and embarrassing, bringing a cheerleading mentality into a professional atmosphere.[1] In a

1. Anne B. Forrest, "The Continental Divide: Coping With Cultural Gaps," *IABC Communications World* (June 1988), pp. 20–23.

similar situation in Japan, an American manager wanted to recognize the contributions of Japanese staff members over the past months and chose a company party as the place to single out individuals for recognition. The result was discomfort and embarrassment, which went unrecognized by the American manager. The Japanese whom the manager's spotlight focused on were as embarrassed for their workmates who were ignored as they were for themselves when singled out. In their minds, it was all a result of team efforts.

While business manners are flexible to some extent—Japanese business associates will be happy to accept your handshake rather than a deep bow from the waist, and Thais are not likely to expect you to perform the *wai*, a shallow bow with hands clasped prayer-fashion in front of the face—in other ways you will be expected to adapt to their habits. Showing up without a business card, for instance, is a major faux pas. It should be presented, as should a gift, with both hands, and with your name facing the recipient. When you receive a card, look at it with interest. Failing to pay attention suggests to its giver that you don't care.

Asia is still a conservative place that honors the dignity of the individual. Don't invade the other person's territory, either physically or psychologically. By that I mean keep your hands to yourself; be prompt; use surnames and titles, unless invited to do otherwise; look for body language and realize that "no" can be expressed in a number of ways that are just as definite, even though the word itself is not used.

Gift-giving has its own rules. Certainly you should avoid "carrying coals to Newcastle." Just as knives and swords are inappropriate for Japan, where such implements are probably the finest in the world, the "made in . . ." label on the bottom of your gift should not say ". . . Japan" if that's where you're heading. Knives (and scissors) are inappropriate gifts for South American countries where they imply that you are cutting off your relationship with the recipient. The suggestion is similar in Thailand.

Just as you shouldn't give a knife to a Thai, don't give a clock to a Chinese. It suggests, in Chinese, a phrase that sounds like "to care for a dying patient." Flowers, which seem innocuous in the United States, may carry many different innuendos in other places. The type and the color have different significations that you should know before you give them, much like white lilies in the United States are appropriate for funerals. In Europe, red roses given to a woman connote a romantic interest, a questionable gesture if she's married. The presentation of a gift can be as important as the gift itself. Properly wrapped and presented, it says that you care. Red is celebration color in Japan; red wrapping there is fine. Somewhere else it may symbolize blood. In the United States, white wrapping paper is an old tradition; in Japan it may suggest mourning. Don't be tempted to take the easy way out and not wrap the gift at all. Presenting a naked gift is almost as bad as presenting a naked guest at the door and suggests an offhand attitude.[2]

Drinking is a popular pastime practically everywhere. When your business partner in Taipei joyously proclaims *"Ganbei"* (gone-BEI) as you join him at his favorite nightspot, it means the same as *kampai* (com-PIE) in Tokyo or *konbae* (guhn-BEH) in Seoul: Bottoms up!

While understanding the dos and don'ts in a foreign culture is important, even vital, being able to think from inside that culture is what you're aiming for. Culture is a collective identity, just as personality is an individual identity. Evaluating behavior and making decisions in a foreign culture must be done not from an American cultural viewpoint, but within the mental framework of the culture itself.

Language in a Multinational Environment

It has been and still is true that English is the common language of business. It is also true, however, that speaking only English can put the American businessperson at a disadvantage in a multicultural setting. Rhonda Snowaert, a spokeswoman for the Coalition for the Advancement of Foreign Languages and International Studies (a two-year nonprofit project sponsored by the Ford, Rockefeller, Hewlett, and James S. McDonnell foundations and based in Washington, D.C. to formulate language-instruction policy) says, "It's not to say that you need to be internationally competent so that you can beat the Japanese, but so that you can understand them and work efficiently in the marketplace."[3]

Perhaps more important than language is sensitivity to different cultural, ethical, and social values. The assumption often still seems to be that everyone speaks English and conducts business the way we do. "Many times, (that) cultural insensitivity will mean the difference between a contract and no contract," says Don Penrose, an assistant professor of German at Gustavus Adolphus College in St. Peter, Minnesota.[4]

When it comes to language, the simplest mistakes can be laughable—unless, of course, your money or your reputation is at stake. One writer tells about a promotion in Germany. The company wanted the world to know about its wide new range of products in Germany and

2. C. Banum and N. Wolniansky, "Glitches in Global Gift Giving," *Management Review* (April 1989), p. 61.
3. Lisa W. Foderaro, "Tongue Untied," *New York Times Special Supplement: As the World Learns*, p. 20.
4. Ibid.

hired an agency to handle it. The translation of the American copy was done by a service bureau and placed in various German magazines. Executives assumed the agency had screened the ad, only to discover after the ads were printed and distributed that "whole new *range* of product" had been translated as "a whole new *stove* of product."[5]

A multinational advertising agency executive, writing on the subject of careful translation, mentioned that all the local problems should be "tabled." In Britain, *tabling* means "discussing it now." In the United States, of course, *tabling* means postponing it.[6]

In a not dissimilar gaffe made in Japan, company executives were in Japan to list on the Tokyo Stock Exchange. They had the requisite mementos made up, to be inscribed with "NCNB Tokyo Stock Exchange, 1987" translated into Japanese. In the nick of time they discovered that the word that had been chosen for "stock" referred to a stockyard rather than a securities exchange.

Language, of course, is vital to communication, but it is seldom just a vehicle for expressing ideas. The cultural values and sense of identity of people are closely knitted into the language they speak.

Belgium, the world's center for global organizations, is a divided country, linguistically speaking. As in Canada, where the Quebequois zealously guard their mother tongue (French), Belgians from the north of the country (Flanders) guard their language, Dutch, and the special identity that accompanies it. In Wallonia, the southern area of Belgium, French is just as protectively used and defended. Meanwhile, English is the language of choice for millions of visitors to the country.

The fact that many Belgians speak English in no way obviates the need for a stranger doing business in the country to be sensitive to the personal, political, and protective attitudes expressed by Belgians in regard to the language they call their own. It is a sensitive subject and one that needs to be dealt with so delicately that it sometimes dictates the restaurants one eats in or the clubs one dances in. Needless to say, it would be an important consideration for public relations professionals there.

Mistakes resulting from language misunderstanding often incur a deeper cultural significance. In one situation, a Japanese staff member ordered filing cabinets. When the American manager saw them, he recognized that there had been a misunderstanding and the office had ended up with fifty, not fifteen, filing cabinets. He pointed out the mistake to the employee as tactfully as possible and directed that it be

5. Henry H. Rodkin, *The Ultimate Overseas Business Guide for Growing Companies* (Homewood, Ill.: Dow Jones-Irwin, 1990), p. 95.
6. Thomas Garbett, *How to Build a Corporation's Identity and Project Its Image* (Lexington, Mass.: Lexington Books, 1988), p. 229.

corrected. The manager, Jim, felt satisfied that he handled the problem diplomatically; the employee, Yoshida-san, when asked how he felt about his new American boss, said, "I never want to work with him again."

Returning the thirty-five cabinets posed a real problem for Yoshida-san, but proper manners and the desire for harmony prevented him from saying so. He was then caught between trying to carry out the instructions of his boss and maintaining good relations with his supplier. The relationship with the supplier had taken years to build up and asking him to take back the cabinets would cause discomfort and mar the harmony. Jim needed to be more sensitive to the clues Yoshida-san was sending him, such as the sign that indicates the impossible is being asked, or the averted eyes that indicate trouble. How one feels *(honne)* and what one says publicly *(tatamae)* are often different. Foreigners need to be able to interpret the difference.[7]

Japan is only one of numerous cultures that place as much importance on the words that are spoken as on those that remain unspoken. The status and position of the speaker, her relationship to the others, the context, and body language add up to human relationships that predominate over words.

Americans use colorful and explicit words; we expect people to say what they mean. In other cultures, saying what you mean may be considered crass and even insulting. The listener is expected to pick up the proper signals. This is often true of developing nations where personal interaction supersedes words and even titles. Face-to-face meetings are important. Letters and faxes may be left unanswered. Communications (and business) are very personal.

Even Americans who are cognizant of the need for awareness of cultural differences tend to assume that people they hire will do fine in another culture if they just speak the language. They ignore the realities of life that say that some people are more acceptable, more responsive, more empathetic to the people of another culture whether or not they speak the language. To know how to behave, to understand the courtesies and subtleties of the culture, are as important, and probably more important, than a knowledge of the language.

Business Abroad Requires Foreknowledge

Alfred H. Fuchs, dean of the faculty at Bowdoin College in Brunswick, Maine, notes that students who plan to do business abroad ought to know "what is expected of the individual and how one behaves—and

7. Jennifer May and David Wagner, "Role Playing for Success," *PHP Intersect* (November 1988), p. 41.

not just Emily Post—but really know the culture, the trade practices and something of the language."[8]

You may not know the local language when you arrive, or even be able to learn it well during your stay, but there are some words that are indispensible: *please* and *thank you*, for instance. Other basics, such as the words for *rest room*, *right*, *left*, and a few others that will allow for simple directions, are easy to learn and will make your daily life easier. Learning the language may seem low on the ladder of priorities at times considering all that you need to do, but Robert L. Carothers, chancellor of the Minnesota State University system, has some wise words to help you keep your priorities straight: "You can *buy* in any language," he says. "You *sell* in the language of the customer." Whether it's words, ideas, brand recognition, product or service, *selling* is what the public relations professional and the marketing executive are ultimately doing.

Spanish and English are the most widely spoken languages in the world in terms of numbers of people who speak them, but the utility of Spanish is still far more limited in the business world than that of English, except in Spanish-speaking countries. English is the international business language, widely used in most parts of the world, including Europe and Asia, as the common language even when it is the second language to both parties. Although Canada, the United States, Australia, and other English-speaking nations are unlikely to ever be members of the EC, English is still regarded as the common means for business communications in Europe.

There is no denying that a knowledge of the local language can be immeasurably helpful. Whether it is vital depends on the country and your particular situation. Certainly for a public relations professional it is more important than for the average businessperson, who can often make-do with only English.

Beyond a certain point, however, it is difficult to understand the subtleties and sensitivities of a culture without a knowledge of the language. One school of thought holds that as the United States diminishes in its dominance, English is likely to become less common for business usage, making command of a second or third language more important for Americans.

Knowing the Language Gives an Edge

Command of other languages for Americans is undeniably increasing in importance as an international mentality spreads, whether or not the United States remains as the dominant economic force worldwide. With

8. Foderaro, op. cit., p. 20.

the growth of world trade and the threat to market share held by the United States, it is ever more important for American businesspeople to be competitive. That means understanding a foreign business partner or a foreign marketplace as it is, rather than how it is perceived through a translator's eyes. It means demonstrating an interest in and respect for other marketplaces by learning how to communicate in the medium of that marketplace.

More basically, willingness to learn other languages shows a sophistication and appreciation of other cultures that is still desperately needed in the United States. Even if the language is not essential to the transaction of business, it has always been an asset and will soon be a necessary part of an international marketer's credibility rating.

Currently, it appears that most corporations feel it is easier to teach a foreign language to a good businessperson than it is to teach a foreign language speaker to be a good businessperson. They choose managers to be sent abroad and then (sometimes) send them to a crash course at language school. Sometimes their judgment is right, but often it is based on the arrogant notion that it is relatively unimportant for the managers to speak the local language—or even know much about the customs, for that matter. It is left to the local people at the other end to speak English and to do the necessary adjusting.

Although more attention is gradually being put on training Americans in an international mentality, we have a long way to go. Glen Germsmehl, coordinator of global studies at Clark University in Massachusetts, reports that the proportion of American universities offering full programs in international studies jumped from 12 percent in 1979 to more than 50 percent in 1989;[9] but a Governors' Association report cites evidence that one in seven American adults cannot locate the United States on a world map.

There is some question as to what a "full program" entails. "The usual approach is to stuff a few courses on international affairs into an already overstuffed curriculum, and then throw in a little area studies or a foreign language," said Harlan Cleveland, former dean of the Hubert H. Humphrey Institute of Public Policy at the University of Minnesota.[10]

Language capability was among the ten most highly rated common denominators for successful performance of expatriates abroad, a study found. Language capability and other skills that demonstrate a familiarity with cultural differences and an ability to see and accept those differences made up a heavy proportion of the list of characteristics attributed to the lower expatriate failure rate among European and Japanese multinationals abroad compared to U.S. multinationals (see Chapter 9).

9. Edward B. Fiske, "The Global Imperative," *New York Times Special Supplement: As the World Learns*, p. 19.
10. Ibid., p. 18.

The President's Commission on Foreign Language and International Studies warned in 1979 that American ignorance of foreign studies was just short of scandalous.[11] Improvement since then has been slight.

Several prominent business schools with an international edge do require proficiency in one foreign language. The vast majority do not. They say it would make no sense to have a student specialize in one language when it is uncertain whether that student would ever work abroad, let alone in the country of his language expertise. Better, they say, to let corporations enroll the employee in an intensive language program before taking an overseas assignment. "We haven't spotted a trend in language requirements," said Sharon Barber, a spokeswoman for the American Assembly of Collegiate Schools of Business in St. Louis, which represents 650 schools.[12]

According to the Department of Education, only one American elementary school in six offers instruction in a foreign language, and only one student in five emerges from high school having studied another language for more than two years.[13] Nevertheless, there is cause for hope. Some schools are noticing the need and trying to meet it. North Carolina, for instance, has mandated that all public school students by 1993 be required to study a foreign language from kindergarten through fifth grade. Stanford University is opening the Stanford Center in Kyoto, Japan, where undergraduate and graduate teaching, research, internships, consulting, and other resources are available. Boston University has operations in fourteen countries. Many other colleges and universities have some kind of linkup or opportunity for students to go abroad, but more are needed—more that are serious about providing students with an international perspective.

If a choice must be made between a high level of professional expertise in public relations/marketing and a knowledge of the language of the region, the choice would be for the former in virtually every case. If a similar choice had to be made between an international outlook with a sensitivity to the culture and professional expertise, the decision would not be the same. The public relations practitioner cannot operate effectively without a good knowledge of his or her environment. Hopefully, these choices will become less necessary as business becomes more finely tuned to the sound of progress abroad.

Importance of Public Relations as Business Abroad Grows

Just as public relations is playing an increasing role in business generally, its role in the international arena is expanding. Part of this pertains

11. Ibid.
12. Foderaro, op. cit., p. 20.
13. Fiske, op. cit., p. 18.

to language. Although certain aspects of public relations practice, such as research, objectives, and methods, remain much the same, the audiences differ culturally, linguistically, and geographically. Words are the first cross-cultural barrier; even translation does not always solve the problems that words may present because the background of cultural understanding and the nuances may be different.

9

Multinational Corporations

Multinational Corporations (MNCs) often have been perceived as movers of foreign frontiers. They've been seen as adventurers, explorers into uncharted lands, settlers, colonists, entrepreneurs. They've braved the desert to dig for oil and established footholds in undeveloped lands to sell their goods in what at times was little more than a trading post.

However, size has often made them inflexible and unable as well as unwilling to adjust to the environments in which they operate. They became behemoths that may not be suited for accelerating global competition.

Multinationals have both ambitious young businesspeople who want to make their mark and the available financial resources to allow them to do so. A hard look at MNCs can reveal lessons to today's bold frontiersperson—the marketer moving into what is a new, changing business arena that continues to develop abroad.

In the past, the Coca-Colas, Mobil Oils, Exxons, and other corporate giants have moved in and set up shop where even intrepid tourists feared to go. They have brought, in many cases, tremendous benefits. They have also been accused of all kinds of outrages, some justified. It is important for the public relations/marketing professional of today to understand some history of American business abroad and how it may have affected the attitudes of people in current target markets. It is also important to realize that some of the biggest, oldest, seemingly most sophisticated corporations make the biggest mistakes.

Familiarity with the failures as well as the successes gives modern public relations and marketing advisors basic information on which to build a case for their own company's entry into another country when that country seems resistant or fearful. It prepares them for problems they may encounter and possible solutions, and suggests strategies that may be useful.

Many companies have taken it on the chin in their attempts to enter Japanese markets. Of course the successes are more widely publicized. One company that courageously learned from initial failure was General Mills, which carefully analyzed food preparation and then adapted its cake mix technology to Japan's number one home appliance, the rice cooker. The effort was a dismal flop—not because the Japanese didn't like cake or didn't like to cook. On the surface it was a genius solution to a specific problem—most Japanese kitchens were too small for ovens so they just didn't bake cakes and cookies. Adapting the mix to an appliance everyone had should have opened new opportunities to General Mills and companies like it. But General Mills failed to take into account the singular place of respect that rice had in the household. Housewives just did not want to use their rice cookers for other purposes. Besides, where would they put the leftover rice until it was eaten?

This example, while comparatively minor in terms of the impact some MNCs have had in foreign markets, illustrates that even major companies with solid resources do not always foresee the effects their decisions may have. International public relations was an unknown phrase twenty years ago. What was considered sophisticated, transnational public relations was really a series of local programs. Sometimes they were strung together by one goal; often their only commonality was the company that staged them.

Then and now, public relations in the broad sense of human relations and image development goes on whether it is intentional and planned or whether it is not. Although it was a minor consideration for many companies in past years, now its value is recognized. MNCs generally operated with little attention to public relations strategy.

Usually, like our country itself, MNCs were giants with endless resources in contrast to needy, small markets to whom and from whom the MNCs brought products and services. In retrospect, what is the kind of influence they have had? How are they positioned to compete for the international trade of the future?

An MNC was defined in the 1960s as "a company which has a direct investment base in several countries, which generally derives from 20 to 50 percent or more of its net profits from foreign operations, and whose management makes policy decisions based on the alternatives available anywhere in the world.[1]

The description seems to support the view of many observers, including that of Harvard Business School's Professor Theodore Levitt, who complains that MNCs have treated the world as though it were

---

1. James C. Baker, "Multinational Marketing: A Comparative Case Study," *Marketing in a Changing World*, ed. Bernard A. Morin (Chicago: American Marketing Association, 1969), p. 61.

comprised of different markets. (Thirty years ago, in what might be considered the heyday of MNCs, the world was certainly comprised of different markets, some linked but others quite isolated.) Certainly *globalization* is today's current catchphrase. Many people—and Levitt seems to be one of them—appear to use it as a synonym for worldwide standardization, or at the very least a concentration on similarities around the world. MNCs will have to become global to survive, he believes.[2]

Markets: Same or Differentiated?

Yet that very recognition of regional differences may be the thing of most value that multinationals have brought to their marketplaces. Many MNCs, either because existing circumstances demanded it or just because of a desire to create a positive image that would make their business more welcome in particular areas, have created programs and projects specifically to benefit certain nations or regional areas in which they do business.

Such visible, successful public relations coups have as their background a basic desire to make a buck, critics claim. True though that claim may be, it does not negate the value of contributions the company may make. Many of the programs undertaken by MNCs, especially those in early years, were never recognized as public relations or given that label. Yet in essence, that is exactly what they were. More recently, the programs have had the right label, but there has been a sad lack of cohesive recording and recognition of the public relations programs of American companies outside the United States. Awareness of such programs is important not merely for professional pride, but for the lessons they teach.

Contributions of Multinationals

Nowhere have such contributions been more concentrated or effective than in certain third world countries. In Brazil, for instance, Pfizer applied its resources as a pharmaceutical giant to assist officials in successfully controlling a pervasive water-born disease, schistosomiasis, which affects the liver. Also in Brazil, Champion International Corporation subsidized meals for its workers to the tune of 13,000 meals a day, in addition to other benefits.

In Gambia, working with a dozen other American companies, Pfizer established a system for distributing pharmaceuticals and improving health

2. "Levitt: Global Companies to Replace Dying Multinationals," *Marketing News*, Vol. 19, No. 6 (March 15, 1985), p. 15.

care. The company helped develop efficient procurement policies, stock-management systems, and distributions networks.

Kaiser Aluminum and Chemical Company and the Reynolds Metal Company worked in Ghana to construct a hydroelectric power project that made the country less dependent on foreign oil. Fluor, a large engineering/construction company, trained more than 20,000 people in South Africa alone, and over 100,000 in various host countries in construction supervision and other civil and structural engineering fields.

Union Carbide's disastrous accident in Bhopal, India, is well known, but few have heard of the technical college the company built and equipped in Zimbabwe. In French West Africa, Warner-Lambert, the first American pharmaceutical company to manufacture there, created Tropicare to provide basic health care training in Cameroon, the Ivory Coast, Senegal, and Zaire. It set up Joint Therapeutic Commissions to administer the nonprofit program.

Chase Manhattan Bank conducted a pioneering agricultural credit program in Panama. Monsanto developed an energy-saving farming system in Kenya, introducing conservative tillage and an environmentally safe, easy-use weed killer.[3]

The above examples may seem to imply that only newly emerging nations benefit from the presence of MNCs. Modern, industrialized nations are also the recipients of public interest public relations programs. Coca-Cola launched an effective clean-up campaign in Japan, educating people to properly dispose of their used cans and other wastage, making a marked difference in many areas by raising public awareness.

Multinationals as Pioneers

Virtually all over the world, multinationals have been in the forefront of foreign influence. They have educated people, created and maintained health standards, built roads and houses. It is true that the education has in most areas been for the purpose of developing a work force to meet the needs of the multinational; that health standards have similarly helped the company by making that work force more reliable and cutting down sick benefits; that roads have been needed to bring in equipment and supplies; that housing has brought the work force nearer the company for what is usually a mutual benefit. But these advances have similarly helped the host nations. Just as importantly, it has confirmed the multinationals' concern and interest in the local culture and welfare to the host countries.

In her well-researched article, Ann McKinstry Micou breaks into

3. Ann McKinstry Micou, "The Invisible Hand at Work in Developing Countries," *Across the Board* (March 1985), pp. 8–17.

four categories the social benefits of private enterprise in less-developed areas:

1. Development of human resources through employment, training, and "indigenization" or the transfer of authority to local managers
2. Strengthening of the knowledge base through research and development and the transfer of technology
3. Raising of the standard of living through the creation of wealth, buildup of local industry, and provision of consumer goods
4. Enhancement of the quality of life through programs that raise health, housing, nutritional, and educational standards[4]

A few studies have produced evidence of the positive influence of MNCs on their host countries. Among them is one done in 1983 by the Center for Public Resources in New York, funded by the Agency for International Development (AID) in Washington, D.C., which documents what private companies have done to raise health standards in some countries. Another, also funded by AID and done by *Business International*, examines the instances in which companies have promoted agriculture near their plants in foreign countries and have accelerated rural development by providing technical advice, training, and seeds. A third study, by Michael G. Royston of the International Management Institute in Geneva, gives evidence that MNCs pollute less than do indigenous companies.[5]

Information of this type can be of great value to a marketer researching entry into a foreign country, especially an underdeveloped one. Officials of the local national area into which a company is intending to move or expand are in all likelihood aware of the reputation of suitor nations and their records for doing good—and bad. Perceptions may be based on previous experience, hearsay, or fact. If the MNC's reputation is good, it can be built on; if it is poor, it will impose difficulties as the company attempts to set up shop. Since developing and strengthening the corporate image is an important goal of the public relations officer, awareness of the weaknesses and strengths will save considerable effort.

While U.S. companies have freely publicized their socially aware public relations programs, their overseas programs almost by definition have received far less attention. Few companies have bothered to put together information assessing their overall impact on host countries, even when the impact has been clearly positive.

For one thing, U.S. organizations such as the Public Relations

4. Ibid., p. 12.
5. Ibid.

Society of America (PRSA), International Business Communicators (IBC), Financial Writers, Women in Communications, and many others welcome discussions, hold seminars, and print articles that serve to record case histories and inform their memberships. Internationally, there is the International Public Relations Association (IPRA), which offers some valuable services, primarily to members. They provide information on topics of concern to the industry; their twice-yearly seminars keep members apprised of developments in the field. They extend special help to third world countries, where educational seminars are held. The IPRA directory is a fine networking and reference source, but it is available only to members. The most recent IPRA membership directory in the PRSA library in New York is from 1986 (see Appendix I).

Even in public relations classes, international information is thin to the point of being accidental, partly because the information has not been collected in an organized manner and partly because international public relations itself is still not yet regarded as an area of specialization. New York University is one of the first, if not the first, university in New York to offer classes in international public relations. It is certainly one of the few in the United States offering it now.

International case histories, unless they are of truly memorable magnitude, are haphazardly recorded for want of good facilities and systems for preserving these stories.

Public relations has been slow to nurture international experts. In virtually every other field they are now common—advertising, accounting, banking, and consulting all have set up systems for rotating people abroad to develop international awareness and familiarity. Yet it is in public relations that the need is greatest. Communications is more vital than any other function for an American company abroad: How to do it, when, to whom and by whom, and how much? How much will it cost? How much will it bring in? All are at the forefront of every manager's thinking.

We know the rule of thumb is that public relations overseas will cost more than it would at home. Language is one reason. Start with two—English and the home country language. Add in some places one or two or three others: (Flemish and French in Belgium; Malay, Chinese, and Tamil in Malaya, as well as British English). Mix in the time factor.

In a country like Japan, where consensus flourishes, a decision may seem to take eons; even where decision making is rapid, there is more time-consuming discussion than is likely to be necessary at home. Add some more dollars.

A few MNCs have attempted to assess in dollars the contributions they have made to local societies—a difficult and sometimes misleading means of evaluation. Case histories such as the above, academic studies, and general research into the impact of MNCs and reports of public relations programs and approaches must be recorded. They need to be systematically documented and compiled for professionals to refer to and use.

Writing for recognized professional, academic, and business publications is one way. Focusing on international issues in classes and seminars is another. Setting up classes in international public relations and instituting employee exchange systems to encourage overseas exposure are other ways.

Computer databases are another area where opening a file on international public relations would allow students and professionals to access data via library information bases. Since virtually no books have been written on the subject, it's not surprising that libraries have no card files on the subject. The preceding cases of MNCs activities abroad would serve as a starting point for readers who seek more information on this topic.

In recording the marketing/public relations experiences of their companies abroad, writers need to resist the temptation to recount only their successes. Balancing plums with downside reports is more helpful to the reader and makes more accurate—and certainly more interesting—reading. Take these steps as you put a new program into place:

1. Outline what you want to achieve, why, and how.
2. Set up a time sheet.
3. Record the steps necessary to get under way; for example, visit the Foreign Ministry to enlist support.
4. List people involved and responsible.
5. Report on the event or promotion and include samples of invitations, press releases, and other materials used.
6. Collect and analyze press reports of programs.
7. Show major budget breakdown and whether you came in over or under.
8. Build a "book" of the public relations/marketing programs that have been conducted.
9. Make sure your company management and staff are aware of the programs that have been held and their effect. Spread the word outside as well.

Why Foreign Governments Fear Multinationals

Despite the positive contributions MNCs make to local societies, they are often feared. They are, after all, large economic powers that can exert serious, long-term, and even unalterable changes in a regional area. Ultimately, they do not owe any allegiance to their host countries.

Further, the host countries often have little negotiating power. The host country has often been selected, not for its marketplace, but for its low labor costs, plentiful work force, existing resources, and other characteristics advantageous to the MNC.

There is also a fear that undue political influence and influence-peddling will be introduced by the multinational. Other fears include favoritism, new standards—from living standards to standards of behavior—erosion of local morals and mores, development of a new power structure or exacerbation of a current unpopular one, and failure to share technology and other developments.

Conflict has certainly developed between MNCs and their host countries in many instances. There are a number of potential areas of conflict: differences in expectations between the MNC and the host country, the company's relative market power, the extent of its diversification, the size of the local subsidiary operation, industries in which it operates, and its managerial style. The length of time the multinational has been in the host country is also a factor in conflict situations.

Political stability in the host country, diversity and degree of democratic influence, the level of economic (and industrial) development, and market/economic conditions are factors on the host country side that can affect its relationship with the MNC. The reputation and desirability of multinational corporations in foreign local areas varies as dramatically as does the desirability of foreign areas in the eye of the multinationals.

MNCs View Themselves Positively

Whether or not they have a strong positive influence, MNCs generally see themselves as contributors. They look at the jobs they create, the wealth they bring in, the international exposure they offer to an otherwise insular and perhaps isolated area, and the educational/training potential they can provide.

In an interesting study intended to examine the conflicting issues and causes of conflict between MNCs and host governments and other publics in six countries, Dr. Anant R. Negandhi interviewed executives of 124 MNCs, governmental officials, and others. Dr. Negandhi found that ownership or national origin of the MNC, the expectational differences between MNCs and host governments, and prevailing market conditions were related to the nature and intensity of conflict between the MNCs and the host governments, as mentioned above. However, the relative size, level of technology employed, level of diversification, period of operation in the host country, and some other internal attributes of the MNCs examined were not found to be significantly related to conflict.[6]

The study's results provide helpful information for public relations managers, who are often regarded as responsible for the corporation's relations in the community. Knowing what has traditionally caused stress can help them advise their companies on more positive ways of handling those areas.

It is also useful to examine the differences between how U.S. MNCs and other national MNCs handle areas of stress with their hosts. Ultimately, of course, the degree of skill with which certain sensitive areas are handled may mean the difference between success and failure of the operation.

The research sample was drawn at random from a listing of United States, European, and Japanese MNCs operating in Brazil, India, Malaysia, Peru, Singapore, and Thailand. The countries were chosen for their diversity in political structures, level of economic and industrial developments, and varied experience with private investors.

Figure 9-1 gives the profiles of the companies studied:

Figure 9-1. Profiles of companies studied to determine sources of conflict and conflicting issues between MNCs and host countries.

Controlling Ownership	Pattern of Equity	Size of Capital Investment
American = 54	Wholly owned = 65	$4.99M to $3M = 64
European = 43	Majority owned = 25	$2.99M to $2M = 14
Japanese = 27	Minority owned = 24	$1.99M to $.5M = 18
	Not available = 10	Less than $.5M = 9
		Not available = 19

Diversification	Employment Size	Period of Operation
5+ products = 53	1000+ = 51	15+ years = 76
2 to 5 products = 31	999 to 400 = 23	6 to 14 years = 35
Less than 2 = 36	399 to 100 = 31	Less than 6 years = 10
Not available = 4	Less than 100 = 11	Not available = 4
	Not available = 8	

6. Dr. Anant R. Negandhi, "Multinational Corporations and Host Governments' Relationships: Comparative Study of Conflict and Conflicting Issues," *Human Relations*, Vol. 33, No. 8 (1980), pp. 517–541.

Interviews and analysis showed that U.S. MNCs have more interface conflicts, while Japanese MNCs have more on the operational level. There seemed to be no significant differences between American and European corporations. The interface problems experienced by United States and European companies centered around the host governments' requirements for dilution of equity and management control, reduction or elimination of royalty payments for technology and know-how, transfer pricing policies, and similar areas.

Facing Japanese companies were low morale and employee productivity, high turnover, absenteeism, and interpersonal conflicts between Japanese expatriate managers and locals.

Differences between the MNCs were not as significant in the Far East as they were in Latin America, except that U.S. MNCs had more negotiational problems in Latin America than European MNCs did.

A common host country demand, especially in developing countries, was for equity participation in the foreign enterprises. Wholly owned and majority-owned corporations tended to have comparatively less conflict than did MNCs with only a minority-equity stake.

MNC Visibility Affects Image

Apparently, the degree of visibility of the MNC can affect the views of citizens and government officials in the host countries either positively or negatively. This is a particularly key issue for public relations professionals, who are generally the ones responsible for visibility and who set the relevant policies. Some activities that may result in high visibility are:

- Extraordinary contributions to the host country
- Use of specialized technologies
- Generation of high employment
- Payment of high wages and provision of extensive employee training
- High level of conflict with the host/home governments
- International publicity
- Operation over a long period of time in the host country
- The pervasiveness/proliferation of end products in daily life

Greater diversification seemed to indicate more negotiational conflict, but diversification itself tended to be regarded in the host country as an indication of the company's willingness to contribute to the host countries' needs. European companies tended to be more diversified than did American companies.

The study found that while the level of investment and sales volume did not seem to be significantly associated with the level of conflict, the number of employees did. Corporations with a larger work force appeared to have a higher level of conflict.

According to the study, an executive's perception of his corporation as relatively very big and possessing a significant amount of leverage had little direct relationship to a higher level of conflict resulting from aggressiveness. However, companies that held a market share of more than 60 percent had more conflict in negotiations than over policy or operations, while a company with only 26 to 59 percent of the market showed a substantially higher rate of conflict over policy than in any other area. A similar parallel is found relative to the size of the investment.

Expectations Are Dissimilar

Research did show a wide gap between the expectations of MNCs and the host governments. This gap clearly created continuous tensions and conflicts. Twenty-three categories were enumerated as areas of possible expectation. The five strongest expectations of the host governments were as follows:

1. Local investors would not be displaced.
2. Local resources would be developed.
3. Local supplies would be used.
4. Local ownership would be increased.
5. A more positive balance of payments would be created.

This was quite different from what MNC executives thought were expectations by the host government:

1. There would be an increase in the quality of goods.
2. Useful technology would be provided.
3. There would be substantial capital inflow.
4. More nationals would be used in executive positions, employment would increase, and raw materials would be brought in from outside.
5. Local resources would be developed.

The MNCs saw themselves as providers of capital, technology, needed raw materials, and better goods and services—contributions that host countries generally considered to be of little importance.

Study results indicated that U.S. companies had larger expectational differences with the host countries than did the European and Japanese MNCs. It's quite possible that one explanation for this is the greater concentration and investment on research into the area usually done by Japanese and European MNCs. American companies have had a tendency to postpone all but the most essential study until after entry.

These expectational differences can have great import to the executive who is organizing operations in the host country and at the same time is placed in the uncomfortable position of having to justify attitudes or events in the foreign market to headquarters.

Disappointment on the corporate side can be just as severe. Executives of MNCs looked to the host countries to:

- Refrain from interference with corporate affairs
- Reduce bureaucratic controls; provide favorable business-government relationships
- Spell out clearly the terms and conditions for foreign investors
- Provide more flexible expansion policies

Needless to say, the inability or unwillingness of host countries to provide the above cause the MNCs some frustration. Here again, public relations can play a role in minimizing expectational differences by laying the proper groundwork prior to entry. This includes following steps outlined in Chapters 2, 3, and 7 with regard to establishing the right contacts at an early stage and building regular communications. It also includes fully educating and advising corporate management as to local area situations and attitudes and working to bring the expectations on both sides more fully in line with each other.

For their part, host countries see their local industries being displaced by foreign-owned companies. They fear control by the MNCs and demands that they may consider unjustified. Many of the developing countries have enacted legislation that requires substantial concessions from the MNCs, such as majority equity, local nationals in top positions, raw materials import reductions, and so on. In doing so, they sometimes have effected changes in the actual organizational structures. More often, the MNCs have taken such demands very lightly.

The views of both hosts and MNCs when sought at a time that conflict had become rather serious were particularly interesting. Host governments complained that they had expected more from the MNCs; that they expected them to assist the local entrepreneurs, establish research and development (R&D) facilities, and introduce products relevant to the local economy.

Most MNCs were aware of these expectations but chose to ignore them under the pretext that "we haven't been asked to do so." They took note of the host country's demands only when the host governments passed regulations to meet their expectations. It seems ironic that such notice should be taken by the parties concerned only after the relationships have deteriorated.

Clarity of expectations should go a long way toward reducing tension and conflict. Most American MNC executives tended to view regulations imposed by the host governments with ideological overtones. As a result, they took a rather belligerent, outspoken stance, undeterred by any embarrassment to the parties involved. The net result of such behavior means that conflict tends to escalate.

Japanese and Europeans Face Conflict Diplomatically

In contrast, Europeans and Japanese—the Japanese especially—maintained a very low profile during periods of stress and conflict. The Japanese displayed a strong propensity to underplay any conflict or resistance to regulations. Rather than go public the way the Americans did, they adopted a very diplomatic stance and attempted to deal with their conflict through influencing the host government's officials.

American MNC executives, after their initial flurry of activity against the imposition of regulations, settled down to follow regulations to legal perfection. By contrast, European and Japanese MNCs generally seemed to interpret quickly and accurately and therefore they acted more in accordance with the spirit of the regulation.[7]

The basic difference between the two extreme behavioral modes of the Americans and the Japanese appears to be the MNC's orientation toward its environment.

Multinationals have often been accused of exploitation, especially by developing countries. Sometimes the claim is justified; sometimes it is invented or exaggerated by national leaders and international pressure groups. Certainly the aftermath of the Union Carbide plant tragedy in Bhopal and less serious but long-remembered other experiences have not helped the companies' reputations.

MNCs have been slow to defend themselves. Many have made major contributions to the economies of their host countries, but few have bothered to gather or publicize such information on an integrated basis. This is part of the public relations professionals' job. Gathering and publicizing such information for his or her own company, and by doing so creating a record of achievement, will stand the company in good stead over time.

In a larger sense, creating a system for establishing awareness means far more than creating a healthy environment for a particular company. It can make a case for capitalism, the profit motive, free markets, and even democracy itself. Numerous examples of exemplary impact of MNCs on local areas are available as previously noted, but there is a lack of sufficiently interested and motivated individuals to collect and compile these data into a useful body of reference work.

7. Ibid., p. 535.

Country and Corporate Goals Should Be Consistent

The long-term goals of the corporations should be related to the needs and goals of the countries in which they are located. This is not merely wise and considerate public relations; it is self-serving to the extent that it helps assure acceptance of the company and in turn, profits. MNCs need to be aware of smoldering resentments and/or misconceptions such as those discussed above and to undertake to dispel them with appropriate education and action.

MNCs seem to be viewed differently by developed nations than by less developed countries (LDCs). Publics in LDCs seem more concerned about the economic impact of foreign companies, while those in developed nations (DCs) focus more on control effects. In both, the heads of local companies seem to take a more favorable view of foreign companies than do those lower in the hierarchy.

Cultural elements seem to rank high in both types of countries also. They frequently appear as factors in correlation analysis, which identifies a key problem: Attitudes toward MNCs are significantly related to a substantial number of factors that vary from country to country.[8] What is clear is that to operate fruitfully over a long term in various host countries, MNCs need to construct an organization that will recognize and handle the fears of the communities they enter. They need to strategize carefully to counteract the negative claims and maximize the effects of their positive inputs. Proper public relations procedures can be invaluable in doing so.

The remaining, implicit question in the pro or con discussion of American MNCs seems to be, "Have they had their day?" While MNCs reflect the traditional structural pattern for an international company, new molds are being designed that may meet the challenging demands of a changing global economy and offer more flexibility, variety, and growth potential.

8. John Fayerweather, "Attitudes Toward Foreign Firms Among Business Students, Managers, and Heads of Firms," *Management International Review* (Germany), Vol. 15, No. 6 (1975), pp. 19–28.

10

Co-Ventures and Joint Ventures

Doing business abroad through a co-venture structure of some sort does not mean that the American entity can hand over its product to the partner to manage and market and then turn its attention back to domestic affairs with a sigh of relief. Involvement with a non-American co-venture partner requires special care and attention. Companies that have the most success with it have learned that collaboration is another form of competition, that you learn all you can from your joint venture partner while keeping as many of your own secrets to yourself as possible. When the time is opportune, you strike out on your own, sometimes in the very same market your partner has controlled. "In an alliance you have to learn skills of the partner, rather than just see it as a way to get a product to sell while avoiding a big investment," says C. K. Prahalad, professor of business at the University of Michigan and an expert on global alliances.[1]

Companies usually have specific strategic objectives in deciding to become involved in a co-venture arrangement:

- Spreading investment risk
- Attaining economies of scale more easily
- Overcoming government trade barriers
- Facilitating market entry
- Attaining vertical integration
- Pooling complementary technologies
- Blocking or co-opting competition, at least temporarily

1. Bernard Wysocki, Jr., "Global Reach: Cross Border Alliances Become Favorite Way to Crack New Markets," *The Wall Street Journal* (March 26, 1990), p. A4.

Any company needs to understand its own objective as well as the objective of the partnership. Unpleasant as it seems at the time of hammering out an agreement that will be positive for both sides, contingency plans must be included in case the partnership does not work out. Be specific and realistic in framing these.

Only recently has the potential contribution of public relations been recognized in searching for and negotiating with promising partners. As part of background research, the identities of major companies in a destination area should become known. Their reputations, their approach to business, their corporate culture all need to be added into the equation of whether or not they are likely to work well with your company and are areas public relations is suited to investigate.

Traditionally, partners have been found through business agents, lawyers, and other means. Emphasis has been on the prospective partner's balance sheet, product line, and resources. "Softer" aspects such as corporate culture, behind-the-scenes reputation, promotional attitudes, and treatment of employees were virtualy ignored. Yet if the personalities and ethical character of companies are dissimilar, their "marriage" is unlikely to be successful. Public relations is charged with managing people as well as facts, and is able to utilize networking and information-gathering expertise to the best advantage of corporations seeking partners.

Outline Expectations of Foreign Partners

Warren Hegg, director of international management consulting at the Stanford Research Institute in California, cautions that successful links with foreign entities require five things:

1. A clear understanding of objectives
2. A well-defined decision-making and management framework
3. Effective monitoring capabilities
4. Patience and willingness to adapt to each other's culture
5. Good training of human resources[2]

Risks there may be, but alliances are on the increase. They are a way to get into markets that may otherwise be formidable, and in most cases are less expensive than going it alone. Tie-ups among industrial giants are legion: AT&T with NEC, AT&T offering its computer-aided design technology for NEC's advanced logic chips; IBM and Siemens for joint research in advanced semiconductor chips; as well as Corning

2. "Culture Clashes Cause Most Global Failures," *Marketing News*, Vol. 21, No. 16 (July 31, 1987), pp. 21–24.

and Ciba-Geigy, Volvo and Renault, Motorola and Toshiba, Texas Instruments and Hitachi, AT&T and Mitsubishi, General Electric and Snecma, the French aerospace company.[3]

The latter alliance was formed in 1974 and gave GE a way to penetrate the market for engines for the Airbus that had been in the grip of Airbus Industrie, the European aircraft consortium. The GE-Snecma partnership produced the most successful commercial jet engine in history, a midsized engine for Airbus 320, Boeing 737, and other planes. In 1989 the venture brought in orders or commitments for orders for engines valued at more than $11 billion.

The joint venture has not been without stress, which continues. Cultural, linguistic, logistical, and monetary problems are some that need to be dealt with, as well as differing attitudes toward personnel and differing approaches to problem solving. Despite the frustrations, the venture has worked well because it is structured well. Investment and revenue are split equally. Senior engine executives on both sides are given broad responsibility. GE handles system design and high-tech work while the French handle fans, boosters, low-pressure turbines, and similar goods. Both do marketing.

On the other hand, the risk of such a joint venture shows up in the well-known alliance between AT&T and Ing. C. Olivetti & Co. AT&T was to sell Olivetti personal computers in the United States while Olivetti would sell AT&T's computers and telephone-switching machines in Europe. But a basic assumption of the arrangement—that the computer and telecommunications industries were converging—hasn't worked out. Although Carlo De Benedetti, chairman of Olivetti, says that the pairing was a total failure because the idea wasn't right, Robert Kavner, a group executive for AT&T, believes the basic flaw was cultural differences. "I don't think we or Olivetti spent enough time understanding behavior patterns," he says. "We knew the culture was different but we never really penetrated."

American companies are not alone in downplaying the human factor in business operations. What people expect, how they behave in the context of both their national and corporate cultures, their degree of flexibility, their willingness to communicate, and their skill in doing so all contribute to the success of a partnership.

Corporations of major size are in the news all the time. Not only do their business successes and failures become public knowledge, but the personalities of top management and internal politics become quite public. Choosing a partner, then, is reduced primarily to intricate negotiations.

For smaller companies, the emphasis may be very different. Identifying possible partners and learning what they are really like can be

---

3. Wysocki, op. cit.

time-consuming and is very likely to be spearheaded by public relations, especially given the advisory management consulting role that public relations is increasingly expected to provide.

Stateless Corporations

A type of organization is taking shape a step beyond that of the MNC, and that is the "stateless" corporation. Stateless corporations, or world organizations, are represented in many countries and have multiple identities and multiple loyalties. They try to resemble insiders wherever they operate and to make decisions with little regard to boundaries.

While American entities have formed some of the greatest MNCs, they are late to evolve into this newest state, which demands a real sense of internationalism. World organizations may have their corporate office in one country, manufacturing facilities in another, marketing and distribution networks in others, and so on. Their various arms may go by different names, making ultimate identity/ownership difficult to determine.

Some that may be considered to be in this group are Nestle, Sandoz, Hoffman-La Rouche, Philips, Electrolux, Coca-Cola, United Technologies, and Du Pont; the first three are Switzerland-based, Philips is from the Netherlands, Electrolux began in Sweden, and the final three are American in origin.[4] Although their home countries are still identifiable to some degree, they tread a thin line between multiple identities and loyalties. They need to be flexible and adaptable and to fit as insiders into any culture in which they operate. Many of them garner over half their profits from areas beyond their "home" borders.

Heads of these stateless businesses cite certain advantages:

1. *Beating trade problems.* As early as 1983, Honda was rolling cars off its assembly line in Marysville, Ohio, built at least in part to beat the threat of sanctions and complaints on the severe balance of trade in favor of Japan exporting to the United States.

2. *Avoiding political problems.* Many companies have pulled out of South Africa to avoid criticisms from within their own country and restrictive or punitive regulations governing hiring and other business practices.

3. *Sidestepping regulatory hurdles.* Pharmaceutical companies and food companies face different regulations governing imports into Japan than they face in, say, the United States. By setting up facilities in Japan, they can minimize restrictive barriers that might have high costs

4. William J. Holstein, Stanley Reed, Jonathan Kapstein, Todd Vogel, and Joseph Weber, "The Stateless Corporation," *Business Week* (May 14, 1990), pp. 98–105.

when the same products are imported. Many countries have different regulations governing imported products as opposed to domestic ones or import quotas and duties.

4. *Achieving labor gains*. Companies look for low-cost, available work forces that have a record of high productivity and a high standard of education.

5. *Balancing costs*. The ability to be flexible can effectively keep costs down. Dow Chemical relies on mathematical equations to decide where to produce. It runs its plants at higher average capacity and keeps capital costs down.

6. *Winning technology breakthroughs*. Areas of technology that are more highly advanced in one country than the other can be combined for the greatest benefit. Know-how can more easily be traded back and forth.[5]

The Need to Recognize Regionality

World organizations (WOs) try to coordinate their efforts over a broad, even a global, area while still tailoring various aspects of their operations, including product, to accommodate the idiosyncrasies of local markets. While their managers still reflect a bias to the home country in most cases, they are becoming increasingly multinational and transferable.

For public relations professionals, these companies offer a real challenge in terms of management and control of the corporate message, transferral and usage of programs from one area to another, human resources management, and consistency. At the same time, many WOs have built in top-level mechanical communications facilities that aid the message transmittal and monitoring functions. Computers with modems, direct phone lines, facsimiles, and satellite or fiber optic broadcast facilities for visual conference calls and even press conferences are not uncommon. However, nothing replaces personal discussions in formulating policy, establishing motivation, or developing morale and loyalty—invaluable factors in promoting a policy or plan.

A deeper challenge, which has barely begun to show its head, is the question of corporate and national loyalties. The strength of many companies has been rooted in a convergence with the interests of their home cultures, from which they gain intangible support in exchange for decisions that keep national interests in mind. Japanese companies are a prime example.

When MNCs enter a new market abroad, they are faced in nearly

5. Ibid.

every case with assuring authorities and then the prospective work force that they have the best interests of the region in mind. As long as home country politics and interest are not clashing with local interests, they stand a good chance of success. As the corporations become increasingly stateless, it becomes increasingly difficult to define their loyalties. Almost by definition, WOs are forced to become either apolitical or ever more divided, and therefore conflicting, in their loyalties. What that means over the longer run in terms of public responsibility and the work of the public relations professional is interesting to speculate.

At the same time, the breadth of their reach and cloudiness of their national identity often means that they can enter markets formerly forbidden to them when they were known to be of a certain nationality. Taiwan and South Korea, for instance, have banned the import of Japanese cars, while Japan has respected the Arab embargo of Israel. But by opening and operating manufacturing facilities in the United States, Honda has been able to surmount the problem. From its Marysville, Ohio, plant it ships cars to all three countries. Similarly, BASF, a German biotechnology company, encountered opposition from the strong green environmentalist group at home. It shifted its cancer and immune-system research to Cambridge, Massachusetts, where it was welcomed. This type of situation is a public relations challenge in the broadest sense, and one that professionals in the field need to anticipate, research, and advise on. It is an area where great opportunity lies in the profession, but also substantial risk and challenge.

Any company multiplies its marketing strength by capitalizing on its name recognition on a worldwide basis. This is certainly the reason behind integrated public relations marketing advertising programs. The force of the psychological impact on the observer advances geometrically as he or she recognizes the corporate image, message, and product around the world. The message, therefore, has to be consistent, but it also has to be individualized for the particular location.

In public relations, the problem is magnified. How do you determine a message for the chairperson to deliver that will be palatable in all markets that receive it and still retain some bite in the bark, so to speak? On the opposite side, how do you impress on top management the speed with which the message is delivered around the world? How do you warn that comments on the company's intention to tighten its belt in view of signals of a downturn in the U.S. economy can instigate workers in Korea to strike for a long-term employment contract to protect themselves from imagined layoffs?

Similarly, a report issued abroad on the financial troubles of a subsidiary can affect the price of the parent company's stock in the United States. Communications need to be considered in light of the effect they may have around the world.

In a world organization where there is a strong effort to customize the identity of the company to the extent that it is accepted as native to the society, how do you then capitalize on its global presence? How do you engineer the interrelation of distinctive markets? Guidelines are needed for managers in local offices as well as head offices. They should outline what subjects can be discussed without prior clearance and what subjects are off limits. They should set corporate policy on certain issues. Public relations plays both a major advisory role and a participatory role as to what information is made public and when.

11

Components for Success Abroad: Assuming an International Marketing Mentality

This chapter shows how an international orientation, management skills and attitudes, and the structural organization of companies can influence their success or failure abroad. Comparing the differences in how American and non-American companies operate in foreign locales will help clarify the issues that contribute to or limit success. We'll also examine, from the foreign nationals' point of view, the plusses and minuses of having foreign (American) corporations resident in their country.

Playing a decisive role in the judgments of how, when, and where to enter foreign markets, public relations/marketing professionals need to understand the risks inherent in bringing two cultures together. They need to bear in mind communications in its broadest sense. That implies that a knowledge of the mistakes others have made as well as a familiarity with research into the problems of businesses in foreign locations will be passed on to corporate management.

Elements of Success in Marketing Abroad

The question "What motivates an American company to open an overseas office?" leads to a quick answer: "To make money." But those who answer quickly may be just the ones who fail to realize that particular goal. Many major companies abroad do not succeed in making money at all.

To give one example, American Express has been in Japan since 1917. When the yen was ¥360 to the dollar, the Japanese economy was cheap; subsidizing the operation there cost the parent in New York little and provided an international image. Non-Japanese cardmembers could be serviced in Japan. Japanese businesspeople could buy special cards for use during travel abroad.

In 1983, when the yen-dollar ratio was approximately ¥270 = $1, American Express, to its credit, decided to commit major funds to develop that market. It introduced the then full line of products of Travel Related Services, which consisted of the Gold and Green cards, Travelers Cheques, and travel services. Providing investment funds still costs roughly half what it costs now.

Until the mid-1980s, most of American Express's foreign revenue came from traveling Americans. The company realized the global potential of its customer base and set about developing a global, as opposed to an export, mentality. (Even in 1989, only 9.3 million of American Express's 33.3 million Card members were non-American, but they brought in 31 percent more revenue per card than did Americans.[1]

By 1986 the company could not come close to breaking even without drastically cutting its advertising budget, which was considered crucial to future success in that marketplace. With the exchange rate dropping fast to about ¥140 = $1 and growth continuing in the Japanese economy, the company found support by the American parent ever more expensive.

Most American companies expect to break even after the second year, though many non-American companies are conservative enough to wait it out for five years, which is the usual period Japanese companies allow for buildup. American Express is unusual in that it has stuck it out so long, but its story is familiar in most other ways. A major international company with a reach around the globe, it made some major mistakes in regard to human resources and other business areas. Finally, it started doing what it had originally pledged not to do: It joined up with major Japanese companies such as Dai-Ichi Kangyo Bank and Nippon Life Insurance Company.

How is the company able to do it? One answer is that its management doesn't have to answer directly to shareholders on that part of the business because the financials aren't broken down on a country-to-country basis. As long as the company as a whole is doing well, shareholders allow it to support a losing venture. Why does it stay? Does it still expect to turn a profit?

1. Jeremy Main, "How to Go Global and Why," *Fortune* (August 28, 1989), p. 76.

Profit Is Not the Only Motive

Clearly, profit expectations are a prime reason for any company to enter or stay in a market. But there are others. In the case of American Express, the operation in Japan supports a profitable business outside the country. Without a strong presence in Japan, millions of Japanese tourists and businesspeople would lack the incentive and confidence to use the company's cards and Travelers Cheques in American and other markets around the world. Less profitable but still vital is the market that must be maintained within Japan for non-Japanese tourists and corporate Card members.

In addition, there is the importance of image. The company's reputation rests strongly on its worldwide identity. If it is not represented in the second largest economy in the world, its claim to global presence is severely weakened. A report by Sanford C. Bernstein & Co., the New York investment research firm, calls American Express's high-quality, upscale image "possibly the most potent asset in all financial services."[2]

In some U.S. companies, status or ego is a strong motivating factor for entering overseas markets. One or more top corporate officers may see such a foreign entry as a feather in his or her cap. Management may be convinced that the status of the company as a whole would be enhanced by creating that extended identity. Public relations may be the main idea rather than a vital component in the decision; the chief executive may want to be credited with globalizing the company. Other reasons may include the advantages of a tax write-off, supply of much-needed cheaper resources, and long-term ambitions for the area in question.

Companies can generally be said to base their decisions for making direct foreign investments on strategic considerations of five main types: They seek (1) a new market, (2) raw materials, (3) production efficiency, (4) knowledge, or (5) political safety. In deciding to move abroad, however, any company must not only consider its own needs but research the needs and attitudes in the local area as well as the impact the company may have.

Certain factors seem to correlate strongly with the ultimate success of the company, such as the ability to understand the foreign market, recognize its needs, and use innovative marketing tactics that mesh domestic strengths with corporate and regional needs. Several specific factors have been found to contribute to or limit the success of companies marketing abroad.

Apathy is a frequent problem. Sometimes it's on the part of local staff who may receive insufficient guidance from parent management or may feel excluded from the mainstream. Expatriate staff may have a

2. Ibid.

similar response for similar reasons. Thus, the head office needs to be involved. Companies need a strategic commitment to succeed. Interest and involvement in the local community are essential. That means that not only locally assigned staff but headquarters officers need to be sensitive and committed to appreciation of local sensibilities. Important to this is the ability to adjust to new and strange ideas, to be flexible.

Flexibility as an important contributing factor to success means a recognition that strategies and policies appropriate for the United States or other foreign markets may need special tailoring for the particular local area. Companies that have a tightly controlled structure in place may not have the adaptability to make the most of particular situations. It is likely that the successful organization of the 1990s will be less structured and more reliant on technology to stay competitive in the midst of business conditions that are changing ever more rapidly. Speed in responding to that change and the competitive pressures that accompany it will be increasingly important factors for success, as will the integration of information and strategies.

Indications are that American companies will have to become increasingly lean, flat, and decentralized; that alliances, partnerships, and co-ventures of various kinds will become more common; and that standardization in quality, pricing, service, and design will receive urgent attention. Companies that manage a high degree of standardization but retain the flexibility to modify themselves to accommodate market conditions are likely to have the greatest edge over their competitors.

Centralization, the other side of the coin, is a factor. In a small organization it can be an asset because decisions tend to be made by the person at the top. In a larger organization, it becomes hard to reach that person. Even if accessible, top management can have only a superficial idea of conditions globally. Making swift decisions becomes unlikely as the decision maker must seek advice or issue poorly considered opinions for lack of full information. The degree of home office control and the competence of the company's executives is of vital importance.

Strong Home Officer Direction vs. Decentralization

The dangers of strong control by the headquarters office have for years been recognized by expatriate managers, who have often considered their major problem to be not the idiosyncracies of business in the foreign area but the challenge of convincing their superiors back home of the validity of their decisions and the unique demands of the local area as opposed to the familiar patterns of the U.S. domestic markets.

Clearly, not everyone agrees that strongly centralized operations can be a real danger. Parker Pen Co. drastically reorganized its international marketing in 1984, moving from total decentralization of advertising decisions to complete centralized control by headquarters. With

80 percent of its sales coming from abroad, the company believed it had made a major marketing mistake by packaging, pricing, and advertising its products differently around the world. In an effort to build a strong, consistent image worldwide in what is a highly competitive market, it consolidated its production facilities and product line and moved into a highly centralized mode that was intended to save management time and money.

In doing so, Parker Pen minimized the downside risk that usually accompanies decentralization. People in local subsidiaries tend to see the differences that exist between themselves and other subsidiaries and between themselves and headquarters. Naturally, they have a point of view quite different from that of headquarters.

Decentralization tends to isolate headquarters from local subsidiaries' decisions; it tends to emphasize the similarities that subsidiaries share and overlook unique aspects. However, headquarters must ensure that activities in one location abroad do not adversely affect either the parent or other "siblings."

Generally, however, decentralization has meant flexibility, which in turn has meant greater strength and success in offices abroad. Growth in globalization may bring changes in this area.

Size is another practical consideration. Although many small companies operate successfully abroad, it is often because they have a very specific market or product. Generally, sufficient size more readily ensures sufficient capital for initiating and sustaining a venture abroad.

The success of enterprises abroad has been found to be directly related to the success of expatriate managers themselves. Influence with the home office is only one aspect of this success, which has many components. We will look at factors that contribute to a manager's success in the next section of this chapter on management strength.

Certainly one aspect should be particularly scrutinized: familiarity with business abroad. To know how to get things done, to understand how markets work, to be alert to business customs, and to be familiar with the infrastructure are part of being a skillful internationalist and, while important to management executives, are particularly important to public relations.

It is impossible to know every market, but a skillful practitioner knows where to probe, what questions to ask, and where to get needed information. Companies need to learn the rules of international trade. More than anything, Americans need a change in attitude and to realize that the United States is becoming a component of the global market.[3] They need to strategically plan their placement abroad in four areas: (1)

3. Charles F. Valentine, "The Art of International Competition," *Business Credit*, Vol. 90, No. 3 (March 1988), pp. 40–42.

testing the waters, (2) learning the language, (3) mapping out a strategy, and (4) beating the competition at its own game.

The companies must have a system of information that keeps them aware of political changes abroad and how their business may be affected. They must have a system in place to train their management teams to be increasingly international in aspect and capability, including the active use of outside directors on the board.

Image has been mentioned so often by marketers and public relations practitioners in recent years that the speaker can almost hear the mental doors slam when the word is mentioned. But a company's image, not only as it is perceived by the marketplace but as it is perceived internally, is an element vital to its success. Companies planning to operate in markets outside their own must see themselves as multinational and be comfortable with that image. The identity of the company must be presented as a single entity in public relations programs, advertising, and internally. Whatever the unique elements of the corporate personality, most cultures are more conservative than our own in valuing a solid, consistent character.

Self-Image Must Be Global

According to Lippincott & Margulies, Inc., concern with establishing a global identity is a contributing factor in the competitive advantage enjoyed by foreign companies abroad. Almost 60 percent of foreign companies surveyed reported that they had increased their focus on global identity considerations over the past two years, but only 36 percent of U.S. companies had increased their efforts for the same period. The need to increase sales and revenues was the key reason for foreign companies to implement global identity programs. Cultural awareness and adaptability cannot be overestimated; corollary to that is good training and utilization of human resources.

Looking over the demands of the 1990s, there is little doubt that strategic planning will focus on projects for the global marketplace. That strategy must include the building of corporate structures that emphasize speed, flexibility, and response to changing demands.[4] Only lean, decentralized organizations can hope to cope with the varied demands of the global marketplace.

Their strategy must be global at the same time it is local. That is, while it must be broad-based and take advantage of whatever economies of size and reach are available, it must also be aware that global does not mean "alike." They must be prepared to back their commitment

4. John Tuman, Jr., "Shaping Corporate Strategy With Information Technology," *Project Management Journal*, Vol. 19, No. 4 (September 1988), pp. 35–42.

with dollars and understand that there is virtually no industry or product in which the United States holds a unique position. Although our natural resources are still rich compared with those of most other nations, one by one our leadership in various industries has been surpassed. Even Wall Street, once the financial center of the world, is taking a back street to Tokyo and London, and facing competition from new stock exchanges in Europe and Asia.

Developing the Management Team

Considering the vital importance of competent, internationally minded executives to the success of overseas operations, current trends are surprising. There seems to be a shift from sending Americans overseas to relying on local management to handle the company's business. Some experts report a dramatic and significant replacement of U.S. expatriates by local nationals. This strong movement may represent a trend that has come and gone for years, although it seems now to be stronger and more persistent than in the past.

The decrease is taken positively as one more indication of the internationalization or globalization of U.S. companies. It assumes that the level of sophistication needed to hire a range of managers from different backgrounds is greater than that needed to select, train, and guide home country managers groomed for placement in positions abroad. That judgment is questionable.

Other reasons are given for the move toward replacing American expatriates with local nationals, including environmental competence and cost reduction. Another explanation is that corporate experience with overseas assignments has been disastrous. The argument is that it is easier to train and promote host and third-country nationals than it is to select high-potential American candidates and expend the resources necessary to give them the attitudes and cultural skills to function abroad.[5]

It is unfortunate and potentially tragic for the United States that no judgment is given for the long run, which is what matters in the end. Among many other arguments, a serious decline in expatriates abroad sacrifices the internationalization of American business personnel and leaves corporate assets somewhat more at risk.

However, the decline in Americans abroad perhaps should not be taken too fatalistically. Certainly over the years the arguments for one decision or the other have changed rather frequently. The question has never been fully answered by any company as to the extent to which

5. Stephen J. Kobrin, "Expatriate Reduction and Strategic Control in American Multinational Corporations," *Human Resource Management*, Vol. 27, No. 1 (Spring 1988), pp. 63–75.

American expatriates should be utilized in overseas offices and up to what level local management should be appointed.

Management by Fad

Observation of American companies in Asia over a period of years reveals a constantly changing policy. At one stage, in one company after another, American top management was deemed necessary, being credited with more drive, more determination, and more technical, marketing, entrepreneurial/whatever know-how than local management had, as well as understanding better the motives of head office orders.

Foreign employees were found to have considerable difficulty understanding the parent company's corporate culture. American management worried that its supervision of local managers was weak and left the company open to risk of lax operations, lowering of ethical standards, corner cutting, and incomplete reporting.

The other side of the flip-flop was that only local management really knew the market, had the contacts, or understood the local work force. The argument can be made that one type is better than another at various stages; the truth is that for the most part the stages have not been designated.

A lone voice is heard in the din, that of Faneuil Adam, Jr., who says:

> To avoid such problems [as mentioned above], a multinational enterprise should strive to establish a worldwide managerial work force by hiring university graduates throughout the world who are confident of the company's career development system. The general manager for a foreign affiliate should be the most qualified individual, regardless of nationality, who has sufficient home head office experience and has demonstrated adaptability to unfamiliar environments.[6]

Expatriate Costs Climb as U.S. Economy Declines

The most frequent reason given for staffing overseas executive spots with local hires is the high cost of keeping expatriates abroad. It is high. Figure 11-1 shows cost-of-living comparisons for an American family of four with a base salary of $75,000 in locations typical of where such a family would reside. Housing costs are based on homes or apartments rented by the expatriate families and vary in size between six and nine rooms according to location. Besides rent, annual expenses for utilities and insurance are included. Transportation costs include fixed and op-

6. Faneuil Adam, Jr., "Developing an International Workforce," *Columbia Journal of World Business*, Vol. 20, No. 4 (1986), pp. 23–25. Reprinted with permission.

Figure 11-1. Annual cost of living worldwide (1990).

	Housing	Transpor-tation	Goods and Services	Total
Tokyo	$143,440	$14,715	$49,549	$207,704
Hong Kong	99,961	9,598	25,649	135,199
Geneva	50,281	9,465	40,245	99,199
Singapore	41,769	14,167	27,807	83,743
London	37,546	11,316	29,212	78,074
Sydney	38,240	10,109	28,167	76,516
Al-Khobar	32,636	10,088	27,219	69,943
Frankfurt	28,491	10,199	30,239	68,929
Buenos Aires	37,447	8,031	21,992	67,470
Mexico City	35,886	7,006	21,115	64,007
Chicago	27,046	8,599	24,943	60,588

Source: Runzheimer International. Reprinted with permission from *Management Review*.

erating costs for one automobile as well as public commutation where appropriate. Costs of goods and services include the total amounts paid (including sales tax) for food at home, food away from home, tobacco, alcohol, household furnishings and operations, clothing, domestic services, medical care, personal care, and recreation.

Taxes are not included. Actual taxes vary greatly depending upon the tax-planning techniques used by companies in accordance with their tax reimbursement policies.

Sometimes the rationale for staffing overseas offices with local executives is based on lack of knowledge of comparable costs. For instance, Japanese executives commonly receive many side benefits such as open-ended expense accounts, golf club memberships, housing, transportation allowances or car and driver, and a bonus equivalent to a full year's salary. The total package can be as high or higher than the cost of an expatriate. In addition, Japan is only one of numerous countries in which it is difficult to dismiss employees once they are hired. A company can be stuck for years with a Japanese executive who was poorly chosen.

Rarely is it explained that figured into the high cost of sending American expatriates abroad is the high rate of failure resulting from inadequate preparation and inappropriate selection. Another reason mentioned among former expatriates but seldom acknowledged by management is the increasing reluctance of managers to move abroad.

There are several reasons for this trend: working spouses who are reluctant to give up career-track positions (implicit in such a move is virtually total dependence on the earning spouse in many ways in addition to financial, in some countries the wife of an expatriate has virtually no legal rights); the unfortunate failure of many companies to provide suitable jobs at home for employees who have put in loyal time overseas before being returned home, and stories of friends who were moved abroad and then returned either to no job at all at the home base or to a significantly lower position.

Almost always, there is considerable financial sacrifice. Although "expats" are often well compensated, they have difficulty guarding their assets and tracking their investments abroad; they may have to sell their homes before they go abroad only to incur considerable expense when they return; and they risk damage or loss to precious possessions whether they put them in storage or ship them to their destination. In addition, moving abroad often means family separation for long periods and sometimes includes complicated educational situations for their children.

American staff abroad encounter a host of other difficulties as well. These include an uncomfortable dependence on the company, a lack of staff support ranging from technical assistance to moral support, lack of opportunity to develop professionally through seminars and courses, legal and political hassles, lack of social acceptance, absence of favorite pastimes, and language problems. There is also the usually remote but always possible risk of political upset in the host country. The danger of being stuck in a foreign country, held hostage, or even tortured or killed may be remote but it is real, as Americans from Japan at the outbreak of World War II or those in Iraq at the time it invaded Kuwait can attest.

The image of American expatriates abroad that lingers in the minds of many of their compatriots at home is that of privileged executives with chauffeur-driven cars, pools in the backyard, private schools for the kids, extended vacations, and ceaseless travel to exotic places.

Modern reality is invariably quite different. The financial incentives and luxury living that spurred prior expatriates to give up the comfort of community, the promotion potential in the parent company, and the opportunity to build equity and deepen roots are seldom a real temptation now. Not only is luxurious living abroad less likely; the sudden jolt that occurs on return is no longer a secret and is not adequately cushioned by most companies.

Thrust into an environment where language, food, and customs are strange, expatriate individuals and families suffer considerable stress and alienation. Cut off from family and community, they often don't even have the counseling and human services, and even the medical services, available to the average American. They sometimes suffer discrimination and other problems. Their children may attend good schools, but at a high price. Special problems go untended and often unnoticed.

Even the protection Americans abroad should expect from their government several generations ago is no longer available. Because tuition costs, airfares to and from the States, housing, and other necessities abroad that are reimbursed by the company are considered taxable income by our government, the total income package, which may seem like a fortune at home, is worth far less abroad. While tax inequities, such as double taxation (by both the foreign country and the United States), have largely been abolished, Americans abroad still pay heavy taxes without utilizing most of the federal, state, and city services that those taxes pay for. They have no one representing their interests in Congress.

The reasons Americans accept assignments abroad are as varied as the individuals themselves. For some it is still seen as an economic opportunity, usually in terms of spending a couple of years in a backwater, difficult situation to put aside some capital for the future. Others are driven by the spirit of adventure. Still others see a real job to be done for their company or for their country. Others may think a couple of years overseas will look good on their résumés.

Whatever the reason, they are America's representatives abroad. They maintain our business presence, bring back a degree of internationalism in their mentality, and see opportunities American business would not be likely to hear of otherwise.

The frontrunners of a global economy are often not much valued by the companies that send them abroad, either. It is well known that they are often given lesser positions when they return, that they are in a politically weak position, and that the information they have gathered is often ignored. This is only the tip of the iceberg. Often they are cast adrift because no specific job has been designated for their return. Is it any wonder that companies are hard-pressed to find talented, ambitious, capable people to go abroad? Is it surprising that despite a pool of educated, ambitious executives, the United States lags in international focus?

Reluctance of Corporations to Invest in Their Own

Companies often argue that it is easier to train and promote host and third-country nationals than it is to select high-potential candidates and expend the resources necessary to impart to them necessary attitudes and cultural skills to allow them to function abroad successfully.[7] The potential expatriate executive should have had sufficient home office experience and have demonstrated adaptability and sensitivity to unfamiliar environments.

Ideally, American companies should consider doing some variation of what Japanese companies do: Hire college students and recent grad-

7. Stephen J. Kobrin, op. cit.

uates, send them to the country in which they will be specializing, and pay for their continued education in that country. Then bring them back after graduation for corporate training and experience before again sending them abroad to work in the overseas offices.

Cultural Adjustment, Morals, and Ethics

Managers can learn to adjust and function at maximal efficiency in unfamiliar cultures with appropriate education and familiarization. There are numerous organizations and consultants who specialize in cultural acclimatization. They can help not only with normal familiarization, but also can be helpful in bridging the gap for managers who are faced with foreign cultural situations that may be inconsistent with their beliefs or the written or unwritten rules of their company.

Some examples come readily to mind. In some cultures, the giving and receiving of monetary gifts or even tangible gifts of some value is an accepted and legal practice in circumstances that would be interpreted in the United States as bribery; often, there is no stigma attached to such a practice and obedience to custom is important in indicating one's sincerity or loyalty. Sometimes the practice is technically illegal but widespread and accepted. Faced with such an apparent conflict, the businessperson needs to make a personal as well as a business judgment.

The Far East, Middle East, South America, Africa, Eastern Europe, wherever, customs may merge with ethics, which then blend with morals, which touch legalities. Practices are as different as the cultures. To make matters more worrisome, some widespread, accepted practices may be illegal, but it may cost you to have the law turn its back. Corruption, bribery, and similar practices (called baksheesh, dash, mordida—the "bite"—or whatever) are commonplace in many areas. In Nigeria, it is recounted, a man who has risen to a respectable position as a construction contractor receives a visit from the elder's council of his home village and is asked to help build some houses there. As a prosperous man, he is expected to take care of relatives, friends, neighbors, and others. When he receives a contract to build a large complex in the capital city of Lagos, he may appropriate some of the cement and other building materials to help build houses in the village. In Nigeria, that's not considered corruption; it's just a part of the culture. [8]

American companies use as a guideline the Foreign Corrupt Practices Act of 1977, the U.S. law that governs conduct of American citizens and corporations abroad. The act is mainly aimed at curbing the efforts of American enterprises to win business through payoffs, but it does leave room for payments to foreign officials to facilitate routine

8. Eugene L. Mendonsa, "Coming to Terms with 'Rubber Time,' " *Business Marketing* (October 1989), p. 67.

government action, from processing visas to providing basic services such as police protection and mail delivery. What this means is that you can pay a customs officer to ensure that he inspects your goods expeditiously, but you cannot pay him for approving it without inspecting it.[9] Even a thorough knowledge of and intention to obey the law sometimes requires a judgment call in borderline situations. Often, there is another solution. Picking a partner whose relationships will open doors is a viable alternative using payoffs. There is no denying, however, that whichever way you cut it, you'll have to pay. The partner with influential contacts will have a high cost attached to him, and for every assistance he gives, he's committing himself to an equivalent future obligation, or is calling in markers. If the rules allow, a direct cash payment often involves less long-term risk. Sometimes it is advantageous to be able to say, "Sorry, I can't do it; I'm restricted by U.S. law."

In Germany and the United States, a written contract is an essential basis for business. Most Americans would find the German way of doing business quite comfortable at this level. But what would the response be in the Arab world, where a man's word is paramount and insistence on a contract may be insulting?

Nepotism is considered a positive, recommendable norm in some places. In others, the hiring, promotion, and remuneration of female employees or minority groups may be counter to local custom or even local law. Practices of this sort may be objectionable or immoral by your own personal standards. Working in foreign countries whose legal, moral, or traditional standards are at variance with those you are accustomed to means that you, as an employee abroad must come to terms in some way with the conflict or suffer increasing frustration and possibly guilt.

Of course such cultural bias influences the products appropriate for introduction into a marketplace and the style with which they are promoted. For example, in most European countries children and well-known personalities cannot be used to market toys and games. Sensitivity to the violent aspects of war toys is high in Holland, Belgium, and Germany. When Parker Brothers, part of the General Mills Toy Group, attempted to convert to global advertising, it tended to target adults instead of children to minimize restrictions that would apply, especially in television commercials.[10]

Steps to Reaching a More Global Attitude

As an expatriate grows into an international mentality in preparation for work abroad, development can be tracked by three ordered stages:

9. Ford S. Worthy, with Shelley Neumeier, "When Someone Wants a Payoff," *Fortune*, Pacific Rim Issue (1989), pp. 117–122.
10. "Multinationals Tackle Global Marketing: Parker Bros., Atari," *Advertising Age*, Vol. 55, No. 36 (June 25, 1984), p. 72.

1. *Functional,* which occurs over an extended period long before the move abroad
2. *Cultural,* which takes place before the move and prepares managers for difficulties they may encounter in the new culture
3. *Political, economic, and social awareness of conditions in the new culture,* which are interrelated and ongoing

A study was done to determine the reasons for lower expatriate failure rate among European and Japanese MNCs than among U.S. MNCs. Success of the foreign executives in an overseas venture was tied to the success of the venture itself. A questionnaire was given to twenty-nine Western European multinationals and thirty-five Japanese multinationals. In-depth interviews were given in seventeen other multinationals to help researchers understand the reasons for the greater U.S. expatriate failure rate.

Common denominators to successful performance, as determined by results of the study, were:

- Orientation toward long-term planning and performance evaluation
- Rigorous training of candidates to prepare them for overseas assignments prior to posting
- Provision of a comprehensive support system to expatriates
- Selection of candidates for assignments abroad on the basis of appropriate qualifications
- Restricted job mobility

Europeans, who have had considerable experience in a variety of markets outside their own, had several particular assets that enhanced their success: an international orientation, a longer history of overseas operations, and language capability, the study found.

American businesspeople, on the other hand, are considered to be comparatively inexperienced in countries outside their own. They often lack language skills and more importantly lack sensitivity to peculiarities of a foreign culture. The study recommended that American companies adopt orientations that were more long-term and more international in outlook.[11] It is clear that rather than being a positive indication of the internationalization of American companies as is sometimes claimed, the practice of replacing American managers with locally hired nationals reduces the international skills and resources of American companies over the longer run.

11. Rosalie L. Tung, "Expatriate Assignments: Enhancing Success and Minimizing Failure," *Academy of Management Executives,* Vol. 1, No. 2 (May 1987), pp. 117–125.

Letting Foreign Nationals Select Executive Expatriates

In selecting the appropriate executive to open or run an overseas office, American companies customarily look at the candidate's record: success in the domestic market, familiarity with the product and company, ability to set up a factory or marketing system, financial expertise; secondary is their ability to learn and deal with the psychology of the local work force and sensitivity to the local environment. Yet the personality of the top executive is more directly relevant to the success of the operation than any other single factor.

According to a study done in 1985, the early return rate of expatriate managers (EMs) can run as high as 79 percent.[12]

In response to queries, host country organizations agreed that selection of expatriate managers for assignments abroad should be based on the following criteria:

- Language proficiency
- Expertise in the specific area needed
- Expertise in the business environment of the host country
- Knowledge of the organization's processes
- Age
- Seniority
- Appearance
- Spouse adaptability
- Position in the organization's hierarchy
- Previous foreign success
- Education
- Country of origin
- Marital status

Language proficiency is given top priority, but American companies are only now beginning to apply it as a qualifying factor in selection. Although not indicated in this study, sensitivity to cultural environment is often cited as of crucial importance by employees of corporate branches overseas. Language proficiency without such awareness is not only quite possible but fairly frequent; cultural sensitivity without language capability is also possible and more desirable, if a choice must be made.

As indicated in Chapter 4, a common language does not necessarily indicate a culture in common as well. Ben Loctenberg, the Australian chairman of ICI Americas, Inc., testified that a common language is no insurance against culture shock. When he went to London, his

12. U. Zeira and M. Banai, "Selection of Expatriate Managers in MNCs: The Host-Environment Point of View," *International Studies for Management & Organization*, Vol. 15, No. 1 (Spring 1985), pp. 33–51.

direct Australian manner commanded no respect. He had to learn the oblique ways of the English before he was able to move ahead.

For example, he says, "If an English boss reacted to a pet project by saying, 'Perhaps you ought to think about this a little more,' what he really means is, 'You must be mad. Forget it.' "

In the United States he told a manager, "Perhaps you ought to think about this a little more." The manager took him literally. Asked why he had gone ahead, the man replied, "Well, I thought about it, like you said, and the idea got better." [13]

Although English has been the major international language in the business, financial, medical, technological, and academic fields for years, American companies abroad still need to have people who understand the local language as well as the culture. A corporate officer who makes an attempt to learn at least the rudiments of the local language sends a signal of interest and concern to the potential marketplace.

Social gaffes that affect relationships so vital to business can often be avoided when basics about the culture are known. Business decisions are grounded in awareness rather than speculation.

Current thinking seems to be that the executive in charge should be the most qualified individual available, regardless of nationality. Idealistically, that is certainly admirable, but in practical terms it may be too general a standard to be of value unless the qualifying criteria are carefully detailed.

Corporate Boards Need Local Representation

An organizational strategy that seems to support the success of non-American MNCs is the practice of placing local nationals on the board of directors. It apparently is one important step in internalionalizing a company, but it has not come easily to many American companies.

In a study of the ways in which companies based in different countries utilize boards of directors in foreign subsidiaries, thirty-six parent companies and ninety foreign subsidiaries in twenty-one countries responded to a survey. A company can hardly claim true internationality if all its directors are domestic and there is little or no representation at the top from the countries in which it does business.

Results indicated that American MNCs used subsidiary boards less often than did Swedish, Japanese, and European MNCs. It also mentioned that most companies could benefit from activating selected boards of subsidiaries; that it is a strategy for coping with local legal and political pressures and for increasing access to information about local economic changes. [14]

13. Jeremy Main, "How to Go Global—and Why," *Fortune* (August 28, 1989), p. 72.
14. Mark P. Kriger and Patrick J.J. Rich, "Strategic Governance: Why and How MNCs

Common Problems Faced by Offices Abroad

American MNCs are learning somewhat painfully of the problems inherent in strong centralized operational control. Managers abroad have often complained about having to convince those back home of decisions regarding situations they cannot hope to understand from afar.

Although managers in foreign areas clearly must deal with certain restrictions that bind the company as a whole, they must be knowledgeable enough to use profitably the unusual characteristics and resources of their local area. One major resource that is often underutilized from lack of knowledge on the part of the expatriate manager is people. Gathering the financial data necessary to run an office or choosing the location for a factory is plum pudding compared with learning the psychology of the local work force and how best to deal with it. "Success on the international scene depends largely on the skills of expatriate employees and the home office managers who supervise and support them," says Marlene Piturro in *Management Review.*[15]

Structured for Success

Companies seem to evolve through three stages in relation to their internationalism. At the first stage of emergence beyond that of a local, regional, or national enterprise are the emerging international companies (EICs). They have little experience in international trading. At the second stage are EICs that have had experience outside of a national base through exporting but not through foreign factories or offices. At the third stage, the companies have become MNCs, with manufacturing and/or offices abroad.

Colin G. Armistead, a lecturer at the Cranford School of Management in the United Kingdom, has formulated the table shown in Figure 11-2 to describe business functions in the various stages of internationalism.

Assuming certain basics, such as sufficient capital to initiate and sustain a venture abroad for a prefigured period of time, what goes into determining whether a company is suitable fodder for the overseas machine? The head of one major multinational, Robert Lambert, states that "any firm with sales in excess of $25 million should consider world marketing." His company, General Foods Corp., conducts international sales through subsidiaries that run as local companies within their foreign boundaries. He may be right. Considering world marketing is

Are Using Boards of Directors in Foreign Subsidiaries," *Columbia Journal of World Business*, Vol. 22, No. 4 (Winter 1987), pp. 39–46.

15. Marlene C. Piturro, "Southeast Asia: Doing Business in Paradise?" *Management Review*, Vol. 77, No. 7 (July 1988), pp. 30–34.

Figure 11-2. Progression of companies to multinational status.

Function	EIC-1	EIC-2	MNC
Marketing	▪ Domestic market mainly	▪ Markets in several countries through export	▪ Widely developed markets in many countries
Human resources	▪ Limited	▪ Some experience outside home country	▪ Experience and management able to operate internationally
Finance	▪ Mainly home based	▪ Financial aspects limited to export	▪ Established systems to maximize parent profitability
Information systems	▪ Home based	▪ Limited outside national boundaries	▪ Integrated across national boundaries
Operations			
1. Sourcing	▪ National and/or foreign	▪ Local and/or international	▪ International sourcing often interfactory
2. Manufacture	▪ EOSs (emerging overseas subsidiaries) may be limited by home markets	▪ EOSs may be limited by local markets and export potential	▪ More developed to gain EOSs along value-added chain

Source: Colin G. Armistead, "International Factory Networks," *European Management Journal*, Vol. 7, No. 3 (September 1989), p. 367.

one thing; readiness for it is another, and is something to which marketing/communications people should be particularly sensitive.[16]

The steps of internationalism are indications of the type and scope of public relations activities that would be appropriate for an organization at any given time. On the assumption that a healthy, well-managed company will grow, the table of business functions suggests what a public relations professional should be considering in the next strategic step toward internationalization.

How well organizations utilize their public relations operations and the contributions those operations can make toward the success of the company were suggested in the results of a study called "Excellence in

16. Stephen J. Kobrin, op. cit.

Public Relations and Communications Management." Excellent organizations, it said, use public relations to "mobilize support and manage conflict with key audiences, while other organizations use it as a propaganda weapon . . . Excellent organizations typically have decentralized structures and participating management. . . ."[17]

Certain Products Sell Well Abroad

As suggested previously, certain products tend to be readily salable abroad, requiring little or no adaptation to the overseas market. Determining which ones they are takes research and a feel for the marketplace, which are parts of the basic preparatory plan.

While research needs to be done for each product or service being considered for a new market, certain general assumptions can be made. Advanced technological know-how, for instance, is in great demand almost everywhere—many countries want many types of it. Products that fill a particular niche have great promise; sometimes certain areas have clearly identifiable needs. Uniqueness is another characteristic that generally promises success, even when it is unfamiliar, but especially if the company has unusual knowledge or experience in connection with the product.

Soft Sheen Products, Inc., claims to have both unique products and special knowledge. The company manufactures more than 165 ethnic hair care products that it markets to black users. President Gary E. Gardner, who is black, says the company expects to capitalize on its extensive knowledge of consumers' needs to outmarket the competition when it goes international.[18] Soft Sheen grossed $81.2 million in 1987 in the highly competitive toiletries field up against such giants as Revlon and Alberto Culver.

Having the right product is a major factor in the quest for success, but it is only a start. The right method of marketing the product is another matter. Realizing that methods that work in the United States may be deadly somewhere else is the first step in developing a successful strategy. For instance, the hard sell so familiar to American TV viewers and characterized in its extreme form by the old Crazy Eddie commercials and many regional used car commercials would bore and probably

---

17. Denny Griswold, Special Report, Part II, *PR News* (June 18, 1990). The study mentioned was begun in 1986 to identify the effect of communication on the bottom line. It is sponsored by the IABC Research Foundation in San Francisco, funded by contributions from individuals, IABC chapters and districts, corporations, grants, and sales of research reports. The study's director is James Grunig, professor of journalism at the University of Maryland.
18. Paul S. Besson, "The Guts to Go Global," *Black Enterprise*, Vol. 18, No. 11 (June 1988), pp. 192–196.

offend a Japanese viewer, who is used to subtlety and humor. By now even the average reader knows that trying to avoid the middlemen in that culture by marketing directly is also likely to lead to dismal results. Promotional methods that have proven successful in the United States are often too direct, too hard-hitting, or too disruptive of normal social interaction in Japan and some other countries.

Similarly, the frequent and heavy emphasis on sex in so many American ads would probably be censored in Pakistan and China, but would seem mild in many European countries. Don't let proximity fool you, or the idea that because Europe is becoming unified one country is similar to another. A commercial that seems innocuous in Paris may be refused airtime in Geneva.

Do Your Homework!

Companies considering moving into operations overseas should be willing to research the culture, language, history, political environment, social and moral structure as well as market competition and the usual financials. Selection of management personnel, proper training of executives, and preparations within the host country prior to entry are also essential. While all these functions do not fall into public relations functional areas, the preparation, background, and consultation on them certainly can be assumed by public relations.

Essentially a problem-solving discipline, public relations is of particular value in opening new doors, in seeing "the trees *and* the forest"[19]— a global perspective but the ability to operate locally.

How the company is structured; what its priorities are; its degree of flexibility, centralization, or decentralization are all elements that contribute to or limit its potential for success abroad. Some companies, though superficially good candidates for business abroad, should not attempt it, at least under their current structure. One of these apparently was Lever Brothers, Ltd., maker and marketer of soaps and detergents. Its brands are global but its structure has been less than optimal for international marketing.[20] Lever encouraged international sales without keeping an eye on the activities of its overseas marketers. It concentrated on domestic strength and forfeited control of its products and product names in the international arena. As a result, it faced a loss of market share to retailers who were producing products under their own labels that imitated Lever's category leaders. Lever's policy was to refuse to supply its products under other labels. Looking now to internationalize,

19. Gavin Anderson, "A Global Look at Public Relations," in Bill Cantor, *Experts in Action: Inside Public Relations*, 2nd edition, ed. Chester Burger (White Plains, N.Y.: Longman, 1989), pp. 413–414.
20. Tom Lester, "Lever Centerary: Cleaning Power," *Marketing* (United Kingdom) (March 10, 1988), p. 26.

it faces stiff competition from Procter & Gamble and may have to lose some domestic strength to recoup abroad.

Procter & Gamble is one example of a company that has long been active internationally. The same factors that have made it a leader in the U.S. market have held it back internationally: rigidity and centralization.

In 1986 it reorganized itself into a matrix structure that put its product lines under international brand managers who reported upward to national general managers, who reported directly to a Eurobrand manager. Even this was again changed and Pampers™, for instance, is run by a general manager for Europe.

In contrast, Unilever allows national companies to develop their own brands and markets. It encourages a bottom-up style of consensus management that seems to work well for the global marketplace.[21]

What is clear is that many companies, both American and non-American, have operated successfully outside their home markets for years. Sometimes they seem to have broken all the rules, in which case being in the right place with the right product no doubt had a strong influence. In most cases, however, they have been successful because in addition to formulating careful plans and sound strategy they have followed the two cardinal rules of public relations: Know your audience and communicate effectively.

Strategize for Success

Since strategic planning for the 1990s will focus on projects for the global marketplace, strategy must build organizational structures that emphasize speed, flexibility, and response to changing demands.[22] In a network of interrelated corporate activities, one researcher includes vision, mission, structure, policy and procedures, and systems. Information technology can be profitably applied to provide a competitive advantage if the company's values and priorities are examined in the light of how they can be enhanced through the application of that information technology.

The words *structure* and *information technology* recur repeatedly in forecasts about the coming global marketplace and winning a competitive advantage. Speed in responding to change is cited as another factor. Added to this is "lean, flat, decentralized organizations with quality, pricing, service, and design."[23]

A "prescription for survival" was given recently in a Japanese pub-

21. Tom Lester, "World Ends," *Marketing* (United Kingdom) (January 14, 1988), pp. 17–18.
22. John Tuman, Jr., "Shaping Corporate Strategy With Information Technology," *Project Management Journal*, Vol. 19, No. 4 (September 1988), pp. 35–42.
23. Jeremy Main, "The Winning Organization," *Fortune*, Vol. 118, No. 7 (September 26, 1988), pp. 50–60.

lication by the chairman of Mitsubishi Research Institute, Inc., and the managing director of Software Economic Center, Inc.[24] They advised:

- Don't abandon your core business, but don't stay locked into it. Diversify from within.
- Move to a managerial style and operations structure that responds selectively to market needs.
- Develop an effective personnel policy based on performance criteria rather than longevity.
- Training in-house specialists in high technology and finance will be crucial factors.
- Go beyond a merely vertical or horizontal corporate structure to something like a net structure or network.
- Ensure the flexibility of the corporation and the good morale of the employees by creating smaller, semiautonomous units and subsidiaries.
- Articulate a strong corporate ideal to strengthen corporate image and unite the company.

In a panel discussion held to discuss factors that contribute to corporate success, it was not surprising that Japanese management people underlined the importance of the human factor, a viewpoint frequently found echoed in research for this book. In the same discussion, the president of Nestle K. K., H. J. Sinniger, focused on the importance of companies' finding and marketing products that consumers want, particularly in view of the increasing segmentation now occurring. Also mentioned were the importance of paying attention to details in marketing, servicing, and providing quality products. But Yoshihiro Tajima, professor of Gakushuin University and author of best-selling books on distribution and marketing, concluded that growth companies are those that have a philosophical perspective of what human beings are.

Masatoshi Ito, president of Ito Yokado Co., Ltd., observed that in any country some employees work hard and seriously. The most important factor in running a business, he said, is trust—that of stockholders, employees, suppliers, and customers. Not a popular view, perhaps, in American MNCs, but the competitive edge for the future, in this writer's opinion.

Retroview

In assessing and preparing to advise your employees as to their readiness to move abroad and steps they should take to ensure success, consider and respond to the following:

24. Kimindo Kusaka and Noboru Makino, "A Prescription for Survival," *PHP Intersect* (February 1988), p. 12.

- What is our purpose in moving abroad? What are our goals?
- What do we expect to contribute to the marketplace?
- What does the destination market expect to contribute and receive?
- What kind of image do we want to project?
- What type of venture is best for us and our products?
- Who will be managing the overseas venture and how will we select that person?
- What will be our policy on information dissemination?
- Have we done a thorough analysis of the target country? Are we familiar with cultural as well as legal, financial, and organizational demands?
- Are we taking steps to develop a global perspective in our organization?
- What level and range of responsibility will the manager have?
- What kind of training will we give American managers responsible for overseas operations and their families?
- What kind of compensation package have we developed?
- At what stage of development is our company in terms of internationalism?
- What are our most promising products for target? Why?

12

The Future Is Outside Our Borders: The European Common Market After 1992

Changes in U.S. domestic markets, the economy, and overseas markets all create an imperative for U.S. business to think on a much broader scale and to seriously consider the risk-reward potential in a move abroad. Unfortunately, the U.S. proclivity to short-term action combined with lack of experience and success abroad as well as the current conservative, risk-avoidance stance in business, make the promise of the EC more of a threat.

The opportunity is there for those who want to grab it. It's also there, increasingly, for public relations. Having moved steadily from a publicity function into a management consultancy/communications management mode, public relations is entering its own heyday. No other functional area in business is as well suited to fulfilling the needs and opportunities facing business at this time. Public relations professionals need to keep current with business potential and understand the expanding—and contracting—markets abroad. We need to be alert to the direction changes are taking, to evolving trends, to danger signals, and to the degree to which we can utilize and develop public relations operations.

Both Europe and Asia offer protean opportunity—changing business, economic, cultural, and in some cases political scenarios—but a dearth of sophisticated public relations facilities to handle them. With the exception of the United Kingdom, public relations in Europe is still evolving from the basic publicity level. In much of Asia, both the need and the opportunity are parallel with their counterparts in Europe. Russia, Eastern Europe, China, and some other Asian countries offer future potential. South America is ripe for the introduction of certain functional public relations areas.

Following is an overview of movements in the European Economic Community and Asia that American public relations professionals need to be aware of. In Chapter 6 we took a quick look at the status of public relations in various countries and the consolidation of public relations firms that is growing out of that. While these are movements in the mechanics of the industry, more important is an awareness of the expanding functional possibilities that corporations now seek from public relations professionals in the international arena.

By 1992 Europe is expected to be forged into a single economic entity. If all goes well, physical, fiscal, and technical barriers will have been largely eliminated as will customs formalities, national requirements/restrictions on goods, and differential indirect tax rates.

The European Economic Community (EC), with twelve member countries and a population of 325 million, is the largest trading block in the industrialized world. It is a greater exporter to third world countries than the United States, Japan, and the U.S.S.R. combined. Even before unification is accomplished, the market is already 30 percent larger than the United States market and almost three times the size of Japan's.[1]

The market is not only large, but rich, with a gross domestic product (GDP) higher than that of either the United States or Japan. When unification is accomplished, which will probably not be by 1992, a product on sale anywhere in the EC would be allowed access to markets anywhere else in the EC.

While many issues still have to be resolved prior to full accomplishment, substantial changes have been made and for many purposes the 1992 deadline is on schedule. Forging a real common market, eliminating import/export restrictions, and applying the same minimum specifications and laws to products from different countries has been no easy task for the Europeans.

The implications for the rest of the world, especially the United States, are enormous. Rich in resources, large both geographically and in numbers of people, industrialized and well-to-do, the United States has for decades been the world's premier market. Opportunities for domestic business have been so substantial as to limit the ambitions of many U.S. marketers to the local scene and ignore more global opportunities. As a result, other countries have gained much from the experience of marketing outside their home grounds.

The EC: Challenges and Opportunities

Finalization of measures to integrate the market is commonly expected to produce the following results: improved market opportunities, in-

1. *European Management Journal,* Vol. 7, No. 3 (September 1989), published by Basil Blackwell for Management Centre Europe.

creasing domestic competition from other EC countries, and rising competition throughout the EC from external sources. There is little question but that the opportunities and threats of the changed marketplace will demand erasure of insularity in Europe.[2] However, there is no evidence that standardization is in any way eroding distinctive national or local differentiation. Planned and implemented changes will

2. Jeremy Thorn, "Exporting: The Community Melting Pot," *Industrial Marketing Digest* (United Kingdom), Vol. 13, No. 3 (Third Quarter 1988), pp. 51–57.

make distribution across borders easier, but will give little boost to marketing. The product, at least in most cases, will still have to be tailored, packaged, promoted, and sold in a manner appropriate to each national marketplace.

Although many markets will continue to stay local, they are likely to get smaller over time. Political, geographical, cultural, and tariff barriers that once bolstered national marketing strategies will become less relevant. Increased travel, proliferation of electronic information, and similar factors will push the homogenization of consumer tastes and preferences. Customers will increasingly cross borders to buy better goods and services; at the same time, differences in quality and price according to geographical area will gradually disappear.

The key word here seems to be service. Of all the values that may present opportunities in the coming European market, service may take top priority, which suggests growth opportunities for both public relations and marketing. Take a look at this: In a study involving 1,055 senior managers from 14 European countries,* 94 percent saw service to the customer as more or even much more important in the next 5 years. Of those, 78 percent saw improving quality and service to customers as the key to competitive success, and 85 percent believed that giving superior service is one of their key responsibilities regardless of position.

Inherent in these views are the opinions that service is more important as a differentiator, that competition is fiercer, and that customers are more demanding. However, only about half think service is a clear and accepted priority throughout their company. In terms of the priorities of service, quality is the most important, followed by problem solving, reliability, after-sales service, speed of delivery, courtesy, and others.

Tools of the Public Relations Trade: Reality and Perception

This information is important to the public relations professional on two sides: reality and perception. Within the company, it is up to the marketing and public relations areas to be aware of such priorities and to attune the company to meet the observed needs; it is also up to public relations to establish and strengthen the external perception of the company as service-oriented. The companies that are most admired rank high because of awareness of what they do and what they stand for. That comes from years of investing in the image through public relations efforts such as promotions, community programs, publicity, and

---

*In a joint venture between Management Centre Europe and John Humble and Company, John Humble did a study from August to December 1988, published in *Service: The New Competitive Edge* by the European Headquarters of the American Management Association International, Brussels.

advertising. Public relations must be the primary instrument in establishing this perception.

Second, the performance of the company must have "substantially lived up to their service and quality promises."* No matter how hard the public relations people work, they cannot create substance from smoke. Both consumers and press are far too sophisticated these days. While skillful promotion is not only desirable but necessary, and while it can and does enhance the product being marketed, there has to be a product and reality must be close to perception.

The best guess seems to be that new markets will form based not on local or national markets as they are now, but based on specialization. They may be in geographical proximity, with similar demographics and economics. The market is predicted to develop into large regional mass-clusters of consumers, medium-size regional niche-clusters, and small local niche markets based on specific locality, life-style, and industry differences. These latter will be highly customized markets, while the medium-size clusters will be mass customized.[3]

The formation of Euromarket groups of this type can have considerable impact for public relations as well as marketing people who must decide which communities and which publications are most useful to cultivate as part of their audience. The degree of standardization in product is an indicator of the degree of standardization that may be possible in communications. Clusters that are limited and exclusive would seem to flag a need for very targeted communications.

Figure 12-1 shows Euromarket groups, their characteristics, and the necessary approach to them.

In organizing the approaches for various functions that would be most appropriate for European markets, the writer has compiled a neatly packaged marketing strategy utilizing the "eight Ps": (1) positioning, (2) product, (3) pricing, (4) place, (5) promotion, (6) public affairs, (7) people, (8) period. This approach gives a good overall view of the likely marketing situation as the Euromarket develops.

The "Eight P" ingredients for future integrated marketing strategy are summarized in Figure 12-2, showing Euromarket groups as described in the previous analysis.

Pricing is likely to be similar across the board for a number of reasons: Customers are likely to be aware of price differences one place to another; customers will be increasingly mobile and able to buy outside their home areas if price or quality makes that worthwhile; mail order and electronic network shopping will be widespread; exchange rates will become more stable; and the Eurounit may come into wide usage.

3. Sandra Vandermerwe, "From Fragmentation to Integration: A Conceptual Pan-European Marketing Formula," *European Management Journal* Vol. 7, No. 3 (September 1989), pp. 267–270.

* Ibid.

Figure 12-1. Euromarket group characteristics and market approaches.

Characteristic Overall Thrust	Regional Mass-Clusters	Regional Niche-Clusters	Local Niche-Markets
Size	Very Large/Large	Medium	Small
Fragmentation	Very Low/Low	Medium	High
Differentiation	Little	Some	Lot
Marketing approach	Mass	Mass Customization	Customization
Degree of standardization	High	Medium	Low

Source: Sandra Vandermerwe, "From Fragmentation to Integration: A Conceptual Pan-European Marketing Formula," *European Management Journal* (September 1989), Vol. 7, No. 3, pp. 267–270.

Generally, the size of the market, the customer, and competitive pressure will drive prices downward. Increased pan-European television and broadcast advertising will make mass promotion practical.

There is some concern in the United States as to how the integrated market will affect its trade interests. A plethora of directives from the European Commission covering service industries provide U.S marketers with specific guidance on requirements for entering the marketplace. They give companies substantial homework to do, but at the same time may, over the long run, cut down on both individual company research and paperwork for doing business abroad. (See Appendix I for organizations and publications that provide information and help on EEC markets.)

The services directives fall into these categories: financial services such as banking, insurance, and mortgage credit; transport services; miscellaneous sectors such as tourism, engineering, and medical practice; and cross-sectional directives.[4]

Beyond the directives, factors such as economic climate, cultural differences, government regulations, and nontariff trade barriers can seriously affect entry.

Certain general Europewide conditions must be accommodated by American companies. Among them are: low economic growth, high employment, low productivity, and high prices.

For instance, it is virtually impossible to fire anyone because of the strong influence and staunchly socialistic attitude of unions and government (although unions are reportedly losing membership in many

4. Brant W. Free, "The EC Single Internal Market: Implications for U.S. Service Industries," *Business America*, Vol. 109, No. 16 (August 1, 1988), pp. 10–11.

Figure 12-2. Eight-P marketing strategies for Euromarkets.

Marketing Strategy 8Ps	Regional Mass-Clusters	Regional Niche-Clusters	Local Niche-Markets
Positioning	• Pan-European • Uniform corporate identity	• Pan-European • Uniformity with some differences when necessary	• Localized adapted to suit market
Product	• Pan-European rationalized brands • Increased choice • Standard marketing names, logos, etc.	• Pan-European rationalized brands • Differentiation and customization • Some adaptation	• Localized products and brands specific to area
Pricing	• Uniform Pan-European • Lower	• Uniform Pan-European, some differentiation • Lower	• Localized depending on circumstances
Place	• Uniform • Consolidated and rationalized systems	• Uniform adapted • Some consolidation and rationalization	• To suit area • Locally based
Promotion	• Pan-European integrated sales and marketing • Some harmonization	• Pan-European • Some adaptation and integration • Some harmonization	• Local done by locals for locals
Public affairs	• Pan-European integration with promotion • Some local activity	• Pan-European where possible • Regional activity	• Highly localized • Some Pan-European activity
People	• Pan-European cultures, people, and organizations linked and integrated • Local contact	• Pan-European approach and linkage • Regional structures and organization • Local contact	• Local people and structure
Period	• Shorter life-cycles and diffusion • Simultaneous marketing Pan-European	• Shorter life-cycles and diffusion • Simultaneous marketing in regions even Pan-European	• Local timing of strategies

Source: Sandra Vandermerwe, "From Fragmentation to Integration: A Conceptual Pan-European Marketing Formula," *European Management Journal* (September 1989), Vol. 7, No. 3, p. 270.

countries). This eliminates U.S. companies' favorite means of cutting costs, solving production and organizational problems, and rationalizing the bottom line.

Other issues that need attention are the evaluation of the current market size and the importance of nonprice factors. Specifically, businesses need to ask themselves:

- Should we export or invest?
- Should we expand existing production capabilities?
- Should we establish a new facility or acquire it by joint venture?
- Which countries will lose?
- Where should investment be made?
- How are EC and non-EC members poised to invest?

These questions are crucial to formulating initial strategy and outlining longer-term goals. Areas in which U.S. companies can be expected to benefit from 1992 in the near range are:

- Economies of scale
- Higher levels of EC-wide trade
- Increasing standardization of products to fit divergent national identities
- Pan-European advertising and public relations, which will take some time to develop and will never totally erase communications tailored to individual locales

(In earlier sections (Chapters 4 and 12) on communications media and methods, we looked at trends and forecasts in communications and how they are developing in the Euromarket. Specific information on both national and international media can be found in the Appendixes I and II.)

Product price differentials between the various EC countries, the importance of transportation and distribution costs, the responsiveness of product sales to price changes, and the costs of achieving competitiveness must also be figured in.

Changing Marketing Methods

Preparing for removal of barriers to trade in 1992, multinational marketers are trying to revolutionize the marketing of products and services in Europe. They plan to save an estimated $200 billion over the liberalization years in a market of 320 million consumers.[5]

5. Kevin Cote, "European Advertisers Prepare for 1992," *Europe*, No. 279 (September 1988), pp. 18–19.

In examining how to approach this new marketplace, it was determined that American business must consider its competition with respect to the following strengths of major geographic business sectors:

United States
- Biotechnology
- Aerospace
- Software
- Electronic systems
- Integrated circuits
- Electronic materials
- Artificial intelligence

Europe
- Telecommunications
- Software
- Automotive plastic
- Chemicals

Japan
- Ceramics (structural/engineering)
- Consumer electronics
- Automotive composites
- Low-cost manufacturing techniques
- Semiconductor equipment
- Electronic peripherals and components
- Image recognition equipment[6]

Within this context and in some cases diverging from it are businesses that are viewed as most likely to gain from 1992. These include:

- Motor vehicles
- Chemicals
- Aerospace
- Electronics
- Food and beverages
- Pharmaceuticals
- Telecommunications
- Financial services

Aerospace and electronics are clearly viewed as opportunities for the American side. After that, the question of opportunities versus risks enters into the discussion. Software, which has to compete with European software, is not on the second list. Neither are artificial intelligence, integrated circuits, or biotechnology.

Given the sophisticated technology of telecommunications in France

6. John Elkins, president and CEO of the Naisbitt Group, in a lecture at Baruch College, April 1989.

and Germany, there is some question as to the ease of entry into that market. The chemical market may also be difficult for a similar reason. German pharmaceutical makers own a large piece of the global pie and offer strong competition to American makers. While the potential of motor vehicles may be very real, the market is highly competitive. The most reasonable approach is to manufacture American cars in Europe, which then raises the spectre of overcoming some of the problems, labor and otherwise, that already face European makers.

Food and beverages would seem to offer good promise, as would financial services. The latter category is predicted by virtually every measure to grow rapidly in the future but will encounter no little competition from home companies.

Specifically on the financial services side, after 1992 consumers will be able to choose the best deal available from the full range of banking, securities, and insurance options offered throughout all member states.[7] Since the end of 1988, the second half of the 1992 project has been in effect—it calls for the end of sovereignty, one of the stickiest problems in the issue of frontier controls, and a customs-free solution to the tax problem.

One industry that seems glaringly absent is that of health care, which appears to date to have taken few steps to move abroad.

Strategic Windows

Whole countries, like whole industries, may perhaps be too broad a target to be considered strategic windows. However, certain specific geographical areas need to be pinpointed as particularly promising. One of these is Spain.

Long in the doldrums, the economy of Spain is looking up. Her gross national product grew by 5.2 percent in 1987, double the EC average, and inflation fell to 4.6 percent at the end of that year. Gold and foreign currency reserves are at an all-time high, exceeding her total public and private debt. The strengthening of the peseta and other indications point to Spain as the fastest-growing consumer market in Europe.[8] Furthermore, her cost of labor is half that of Germany, while her production output is more than half and growing rapidly.

Now, in Spain's fourth year of membership in the EC, imports have also been growing. Plastics top the list in import growth, followed by chemicals. Petrochemicals and fertilizer sectors have become stronger

7. Roger Gray, "Europe 1992: Liberalization of Capital Markets," *Management Accounting* (United Kingdom), Vol. 66, No. 5 (May 1988), p. 7.
8. Tom Burns, "Spain: Spain's Economy Is Booming With EC Membership," *Europe*, No. 277 (June 1988), pp. 34–36.

competitors in EC markets. There are no quotas on Spanish products sold to EC countries, an advantage that affects foreign manufacturers as well. Also, EC duty on goods made in Spain is substantially less than that applied to most other members. Plans are to boost electronic and other high-tech exports.[9]

Since the election of Felipe Gonzalez in 1986, Spain has attempted to control inflation while expanding the economy. The current administration has big ambitions for the country and is endeavoring to utilize the upcoming Olympic Games in Barcelona, Barcelona's birthday, and other national events as pivotal events to attract businesses and tourists to the country.

Although Spain's development lags behind that of France and other EC countries, it is a ripe market for certain products. As mentioned, there is a clear move by women 25 and older (who are usually married) to enter the work force.

Electricity is readily available in virtually every area of the country, as is refrigeration. Fast foods for domestic use are not popular, possibly because their availability and selection are very limited. Even in other EC countries, frozen and other quick foods are not in wide use. French women, for instance, spend an average of three hours daily in the kitchen as opposed to a half hour a day for American women.[10]

In 1988 Vale Foods, a small, American, limited liability partnership headquartered in the United States, introduced frozen convenience foods, principally high-protein commodities, into Spain. The company considered its entry a move to open new markets specifically designed to appeal to the recently and more widely employed Spanish working woman. Vale planned to develop local markets in the short term and aim for sales on a national basis prior to 1992.

Vale Foods test marketed by importing selected products from the United States. They met with fair success. However, they are optimistic and intend to produce and package new products in Spain designed specifically for that market, believing that it not only will be more economical but that they will gain by providing jobs and will be better equipped to design food products acceptable in their target market.

Similarly, Portugal is showing economic growth and declining inflation. It has begun privatizing some public companies, removing restrictions on employee dismissals, and streamlining the direct income tax system.

Lower U.S. prices make our businesses competitive in specialty chemicals, industrial machinery, computers, telecommunications, and

9. Eduardo Cue, "Spain: A New Mecca for High-Tech Companies," *Business Week* (Industrial/Technology Edition), No. 2880 (February 11, 1985), pp. 116H,L.
10. Elkins, loc. cit.

some other areas. The increase in construction and mining projects should also affect some U.S. businesses favorably.[11]

Though they are not yet part of the EC, developments in Eastern Europe and even Russia suggest the possibility of new markets in both areas soon. The bureaucratic tangle and socialistic consciousness that has built up over the years will take some time to sort out, but the lure of the capitalist dollar promises to have a strong influence.

Issues and Trends

With the approach of the deadline for unification, anxiety increases concerning certain issues. One that seems to have gotten remarkably little press, considering the impact it could have on U.S. companies, is the inability of American lawyers to argue before the European Commission and European courts. A 1989 directive required member states to recognize diplomas of higher education across the EC, although diploma and licensing requirements differ appreciably. Law firms seeking to practice in the EC will still be subject to the regulations of individual lawyers' countries.[12]

Language and a common currency are other important unresolved issues. Many Europeans speak more than one language, a factor that helps facilitate business interchange. English is also widely used, a fact that is very convenient for Americans. However, no real agreement exists on language apart from an acknowledgment that an official business language might be a good idea. The common currency issue has a somewhat greater degree of urgency; although the ECU (European currency unit) exists, it is not yet in wide usage inside the EC.

Standardization on other fronts is also an issue. The EC Commission has said that central securities depositories must cooperate and draw up common standards. They are a natural starting point for the settlement of international transactions because of their official status and comprehensive functions. Because depositories must offer each other a reciprocal custom service, they need to have similar legal structures.

Stock exchanges will be asked to help develop a depository receipt accepted all over the EC. Depositors will have to keep the currency accounting and will have to open cash accounts with each other.[13]

Despite sophisticated telecommunications in many European countries, communitywide Europe remains a patchwork of divergent tariff, certification, and procurement policies. Equipment and service

11. "Portugal: U.S. Firms Need to Market Aggressively to Counter Strong EC Competition," *Business America*, Vol. 109, No. 12 (June 6, 1988), pp. 22–23.
12. Josephine Carr, "Contrary to the Spirit of 1992?" *International Financial Law Review* (United Kingdom), Vol. 7, No. 8 (August 1988), pp. 10–12.
13. Jorg-Ronald Kessler, "Stand Up and Be Standardized," *Banker* (United Kingdom), Vol. 138, No. 747 (May 1988), pp. 59–62.

are irregular.[14] The flow of communications and the rapid exchange of information will have to be standardized.

Requirements for Success

While it is generally accepted that barriers in Europe will drop for European companies, many analysts consider them likely to increase for U.S. companies as protectionist pressure mushrooms. The benefits of being small—flexibility, adaptability, and creativity—will be appreciated in Europe and will allow the company to react quickly to changes. The best approach may be to choose a small national market soon, get established, and wait until this market becomes integrated into the larger Pan-European market.[15]

Others believe that U.S. companies will benefit from freer movement throughout Europe as crossing borders becomes easier. The changes necessary to accomplish unification will cause restructuring in European countries, which in turn will cause gains in productivity, economies of scale, and new product development. Durable corporate alliances may become the only way to successfully compete in business there, at least for non-EC companies.[16]

Certainly in examining the inherent possibilities in the European market, it is essential for companies to analyze their current structure and operations to determine their preparedness for entering the EC. *Europe 1992*, a publication of the European Commission (1988), describes how to get the ball rolling. The procedure it recommends, while thorough enough to meet the needs of large companies, will probably prove too cumbersome for smaller ones with more limited resources but enough flexibility to allow greater freedom to learn as they go.

For such smaller enterprises, three lecturers from the University of Glasgow Business School have developed a Small Company European Analysis Technique (SCEAT).[17] It was designed to construct an initial analysis of a company in relation to 1992, but it assumes a certain familiarity with regulations and implications associated with the market.

The model provides steps to guide a company toward awareness of its readiness to participate in the market. It is not a substitute for the strategic planning for formulation of goals described in Chapter One,

14. Denis Gilhooly, "European Telecommunication—Fact or Fiction?" *Telecommunications* (International Edition), Vol. 21, No. 10 (October 1987), pp. 46–58.
15. George V. Priovolos, "Small Business Can Benefit From European Changes If They Take Precautions," *Marketing News*, Vol. 22, No. 20 (September 26, 1988), p. 6.
16. Philip Revzin, "U.S., European Firms Prepare for 1992 Market Deadline," *Europe*, No. 275 (April 1988), pp. 16–18.
17. Robert Paton, Geoff Southern, and Martin Houghton, "European Strategy Formulation: The Small Company European Analysis Technique (SCEAT), *European Management Journal*, Vol. 7, No. 3 (September 1989), pp. 305–309.

but for some companies may be a valuable, targeted adjunct to that. It is an analysis technique for determining an organization's awareness of the implications of 1992 and what must be done to prepare for the single market. It does not substitute for overall corporate planning, nor for public relations strategizing.

Following are the principle steps in the model:

Step 1: Business/Euro presentation
Step 2: Primary issue generation—brainstorming
Step 3: Primary issue evaluation and classification
Step 4: Issue explosion—brainstorming generation of associated factors/questions
Step 5: Classification and evaluation of the "issue explosion"
Step 6: Statement generation—brainstorming
Step 7: Statement ranking and evaluation
Step 8: Statement integration
Step 9: Allocation of tasks
Step 10: Report back

During Steps 2 through 6, it is likely that new issues or questions may arise that necessitate moving back to previous steps to reevaluate before again proceeding. Steps 7 and 8 may also require some back-and-forth movement. By the time Step 10 is reached, it will be necessary to incorporate findings into previous steps.

The developers of the model assign the job of the initial presentation to the chief executive or a senior member of the management team. Of course, it is reasonable for the top public relations executive, if that person has sufficient seniority, to be the presenter unless the chief executive wishes to do so personally.

The developers of the model also stress that all participants already should have been provided with relevant background information. If the senior public relations professional is not a member of senior management, she should certainly play a key preparatory role in gathering information and constructing the presentation. It is also reasonable that the public relations professional should be the facilitator that conducts and oversees the SCEAT. Depending upon the resources of the organization, he or she may be the most appropriate one to conduct the brainstorming session in Step 2.

Once the primary issues are generated, they should be evaluated and categorized into general headings such as finance, communications, and marketing, according to the developers. Participants then write questions or comments concerning the issues raised which probe the validity and implications associated with the issue headings.

The group is then divided into "syndicates" to review the material and discuss critical points. They then, in Step 6, generate statements associated with the previously classified questions and comments. In the next step, the group reconvenes and each issue, with its associated statements, is posted. Every statement is prioritized and ranked for agreement or disagreement by the group. A semifinal report is then developed.

By Step 8 the management team is ready to consider the findings and eliminate those that are unfavorable. A tentative strategy is formulated and an action plan constructed. The chief executive should be ready to allocate tasks. Except for the report back, the SCEAT event is now complete.

Developers say the SCEAT model is designed to be run over a period of three to five hours, excluding the final stage, which lasts about two hours. Among the duties of the facilitator is to ensure that the syndicate groups have generated statements, not questions. By the ninth step, the participants are beginning to "own" the project and are in a position to work together to develop strategy. The support of top management is essential to their success. The model is designed to be a diagnostic tool that particularly targets the EC, is consistent with but does not substitute for overall corporate missions, and creates an awareness of issues. Public relations strategy would be formulated separately from this SCEAT exercise, but the information developed in SCEAT would be useful in fine-tuning it.

Numerous publications have been made available to inform and prepare marketers and manufacturers for the European Economic Community. Some of these are:

The Single Market: The Facts
Progress on the Commission White Paper
A Single Market Checklist for Small Firms
Single Market News

They are published by DTI, Internal European Policy Division, Room 405, 1–19 Victoria Street, London SW1H OE1.

See Appendix I for others. Another help to businesspeople is the Euro-Info Centres Project, which has about 187 centres throughout Europe and the U.K. at which you can get across to Brussels data bases and information on prospective EC partners. Most are located in Chambers of Commerce or industrial development agencies.

There are also thirty Business Innovation Centers (BICs) that offer business development services and venture capital provision. Information on them can be obtained from the Commission of the European Communities, Directorate General for Information, Communication, Culture, Rue de la Loi 200—B-1049, Brussels, which also publishes a variety of pamphlets and brochures on various aspects of the community: finance, labor and human rights, the role of women, competition, regulations and restrictions, communications, administration, and so on.

The U.S. centers for information on the EC are: 2100 M Street, NW, Suite 707, Washington, D.C. 20037 (Tel. 202-862-9500) and 245 East 47th Street, Dag Hammarskjold Plaza, New York, New York 10017 (Tel. 212-371-3804).

Also, the Chartered Accountants of England and Wales have published a leaflet "Get Your Business into Europe," which is helpful to both accountants and client companies. Eibis International Ltd., London, publishes "Pressing Ahead to 1993," which gives advice to exporters on how to prepare product literature and publicity for publication in the European Press.

Southeast Asian Nations

Pacific Rim nations have staged an impressive surge of growth in recent years. In the 1990s this region will become a market as big as Europe or North America (see Appendix III for more details). Led by Singapore, Hong Kong, Taiwan, and South Korea, and backed by ASEAN (Association of Southeast Asian Nations), Asia is fast moving into world economic status comparable with the best, but it still offers unusual opportunities for savvy Western marketers.

Of the first four, Hong Kong is probably the most familiar to Americans. Long the mecca for shoppers, investors, and traders of all sorts, Hong Kong, with the threat of reversion to the People's Republic of China in 1997 hanging over its head, is gradually evolving a new personality. But it's still an advantageous base for operations in Asia.

With English the official business language (but Cantonese is a big help) and the English influence an important cultural factor in the British Crown Colony, Hong Kong is a relatively easy foreign environment for an American to operate in.

Newspapers, magazines, and radio and TV stations use English and Chinese, although Chinese predominates. Despite its identity as an international city and port, the resident community has many characteristics of a small town. It's important to know the people, what they do, and where their influence lies.

Singapore, with a past similar to Hong Kong's as a British Crown Colony, has something akin to Hong Kong's level of comfort for an American, although its culture has evolved into something quite different. Almost thirty years after gaining status as an independent island nation, Singapore, under the steady guidance of Prime Minister Lee Kuan Yew, is an important economic power in the region, with its star for the future continuing to rise.

In this cultural mix, English is the language for business: Media use English, but also use Chinese, Malay, and Tamil. Although governance is strict, a real sensitivity to the various ethnic groups is re-

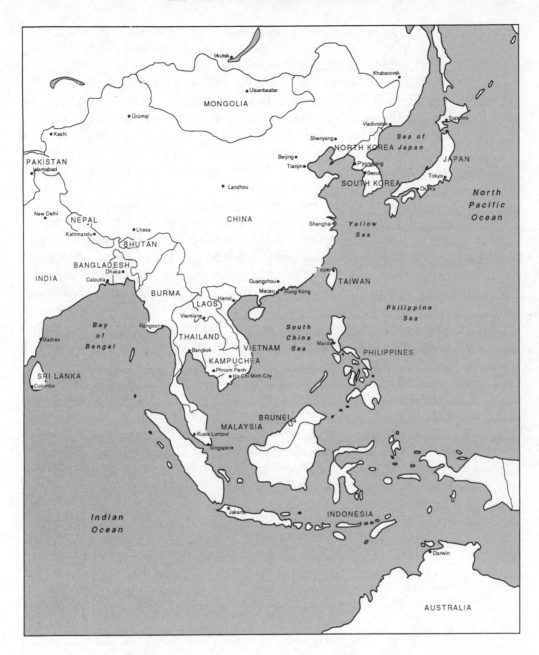

quired here. There is considerable stress among them, as there is in Malaysia, but it has been handled well.

The Chinese-influenced culture that Hong Kong and Singapore share is even more evident in Taiwan, which seems to have made some sort of peace with China, at least for the time being. The people of Taiwan, many of whom did not start out as Taiwanese but came from the mainland, have managed its conflicts, both internal and external, and built its industry to strength. The division between the original owners of the island, the Taiwanese, and the mainland invaders who have settled there, also requires a particular sensitivity.

Korea is another Asian area demanding considerable attention. Although its political future is judged uncertain by many, for the time being it is reasonably stable. The Republic of South Korea has a highly literate, motivated, hardworking labor force. There is a good supply of skilled workers and technicians, which is increasing with the vocational and training programs now in place. Qualified executive and supervisory personnel are in short supply.

Less than 10 percent of workers are union members and the unions generally have little power. Nonunion companies tend to be paternalistic in nature. Foreign companies investing in Korea under the Foreign Capital Inducement Law are covered by the Labor Disputes Mediation Law, which means that labor disputes are guaranteed to be mediated and solved by the government within twenty days. Foreign companies are given special protection from unwarranted labor disputes; a foreign investor who wants to enter into collective bargaining is subject to a special regulation requiring the Ministry of Labor to decide the issue in question within thirty days.

The work week is certainly beneficial to the employer—forty-four to forty-eight hours is common depending upon the industry, and even sixty hours is acceptable if it is provided for by contract.

Since 1987, when the country shifted toward a more democratic government, workers have become stronger and have yearly staged long annual strikes for higher pay. Still, wealth is concentrated in owner-founder families of the large corporations *(chaebol)*, which are similar to the Japanese conglomerates known as *zaibatsu*, which formerly had a stranglehold on business. Their descendants are still the powerful trading houses. The *chaebol* exert a profound influence, some of it positive. The threat of North Korea is a sword dangling over the country.

The business climate of countries belonging to the Association of Southeast Asian Nations (ASEAN)* is characterized by high literacy rates, skilled craftsmanship, an entrepreneurial spirit, and a tradition of service.

All of them, though for the most part they have not yet reached the status of newly industrialized countries (NIC), have communities of experienced businesspeople with a history of trading with other nations. Their credit ratings are good; they have a strong work ethic.

The political climate, once in upheaval, has stabilized since the 1970s, making the area the most stable in the developing world. Geographically, these nations occupy a strategic location that contains all the straits crucial to trade between the Indian and Pacific oceans.

*Brunei, Indonesia, Malaysia, Singapore, Thailand, and the Philippines.

ASEAN nations have combined their mutual interests under a united front by which they leverage their international voice as one. They purchase collectively to strengthen bargaining and to lower costs, buying more from Japan than any single country does.

As these nations strengthen their own economies and infrastructures, American business would be wise not only to recognize these increased attributes but to understand the dignity with which business is undertaken and to respond to that. American business should also realize that awareness of American corporations and brands is usually low and demands a sustained campaign for successful promotional activities.

The ASEAN area offers particular opportunities in construction and related fields, and in insurance because of the burgeoning economies. Financial services is a relatively recent development and another area of growth. Comparatively speaking, the United States and Japan hold stronger positions in this area than other nations do, claiming half of the business, whereas European businesses have not made as strong inroads.

The EC has no doubt absorbed attention from European companies that might otherwise be devoted to Asia, and the history of political turmoil, which has become more stabilized, may be the reason. Also, the United States has been an attractive market for Europe as have South America, the Middle East, Africa, and Eastern Europe.

While China still holds promise for the future, it is a country that is developing more slowly than previously expected and more slowly than are the smaller nations of the East. The People's Republic of China is also drawing investment and construction from companies that are willing to build a base for prospective future business.

With a small window allowing private enterprise, another allowing advertising, and increasingly decentralized decision making, marketing in China is, however, inhibited by strong regionalism and a primitive transportation system. The uncertain political climate, which is reflected in a somewhat unpredictable business environment, requires real commitment and patience from the outside investor. The country's future potential and the current low wage requirements, which China shares with the Republic of the Philippines, make the nation a place of continuing interest for many businesses.

Referring to China, an article in *Advertising Age* admonishes: U.S. marketers should avoid false expectations and inpatience. Other important rules are to carefully prepare, choose the right partner, limit exposure, and establish a strong corporate presence, which indicates long-term commitment.[18]

---

18. Lynne Reaves and Arne J. De Keijzer, "China: A New Frontier for Advertisers/ Guidelines for U.S. Marketers Planning to Expand in China," *Advertising Age*, Vol. 56, No. 72 (September 16, 1985), pp. 74, 78.

Left behind in the Asian race for economic recognition are the countries of what was formerly called Indochina: Vietnam, Laos, and Cambodia (Kampuchea). Other Asian nations are slowly investing in the area, attracted by natural resources and long-term potential, but Americans are still barred by law from investing in Vietnam.

The lack of basics such as good roads, convertible currencies, and stable politics suggest that considerable time will pass before these nations attract substantial outside investment. Nevertheless, both Vietnam and Laos are making moves in an effort to attract business.

Modern communications equipment—telephones, computers, printers, facsimile and telex machines, cable, direct dial technology— are all available in Vietnam. Getting through on the phone lines, or completing fax transmissions, is something else. Reports are that it can't be done.

Perhaps it's no wonder that when sending a telex, it currently costs $12 (in U.S. dollars), over half the average monthly salary. It is perhaps not surprising that communications are kept to a minimum. Don't count on letters, either. Paper is in chronically short supply.[19]

The situation is less encouraging in Laos, where the existing equipment for international communications consists of nine lines to Bangkok, one radio phone (which has to be booked six hours ahead), and a handful of unauthorized fax machines.

Thai, French, and Australian entrepreneurs have been venturing in, but the going is rough. At the Ministry of Trade and External Economic Relations, the first stop for prospective joint venturers, the director was asked for a list of operations: "We certainly do have a record of existing ventures," he said, "but I do not have it in my possession and my colleague who does have a list does not have a phone."[20]

In the planning stage is a new satellite-linked telecommunications system sponsored by the Australian government. It may take some time.

19. Colin Mackay, "Vietnam: Joint Ventures," *Asia Money*, No. 3 (December/January 1990), p. 30.
20. Ben Davies, "The Lawless Jungles of Laos," *Asia Money*, No. 3 (December/January 1990), p. 34.

13

Globalization:
Realism vs. Fantasy

Globalization is the catchword of the 1990s. Companies hoping to succeed in the evolving interconnected markets will seek a combination of coordinating mechanisms to accomplish their goals. At the same time they will be seeking to minimize interference in the freedom exercised by nationally based operating units.

Globalization implies a definite shift in the perceptions of both competitors and marketplaces. Foremost among them are corporate intelligence and information gathering, functions of the public relations and marketing units.

Organizational structure is another area to be considered, along with economies of scale, costs, and strategies. Competitors that have a real impact in the global arena will be those that are capable of coordinating their worldwide resources for global objectives.

Proponents of global marketing argue that modern, worldwide communications have made consumer demands universal and cultural differences meaningless. An evident trend toward globalization of telecommunications products, with products taking on a common appearance and providing increasingly common functions, underlines this perception.

Experience and observation strongly suggest that it's not so. In fact, although more products are being marketed on a global or international basis, most are tailored to the particular marketplace as are the ads that push them. Forces that call for customization over standardization are customer demand in different nations for different product features, consumer resources, and different environmental factors. The most successful marketers examine and answer these forces.

McDonald's Corp. sells beer in Germany, mango shakes in Hong Kong, and a different hamburger in Japan from what it sells in the

United States. Even when the product itself is standardized, the branding, positioning, and promotion may be different according to local conditions.

When Coca-Cola tested its Diet Coke in Japan and Europe, which had been highly successful in the United States, it found that the word *diet* conveyed medicinal connotations. By calling the drink Coca-Cola Light, it was able to successfully market the product.

In a similar vein, while claiming the traditional beverage is the same all over, Coca-Cola carefully tailors its television commercials to the viewers in specific markets. One commercial, which featured 1,000 children singing, had at least twenty-one different versions around the world, each of which highlighted a child from a different market. A study by *Business Horizons* in 1987 found 50 percent of American companies in the EC nations tailoring their advertisements to national markets as against only 17 percent that had done so in 1973.[1]

Nevertheless, global marketing emphasizes consumer similarities across geographic borders and reaches for marketing strategies that can be standardized while local differences are minimized. To the extent that is achieved, cost efficiency is increased.

Steps toward building that efficency are: (1) to establish the product as a world brand by maximizing name, feature, and image standardization worldwide; (2) to identify global segments that share the same psychographic characteristics; and (3) to place the brand toward either end of the high-technology/high-touch spectrum. This strategy encourages consumer involvement and offers common symbols and language based on high technology or on human emotion and product image.[2]

It's sometimes surprising that even products that would seem the most universal, or demanding of the most minimal changes, often still require appropriate adjustments to the national taste. Mattel's Barbie Doll was a runaway success when introduced to the U.S. market some years ago. When introduced into Japan, however, it fell flat. To a little girl a doll is a doll is a doll, right? Wrong. When finally reintroduced several years later in a more petite size, with dark hair and different body configurations, the doll became a resounding success.

Similarly, the television nighttime soap *Dallas* was a smash hit in the U.S. domestic market and even in some markets abroad before it was bought and screened on Japanese television. It was a flop. Too morally ambiguous, the viewers said. They were confused about who was good and who was bad and why the characters did some of the things that American viewers loved to see them do.

1. Julie Skur Hill and Joseph M. Winski, "Goodbye Global Ads: Global Village Is Fantasy Land for Big Marketers," *Advertising Age*, Vol. 58, No. 49 (November 16, 1987), pp. 22–36.
2. Teres J. Domzal and Lynette S. Unger, "Emerging Positioning Strategies in Global Marketing," *Journal of Consumer Marketing*, Vol. 4, No. 4 (Fall 1987), pp. 23–40.

Marketing elements that need particular attention for adaptability to a new marketplace include: packaging, labeling, materials, colors, name, product features, advertising themes, media, execution, price, and sales promotion.[3] In addition, laws governing marketing practices and even advertising in various countries are quite different.

Domino's Pizza, a U.S. company founded by an Irishman, sells Italian pizza in 10 countries. It makes only two sizes of pizza, and in every location it guarantees to deliver in 30 minutes. Its employees wear the same colorful uniforms and use the same standardized equipment all over. But Domino's works hard to satisfy local tastes.

It uses "cultural" toppings on its pizzas: sweet corn in the United Kingdom, tuna fish in Japan, salami in Germany, prawns in Australia. Domino's looks for situations where this kind of standardization/localization can be maintained. It plans to enter seven more countries soon and every year between now and 1995 plans to double its number of global outlets.[4]

Another company that has successfully dealt with the standardization/customization marketing mix is Nissan. Discovering that it would have to design forty-eight different models to meet the market demands of the United States and Canada, Europe, and Japan, Nissan undertook to study the real requirements of the marketplace. It found that in the United States you need a sporty model as well as a four-wheel drive. In the United Kingdom, where the market is influenced by tax policy, the corporate car is popular.

So Nissan built "lead country models" to meet specific national market tastes. Once the lead models are right, local managers suggest minor changes that are needed to sell the cars locally. Success has been attributed to good research, localizing the product, and listening to the customers.[5]

Public relations assistance is becoming more, not less, important in an environment of global marketing in order to fine-tune the product and/or the presentation and differentiate it from the competition.

Standardization in Public Relations

Increasingly there is a distinction being made between international and global public relations and marketing. One expert says that international public relations practitioners implement distinctive programs in multiple markets, with "each program tailored to meet the often acute dis-

3. Phillip Kotler, "Global Standardization—Courting Danger," *Journal of Consumer Marketing*, Vol. 3, No. 2 (Spring 1986), pp. 13–15.
4. Preston Townley, "Going Global in the 1990s," *Vital Speeches of the Day*, given April 11, 1990, in Quebec, Canada.
5. Ibid.

tinctions of the individual geographic market." Global public relations, he says, "imposes an overall perspective on a program" that may cover several markets, recognizing similarities and adapting to differences.[6]

There are three prime factors that have contributed to globalization moves by public relations firms themselves: (1) the need of American companies for new markets to grow profits; (2) the trend toward globalization of the media; (3) the increasing sophistication of the public relations abroad.

In business usage, *standardization* is often a synonym for *globalization*. Yet globalization is a concept involving worldwide promotion that may be tailored to the individual marketplace in varying degrees. Standardization in business generally is widely accepted to mean identical product lines, packaging, promotion, and possibly pricing and distribution. The primary reason given is usually cost efficiency, followed by simplification and consolidation (alternate words for cost savings; really fewer resources are needed), and last by strengthening the corporate image through repetition. It might otherwise be softened by variety of color or design.

Certainly marketing and public relations need to be highly sensitive to differences that might mitigate the success of their efforts. While it can be argued that in the United States and elsewhere marketers have been able to widen their markets by standardizing products, they have also discovered that some of the standardization they assumed could be done has not worked.

For public relations an almost opposite situation could be argued. As communications have become more sophisticated, the world in which they operate has become wider. The time spread on virtually any project has shortened, and standards of expectation as far as delivery of the message, veracity, accuracy, attractive packaging, and even quantity have risen. The result is that rather than standardizing the messages, communicators often find they have to carefully fine-tune it to fit the market.

Agencies are developing global networks, and may be in the forefront of industries that are doing so. The reason is, of course, to meet the needs of their major, multinationals clients. If standardization on a grand scale were workable, the need for offices around the world would be minimized and basic information could be disseminated from the home office. Clearly that is not the case at this time.

International, and in some cases global, networks have been developed by public relations agencies in a number of ways:

- *Growth*. Like a corporation, the agency sets up wholly owned offices or subsidiaries abroad as it grows.

6. Gavin Anderson, "A Global Look at Public Relations," in Bill Cantor, *Experts in Action: Inside Public Relations*, 2nd edition, ed. Chester Burger (White Plains, N.Y.: Longman, 1989), p. 413.

- *Acquisition*. Mergers and joint ventures.
- *Purchase*. A fast way to grow. One agency buys out another; usually a major agency buys a smaller local one.
- *Affiliation*. Independent local agencies are tied by contractual agreement, or agencies agree to assist each other as needed.

Although many writers cite the aggressive movement of corporations into the international area as the primary reason for the spread of agencies, many corporations are seeing the need for public relations to play a major role in their advancement. Among corporate representatives going abroad to move the company into a new marketplace, public relations professions are often first or close to first.

Shandwick (which owns Golin/Harris, Dorf & Stanton, Rogers & Cowan, Rand, Rubinstein, Wolfson, IPR, and many others) owes its expansion to acquiring independent agencies around the world. It's an expensive way to go, but one that assures a strong, far-reaching organization. The acquired agencies retain a large degree of independence.

In one sense, public relations operations can be standardized in much the same way MacDonald's is in the fast food market. The agency has greater influence over quality control, can use many of the same methods, formats, products, styles, and distribution channels, but must tailor the message and the program to the target market. Similarly but to a lesser degree it can tailor its services and its output to the culture of the client.

Burson-Marsteller (owned by Young and Rubicam) and Hill & Knowlton (owned by WPP Group since 1987), both heavy presences abroad, use several methods for establishing a strong global presence. The choice seems to be made on the basis of agency availability, need, and prospective business.[7] Burson-Marsteller relies on a matrix structure to exercise strong control over its satellite offices. It offers clients the capability of servicing global needs.

Hill & Knowlton, a publicly owned company, buys companies outright and puts its own name on them to ensure full control. It also has a network of affiliates. Each type of organization has its merits, of course. From the standpoint of control over a major international campaign, there is little doubt that the ownership structure has strong advantages.

Priorities can be set by top management, ensuring that for a major client the worldwide release of information or initiation of a program can be exercised almost simultaneously around the globe. Depth of expertise, which usually incorporates marketing specialists, is another ad-

7. Joan Reisman, "Taking on the World," *Public Relations Journal* (March 1990), pp. 18–26.

vantage, as is flexibility in moving management from one location to another according to where it is most needed.

A public relations practitioner in this type of organization is more likely to have a broad view, and to think, for instance, of the effect the release of news in one country may have in another, and to realize that managers in other areas need to be kept informed of news, developing conditions, or programs. Consistency in reporting is essential to the credibility of both the agency and the client.

Looser associations that rely more heavily on skills of local practitioners can be particularly valuable in areas where government involvement in business is a fact of life, and where long-term "old boy networks" are necessary to conduct most business. They may understand the organization of the press, government organs, or certain industries that would take outside management an inordinately long time to comprehend and therefore be far more efficient in accomplishing certain tasks.

Despite the wide wingspan of the world's three largest agencies, public relations is still basically an industry of entrepreneurs. It has been estimated that all the giants hold only about 10 percent of the business worldwide.

Even in the large agencies with large clients, the majority of work is done on a local basis. Small wonder, then, that small and midsize agencies continue to proliferate. Many of them form networks to enhance their spread and to meet the growing demand for broad-based public relations.

Among the leaders are The Pinnacle Group, Public Relations Exchange International, and WorldCom. Pinnacle, the oldest, maintains a headquarters in Minneapolis and has twenty-three offices outside the United States.

Public Relations Exchange International is set up similarly to Pinnacle, with members operating independently but cooperating on certain issues and for clients. The WorldCom Group, Inc., like the others, accepts only one firm per market. Every shareholder is equal and is expected to participate in meetings.[8]

The list of public relations agencies available abroad numbers in the hundreds. Several publications list the important ones in each market. Another information source is the many public relations professional organizations abroad. Some of them are listed in Appendix II. They are good referral sources.

Marketing, Standardization, and Globalization

Considerable doubt is cast on the value of more pervasive standardization with recognition of the apparent move by corporations to decen-

8. Ibid.

tralize as they move abroad. The tendency for them to hire top managers locally, noted in Chapter 7, suggests continued dependency on localized public relations activities. Protecting the image of the corporation and its interests must be done, however, from the parent.

Commercially, nations are becoming more similar. Professor Theodore Levitt of Harvard Business School says the new global corporations will have to recognize and utilize these similarities in order to survive and profit. He observes that a successful global marketing strategy requires a common brand name, packaging, and communications; that companies that market globally enjoy enormous cost advantages over competitors that market and produce in narrow segments; and that modern communications facilities have created a worldwide commonality of interest that has surpassed national interests.

Regardless of national origin or culture, he claims, people involved with the same products go to the same schools, study the same subjects, read the same books, and attend the same conferences.[9]

Few would deny that the world is getting smaller, but to assume that people who use the same product have the same culture, ideas, or other entrenched similarities is gross oversimplification. It is in fact astounding how not only countries, but areas of our own country, have retained their special uniqueness.

There are products that are marketable across boundaries, and others that can be made so by means of heavy-cost advertising; there are others that must be tailored to the marketplace. That this need remains in no way negates the concept of globalization. All people are not alike and probably never will be.

A panel in which Professor Levitt participated some years ago with representatives of major advertising agencies with offices in the United States and abroad defined the problems in shifting from a multinational to a global outlook. They mentioned withdrawing autonomy from personnel accustomed to operating independently, finding universal advertising themes and brand positioning, programming air time to take advantage of global facilities, legal barriers, and coping with the role of print media in global marketing.

Yet the idea that a company can operate as if the entire world were a single entity is something more aptly discussed under reality versus fantasy. Managing from the home office on a global basis by definition means overlooking cultural details in various overseas markets. This can sometimes lead to serious oversight that to be avoided requires an unusual international awareness at the home office.

Even the most universal advertising themes, such as Coca-Cola's crowd of children from around the world, was adjusted to the place of exposure by having, for instance, a higher proportion of Oriental

9. Levitt: Global Companies to Replace Dying Multinationals," *Marketing News*, Vol. 19, No. 6 (March 15, 1985), p. 15.

children represented in the scene in the Oriental markets where it was played and more black children in African and American minority-group markets.

The implication is, of course, that globalization usually does not mean standardization to the point where a picture like the one mentioned above can be the same for all markets. Even though the underlying message, and the theme and the purpose are the same, the style of communication is different and is critical to the success of the promotion.

Virtually all agencies and advertisers recognize the difficulty in selling a product the same way everywhere, but by the same token they are trying to position themselves to accommodate global marketing. In determining whether such a global stance would be effective for a particular brand, most agencies agree that market development and competitive strategies must be at similar stages from country to country; that consumer target markets should be similar; and that consumers must share similar desires, needs, and uses for the brand.[10]

Products with visual appeal, high technology, and products promoted with image campaigns are most successfully marketed across borders. A bevy of products have been touted as globally marketed, but few, unfortunately, without some customization.

Even Coca-Cola, long viewed as the most generically marketed of all products, which could be found around the globe in the most unexpected places (in 1968 I bought it in the backwoods of Cambodia where there were no roads and no running water), tailors the package, if not the product, to the marketplace. Originally the package was the familiar, universal glass bottle.

As it spread across countries, the logo was adapted to the local language and eventually the container was adapted to local tastes. In Japan the popular can design is tall and slim, but holds a little over half what the usual 12-ounce American size holds. An alternative is the squat, 250-mililiter can, which holds about 8 ounces. The bottle is still widely used in far-flung areas where rebottling is still cost-efficient.

Some would certainly argue that the product is tailored to the marketplace as well. For years, drinkers have claimed that Coca-Cola was sweeter in some geographical areas, or stronger. Although the change is only in the name, Diet Coke is not sold in Japan, but Light Coke is.

Trivial Pursuit, a vastly popular table game in the United States, has been marketed by its U.S. distributor, Selchow & Righter Co., around the world, but only by first translating it into the local language and then by tailoring the questions to the culture.

Grendene S.A. from Brazil makes plastic sandals that it sells world-

10. Rebecca Fannin, "What Agencies Really Think of Global Theory," *Marketing & Media Decision*, Vol. 119, No. 15 (December 1984), pp. 74–82.

wide. Touted as successful global marketing, the product has been copied in many countries with minor changes, but changes nonetheless.

Concern with establishing a global identity is a contributing factor in the competitive advantage enjoyed by non-American companies operating outside their home markets, according to a study released by Lippincott & Margulies, Inc. Almost 60 percent of foreign companies surveyed reported that they have increased their focus on global identity considerations over the past two years, but only 36 percent of U.S. companies had increased their efforts for the same period.

The need to increase sales and revenues was the key reason for foreign companies to implement global identity programs. The two U.S. companies perceived as having the most notable global identities were IBM and Coca-Cola.* The study noted that although most foreign companies adapt promotional activities to U.S. styles when in the United States, companies seldom adapt to foreign styles when they move abroad.[11]

The factors that contribute to success in a company's domestic market do not necessarily make for success abroad, as mentioned earlier. The fact that local markets are becoming divergent and tolerate the coexistence of foreign goods alongside domestic goods does not lead to the conclusion that markets are becoming global.

True global marketing is possible with homogeneous worldwide needs and resources.[12] The main feature of globalization will be that companies will seek a combination of coordinating mechanisms that will accomplish their goals while minimizing interference in the freedom of nationally based operating units. The goal of globalization, after all, is to do things of value to the company and "ultimately to its various subsidiaries and divisions which no division or subsidiary would ever be motivated to do for itself."[13]

Specific areas need to be considered and acted upon prior to a company's going global. These include establishing a system of corporate intelligence and information gathering and disseminating, outlining and selecting choices for strategic action, developing economies of scale and structure on a global basis, calculating costs and payoffs, and organizing corporate structure to accommodate global business activities.[14]

11. "Foreign Companies' Global Awareness Cited in Study," *Marketing News*, Vol. 22, No. 16 (August 1, 1988), p. 14.
12. Jagdish Sheth, "Global Markets or Global Competition?" *Journal of Consumer Marketing*, Vol. 3, No. 2 (Spring 1986), pp. 9–11.
13. Thomas Garbett, *How to Build a Corporation's Identity and Project Its Image* (Lexington, Mass.: Lexington Books, 1988), p. 220.
14. James Leontiades, "Going Global—Global Strategies vs. National Strategies," *Long-Range Planning* (United Kingdom), Vol. 19, No. 6 (December 1986), pp. 96–104.

---

* It should be noted that both of these companies engage in little more than administrative advice in their overseas offices, most of which are subsidiaries owned 50 percent or less by the parent.

James Bolt, founder and president of Executive Development Associates, a consulting firm, put together a paper aimed at preparing a Fortune-200 company's executives for global competition. In it he gave his criteria for what makes companies successful global competitors:

1. They perceive themselves as multinational, understand that perceptions' implications for their business, and are led by a management that is comfortable in the world arena.
2. They develop an integrated and innovative global strategy that makes it very difficult and costly for other companies to compete.
3. They aggressively and effectively implement their worldwide strategy, and they back it with large investments.
4. They understand that technological innovation is no longer confined to the United States, and they have developed systems for tapping technological innovation abroad. How?
   a. By scanning and monitoring
   b. Through connections with academia and research organizations
   c. By implementing programs to increase the company's visibility
   d. Through cooperative research programs
   e. By acquiring or merging with foreign companies that have extensive innovative capabilities
   f. Through acquisition of external technology by licensing
5. They operate as though the world were one large market, not a series of individual countries.
6. They have developed an organizational structure that is well thought out and unique.
7. They have a system that keeps them informed of political changes abroad and the implications for their business.
8. They recognize the need to make their management team international and have a system in place to accomplish the goal.
9. They give their outside directors an active role in the affairs of the company.
10. They are well-managed, which means that there is a bias for action; that they are close to the customer; that they value autonomy and entrepreneurship; that they recognize that productivity comes through people; that their philosophy is hands-on, value driven; that they stick to the businesses they know; that they adhere to "simple form, lean staff," and that they are both centralized and decentralized.[15]

15. James F. Bolt, "Global Competitor: Some Criteria for Success," *Business Horizons* (January–February 1988), pp. 34–40. Copyright 1988 by the Foundation for the School of Business at Indiana University. Used with permission.

Furthermore, says Bolt, "Any corporation seeking to expand globally would do well to ask itself how well it measures up to the Peters-Waterman[16] criteria for excellence."

Bolt's criteria would invite criticism from few, although an explanation must be added for No. 5. There is still great diversity in markets as previously described. Every company or product is not appropriate for following a MacDonald's or Kentucky Fried Chicken approach to operations and sales.

All ten criteria are clearly the concern of public relations professionals who make the world their marketplace. They are good guidelines for ambitious public relations agencies as well as corporate public relations and marketing executives.

16. Thomas J. Peters and Robert H. Waterman, Jr., *In Search of Excellence* (New York: Harper & Row, 1982), pp. 89–318.

APPENDIX I

Resource Organizations and Publications

Listed on the following pages are research sources including organizations and publications that can provide information on markets, the media, public relations, publicity, and cultural matters. While some are also useful for information dissemination, organizations particularly useful for that will be covered in Appendix II.

International Calling

Throughout the four appendixes in this book, you will encounter telephone numbers and fax numbers that you may wish to use. Many of these numbers will be for organizations overseas. Therefore, following is a list of country codes and city codes for access to overseas telephones. Of course, numbers beside countries are country codes, and numbers beside cities are city codes. Those country entries with no cities listed under them do not require city codes. Those cities with no codes indicated also require no city codes. Also, please keep in mind that military bases (Korea, for example) cannot be dialed directly.

Andorra	33	Melbourne	3	**Belgium**	32
All points	078	Perth	9	Antwerp	31
		Sydney	2	Brussels	2
Argentina	54			Charleroi	71
Buenos Aires	1	**Austria**	43	Ghent	91
Cordoba	51	Graz	316	Liege	41
La Plata	21	Innsbruck	5222	Malines	15
Rosario	41	Linz	732		
		Salzburg	6222	**Belize**	501
Australia	61	Vienna	222		
Adelaide	8			**Brazil**	55
Brisbane	7	**Bahrain**	973	Belo Horizonte	31

Brasilia	61
Porto Alegre	512
Recife	81
Rio de Janeiro	21
Sao Paulo	11
Chile	56
Concepcion	42
San Bernardo	2
Santiago	2
Talcahuano	42
Valparaiso	31
Vina del Mar	31
China, Republic of	886
Hualien	38
Kaohsiung	7
Pingtung	87
Taichung	42
Tainan	62
Taipei	2
Colombia	57
Barranquilla	5
Bogota	
Bucaramanga	71
Cali	3
Cucuta	70
Costa Rica	506
Cyprus	357
Famagusta	31
Kythrea	2313
Larnaca	41
Limassol	51
Nicosia	21
Paphos	61
Denmark	45
Aalborg	8
Aarhus	6
Copenhagen	1 or 2
Esbjerg	5
Odense	9
Randers	6
Ecuador	593
Ambato	2
Cuenca	4
Guavaquil	4
Machala	4
Manta	4
Quito	2
El Salvador	503
Fiji	679
Finland	358
Eppo-Ebbo	15
Helsinki	0
Jyvaskyia	41
Kuopio	71
Lahti	18
Oulu	81
Pori	39
Tampere	31
Turku	21
Vantaa	14
France	33
Aix-En-Provence	42
Bordeaux	56
Le Havre	35
Lyon	78
Marseille	91
Nice	93
Paris	1
Rouen	35
Toulouse	61
Tours	47
German Democratic Republic	37
Berlin (East)	2
Dresden	51
Leipzig	41
German Federal Republic	49
Berlin (West)	30
Bremen	421
Cologne	221
Dusseldorf	211
Essen	201
Frankfurt	611
Hamburg	40
Munich	89
Nuremberg	911
Stuttgart	711
Greece	30
Athens	1
Corinth	741
Elefsis	1
Iraklion	81
Kavala	51
Larissa	41
Piraeus	1
Rhodes	241
Salonica	31
Volos	421
Guam	671
Guatemala	502
Amatitian	
Antigua	
Guatemala City	2
Quatzaltenango	
Villa Nueva	
Haiti	509
Port Au Prince	1
Honduras	504
Hong Kong	852
Castle Peak	12
Hong Kong	5
Kowloon	3
Kwai Chung	12
Lantau	5
Ma Wan	5
Peng Chau	5
Sha Tin	12
Tai Po	12
Tsun Wan	12
Iran	98
Abadan	631
Esfahan	31
Mashad	51
Tabriz	41
Tehran	21
Iraq	964
Baghdad	1
Basrah	4021
Mosul	6081
Ireland	353
Cork	21
Drogheda	41
Dublin	1
Dundalk	42
Galway	91
Kilkenny	56

Sligo	71	Liechtenstein	41	Papua	
Tralee	66	All points	75	New Guinea	675
Waterford	51				
Wexford	53	Luxembourg	352	Peru	51
				Arequipa	542
Israel	972	Malaysia	60	Chiclayo	7423
Ashkelon	51	Ipoh	5	Cuzco	8423
Batlam	3	Kuala Lumpur	3	Lima	14
Beer Sheva	57			Piura	7432
Hadera	63	Mexico	52	Trujillo	44
Haifa	4	Acapulco	748		
Jerusalem	2	Guadalajara	36	Philippines	63
Nazareth	65	Mexico City	5	Angeles	55
Netania	53			Bacolod	34
Rehovot	54	Monaco	33	Cebu	32
Tel Aviv	3	All points	93	Davao	35
				Iloilo	33
Italy	39	Netherlands	31	Manila	2
Bari	80	Amsterdam	20		
Bologna	51	Eindhoven	40	Portugal	351
Florence	55	Haarlem	23	Barreiro	19
Genoa	10	Rotterdam	10	Braga	23
Milan	2	The Hague	70	Coimbra	39
Naples	81	Utrecht	30	Lisbon	19
Palermo	91			Porto	29
Rome	6	Netherlands		Setubal	15
Turin	11	Antilles	599		
Venice	41	Bonaire	7	San Marino	39
		Curacao	9	All points	541
Japan	81	Saba	4		
Gifu	582	St. Eustatius	3	Saudi Arabia	966
Hiroshima	822	St. Maarten	5	Jeddah	21
Kanazawa	762			Mecca	22
Kobe	78			Medina	41
Kyoto	75	New Zealand	64	Riyadh	1
Nagoya	52	Auckland	9		
Osaka	6	Christchurch	3	Singapore	65
Sapporo	11	Dunedin	24		
Tokyo	33	Hamilton	71	South Africa	27
Yokohama	45	Palmerston North	63	Bloemfontein	51
		Wellington	4	Cape Town	21
Kenya	254			Durban	31
Nairobi	2	Nicaragua	505	East London	431
		Leon	31	Johannesburg	11
Korea	82	Managua	2	Pietermaritzburg	331
Inchon	32			Port Elizabeth	41
Kwangju	62	Norway	47	Pretoria	12
Masan	551	Bergen	5	Uitenhage	422
Pusan	51	Drammen	3		
Seoul	2	Oslo	2	Spain	34
Taegu	53	Skien	35	Barcelona	3
		Stavanger	45	Bilbao	4
Kuwait	965	Trondheim	75		

Cadiz	56	Montreux	21	Bristol, England	272
Granada	58	Neuchatel	38	Cardiff, Wales	222
Las Palmas		St. Gallen	71	Coventry, England	203
(Canary Islands)	28	Wintethur	52	Edinburgh, Scotland	31
Leon	87	Zurich	1	Glasgow, Scotland	41
Madrid	1			Liverpool, England	51
Malaga	52	**Tahiti**	689	London,	
Palma de Mallorca	71			England 71 (or 81)	
Pamplona	48	**Thailand**	66	Manchester, England	61
Santander	42	Bangkok	2	Nottingham, England	602
Seville	54			Sheffield, England	742
Valencia	6	**Turkey**	90	Southampton,	
		Ankara	41	England	703
Sweden	46	Istanbul	11		
Boras	33	Izmir	51	**Vatican City**	39
Eskilstuna	16			All points	6
Goteborg	31	**United Arab**			
Helsingborg	42	**Emirates**	971	**Venezuela**	58
Karlstad	54	Abu Dhabi	2	Barcelona	81
Linkoping	13	Ajman	6	Barquisimeto	51
Lund	46	Al Ain	3	Cabimas	64
Malmo	40	Aweir	49	Caracas	2
Norrkoping	11	Dubai	4	Ciudad Bolivar	85
Stockholm	8	Fujairah	91	Coro	68
Sundsvall	60	Jebel Dhana	5	Cumana	93
Uppsala	18	Khawanij	49	Maracaibo	61
Vasteras	21	Ras-Al Khaimah	7	Maracay	43
		Sharjah	6	Maturin	91
Switzerland	41	Umm-Al-Quwain	6	Merida	74
Baden	56			Puerto Cabello	42
Basel	61	**United**		San Cristobal	76
Berne	31	**Kingdom**	44	Valencia	41
Fribourg	37	Belfast, Northern			
Geneva	22	Ireland	232	**Yugoslavia**	38
Lausanne	21	Birmingham, England	21	Belgrade	11
Lucerne	41	Bournemounth,		Zagreb	41
Lugano	91	England	202		

For Antigua, the Bahamas, Barbados, Bermuda, the British West Indies, the Dominican Republic, Jamaica, Puerto Rico, and the U.S. Virgin Islands, simply dial the area code 809 and the number you are calling.

How to Dial Overseas

When dialing a number overseas, first dial 011; this is the international access code. Then simply dial the appropriate country code, city code, and the local number you are calling. It usually takes about forty-five seconds for an overseas phone call to start ringing from the time you have completed dialing. Here's a little trick to keep in mind, however: If you have a touch-tone telephone, press the pound button (#) after dialing your overseas phone number. This will speed things up a bit.

World Time Differences

Whether you are traveling or calling overseas or just out of town, it is always a good idea to keep in mind what time of day it is where you are going or calling. The chart on the next page can be useful to you in determining times of day around the world. The chart is based on the time of day being noon Eastern Standard Time. The standard time in other cities around the world can be computed as New York City plus or minus the factor shown.

Communications and Information Services

American Marketing Association
(world's largest professional marketers association)
250 South Wacker Drive, Suite 200
Chicago, Ill. 60606
Tel: (312) 648-0536

American Society of International Law
(conducts research and study on international law)
2223 Massachusetts Avenue, N.W.
Washington, D.C. 20008
Tel: (202) 265-4313

Business International Corp.
(does political risk studies)
215 Park Avenue South
New York, New York
Tel: (212) 460-0600

Business Environment Risk Information
(does political risk studies)
1808 Swann Street, N.W.
Washington, D.C. 20009
Tel: (202) 462-0007

S. J. Rundt and Associates
(does political risk studies)
130 East 63rd Street
New York, New York 10021
Tel: (212) 838-0141

Dow Jones News/Retricval
(online news provider including Wall Street Journal text, Dow Jones reports, securities quotes, and other business, financial, general news)
P.O. Box 300
Princeton, N.J. 08543
Tel: (609) 520-4000

Dun & Bradstreet Corporation, The
(business statistics, small business information, business surveys)

World Time Difference

(Chart is based on time of day being noon EST. Compute standard time in other cities as New York City plus or minus factor shown.)

Alexandria	+ 7	Damascus	+ 7	Madrid	+ 6	Seattle	− 3
Amsterdam	+ 6	Delhi	+ 10½	Melbourne	+ 15	Seoul	+ 13
Anchorage	− 5	Denver	− 2	Mexico City	− 1	Shanghai	+ 13
Athens	+ 7	Dublin	+ 5	Miami	0	Singapore	+ 13
Atlanta	0	Fairbanks	− 5	Monrovia	+ 4¼	Stockholm	+ 6
Auckland	+ 17	Frankfurt	+ 6	Montreal	0	Sydney	+ 15
Baghdad	+ 8	Geneva	+ 6	Moscow	+ 8	Tehran	+ 8½
Barcelona	+ 6	Glasgow	+ 5	New Orleans	− 1	Tel Aviv	+ 7
Berlin	+ 6	Halifax	+ 1	Nome	− 6	Tokyo	+ 14
Bombay	+ 10½	Hong Kong	+ 13	Oslo	+ 6	Toronto	0
Boston	0	Honolulu	− 5	Paris	+ 6	Tucson	− 2
Brussels	+ 6	Houston	− 1	Beijing (Peking)	+ 13	Valparaiso	+ 1
Buenos Aires	+ 2	Istanbul	+ 7	Phoenix	− 2	Vancouver	− 3
Cairo	+ 7	Jerusalem	+ 7	Portland	− 3	Vienna	+ 6
Calcutta	+ 10½	Juneau	− 3	Rio de Janeiro	+ 2	Vladivostok	+ 14
Caracas	+ 1	Kinshasa	+ 6	Rome	+ 6	Warsaw	+ 6
Chicago	− 1	Lisbon	+ 6	San Francisco	− 3	Washington, D.C.	0
Copenhagen	+ 6	London	+ 5	San Juan	+ 1	Yokohama	+ 14
Dallas	− 1	Los Angeles	− 3	Santiago	+ 1	Zurich	+ 6

299 Park Avenue
New York, N.Y. 10171
Tel: (212) 593-6727

International Advertising Association
(researches such topics as worldwide restrictions and taxes on advertising)
342 Madison Avenue, Suite 2000
New York, N.Y. 10017
Tel: (212) 557-1133
Fax: (212) 983-0455

CCH Electronics Legislature Search System
(state and federal legislative tracking)
Commerce Clearing House, Inc.
4025 West Peterson Avenue
Chicago, Ill. 60646
Tel: (312) 583-8500

Mead Data Central, Inc.
*(provides LEXIS and NEXIS services on legal, medical, news, and business
    information)*
P.O. Box 933
Dayton, Ohio 45401
Tel: (513) 865-6958

Public Relations Society of America
*(library and information on all aspects of public relations; arranges interviews
    with experts and society leaders)*
33 Irving Place, 3F
New York, N.Y. 10003
Tel: (212) 995-2230

Radio Advertising Bureau
(provides marketing and business information on radio advertising)
304 Park Avenue South, 7F
New York, N.Y. 10010
Tel: (212) 254-4800, ext. 425

The Socio-Economic Research Institute of America
*(global trends organization giving data about domestic and international me-
    dia, politics, family, and education)*
Salisbury Turnpike
Rhineback, N.Y. 12572
Tel: (914) 876-6700

Television Bureau of Advertising
(marketing arm for TV)
477 Madison Avenue

New York, N.Y. 10022
Tel: 212-486-1111

U.S. Federal Communications Commission (FCC)
   (regulates interstate and international communications by radio, television,
      wire, satellite, and cable)
   1919 M Street, N.W.
   Washington, D.C. 20554
   Tel: (202) 632-5050

VU/TEXT Information Services
   (largest U.S. newspaper databank gives journalists instant access to current
      local coverage of events, people, and business)
   325 Chestnut, Suite 1300
   Philadelphia, Pa. 19106
   Tel: (800) 323-2949 and (215) 574-4406

Washington On-Line
   (Congressional Tracking System)
   1029 J Street, Suite 450
   Sacramento, Calif. 95814
   Tel: (916) 447-1886

Western Union Corporation
   (provides domestic and international message/financial delivery services, elec-
      tronic mail services)
   One Lake Street
   Upper Saddle River, N.J. 07458
   Tel: (201) 818-5790

General International Information

Organizations

New York State Department of Economic Development
   International Division
   1515 Broadway
   New York, N.Y. 10036
   Tel: (212) 827-6200

   International Chamber of Commerce (ICC) United Kingdom
   Centre Point, 103 New Oxford Street
   London WC1A 1QB
   United Kingdom

Department of Commerce's
   International Trade Administration (ITA)
   U.S. and Foreign Commercial Service
   Planning & Management (of Export Services)
   14th Street and Constitution Avenue, N.W.
   Washington, D.C. 20520
   Tel: (202) 377-4996

Export Promotion Services (same address as ITA) has seventy offices nationwide and eighty to ninety offices overseas.
Tel: (202) 377-8220

N.Y. Office of Export Promotion Services
26 Federal Plaza, Room 3718
New York, New York 10278
Tel: (212) 264-0634

ITA has three main divisions:

1. Industry specialists
2. Country desks
3. U.S. and foreign trade promotion

For more information, call the main ITA number: (202) 377-2000.

Department of State's Agency for International Development (AID)
(Runs an Exporting Program that produces a Procurement Information Bulletin and offers help through its Financial Management Office. AID has about eighty missions internationally. Americans in the United States who need help can contact):
AID
Washington, D.C. 20523-1414
Tel: (703) 875-1551

also:

Small and Disadvantaged Utilization
(703) 875-6823

EC 1992 Unit
(lobbies the federal government on market-related issues)
U.S. Department of Commerce
14th Street & Constitution Avenue, N.W.
Washington, D.C. 20230
or
Single Internal Market: 1992 Information Service
Office of European Community Affairs
U.S. Department of Commerce
Room 3036
(above address)
Tel: (202) 377-5276
Industry experts are available in the following areas:
Textiles and apparel: (202) 377-2043
Service industries: (202) 377-3575
Information technology, instrumentation, electronics: (202) 377-4466
Chemicals, construction industry products, basic industries: (202) 377-0614
Autos and consumer goods: 202-377-0614
Construction projects and industrial machinery: (202) 377-2474
Aerospace: (202) 377-8228

European Community Information Service
2100 M Street, N.W., 7 Floor
Washington, D.C. 20037

ITA (International Trade Administration) European Desks:
- Belgium and Luxembourg: (202) 377-5401
- Denmark: (202) 377-3254
- France: (202) 377-8008
- Federal Republic of Germany: (202) 377-2434
- Greece: (202) 377-3945
- Ireland: (202) 377-4104
- Italy: (202) 377-2177
- Netherlands: (202) 377-5401
- Portugal: (202) 377-3945
- Spain: (202) 377-4508
- United Kingdom: (202) 377-3748
- Delegation of Commission of European Communities: (202) 862-9500

Foreign Press Center(s)
110 East 59th Street, 2F
New York, N.Y. 10022
Tel: (212) 826-4721
Fax: (212) 826-4657

898 National Press Building
Washington, D.C. 20045
Tel. (202) 724-1640
Fax: (202) 724-0122

Los Angeles Media Liaison Office
Federal Building
11000 Wilshire Boulevard
Los Angeles, Calif. 90024
Tel. (213) 575-7693
Fax: (213) 575-7692

GATT Inquiry Point/Technical Office
Office of Standards Code and Information
National Bureau of Standards
Administration Building, Room A629
Gaithersburg, Md. 20899
Tel: (301) 975-4040

International Public Relations Association
Case Postale 126
CH-1211 Geneva 20
Switzerland
Tel: 41-22-292821
Telex: 428380 cre ch

International Trade Administration
(trade and industry information)
14th Street and Constitution Avenue, N.W., Mezzanine 1012

Washington, D.C. 20230
Tel: (202) 377-2867

Kienbaum and Partner
  (EC market entry studies, location studies, executive recruiting, compensa-
    tion)
  Fuellenbachstrasse 8
  D-4000 Dusseldorf 30
  (West) Germany
  Tel. (211) 4555 217

National Center for Standards and Certification Information
National Bureau of Standards
  14th Street and Constitution Avenue, N.W., Mezzanine 1012
  Washington, D.C. 20230
  Tel: (202) 377-3462

OECD (Organization for Economic Cooperation and Development)
  (inquire of Client Services Unit, Publications Service, for information and
    publications)
  2, rue Andre-Pascal
  75775 Paris Cedex 16

Office of Service Industries
  U.S. Department of Commerce, Room 1128
  14th Street & Constitution Avenue, N.W.
  Tel: (202) 377-3575

Overseas Press Club of America, Inc.
  52 East 41st Street
  New York, N.Y. 10017
  Tel: (212) 983-4655

Public Relations Society of America
  33 Irving Place
  New York, N.Y. 10003
  Tel: (212) 995-2230

U.S. Chamber of Commerce
  International Division
  1615 H Street, N.W.
  Washington, D.C. 20062
  (Publishes *Nation's Business*. Organizations overseas are called: American
    Chamber of Commerce [country].)
  Tel: (202) 659-6000

U.S. Chamber of Commerce of New York
  Northeast Region
  711 Third Avenue
  Suite 1702

New York, N.Y. 10017-4046
Tel: (212) 370-1440

U.S. Small Business Administration
Office of International Trade
1441 "L" Street, N.W.
Washington, D.C. 20416
Tel: (202) 653-7794
Fax: (202) 254-6429
(offices in major cities)
S.B.A. general number: (202) 653-6600

Wordnet
8 Agawam Road
P.O. Box 164
Acton, Massachusetts 01720
Tel: (508) 264-0600

Publications

Bacon's International Publicity Checker, Western Europe (1989)
Bacon's Information Systems
332 South Michigan Avenue
Chicago, Ill. 60604
Tel: (312) 922-2400

Business America
(articles and statistics on foreign trade development, markets, trends, calendar of upcoming trade promotions abroad sponsored by the U.S. government)
Superintendent of Documents
U.S. Government Printing Office
Washington, D.C. 20402
Tel: (202) 783-3238

Chase's Annual Events
(an almanac and survey of holidays)
Publisher:
Contemporary Books, Inc.
180 North Michigan Avenue
Chicago, Ill. 60601
(ISBN 0-8092-42-92-3)

The Commerce Business Daily
(for leads on business opportunities reported by the International Trade Administration's Foreign Commercial Service)
Superintendent of Documents
U.S. Government Printing Office
Washington, D.C. 20402
Tel: (202) 783-3238

Consumer Europe 1991
(for consumer goods, statistics, product sales and production, and historical trends)
Publisher:
Gale Research
835 Penobscot Building
Detroit, Mich. 48226
Tel: (800) 877-4253
    (313) 961-2242

Diplomatic List (State Publication No. 7894)
(addresses of foreign embassies in Washington and diplomatic staff members)
Superintendent of Documents
U.S. Government Printing Office
Washington, D.C. 20402
(202) 783-3238

Directory of Foreign Press in the U.S.
Foreign Press Center (USIA)
110 East 59th Street
New York, N.Y. 10022
Tel: (212) 826-4721

also:

Washington Foreign Press Center
898 National Press Building
Washington, D.C. 20045
Tel: (202) 724-1640
Fax: (202) 724-0122

Los Angeles Media Liaison Office
Federal Building
11000 Wilshire Boulevard
Los Angeles, Calif. 90024
Tel: (213) 575-7693
Fax: (213) 575-7692

Directory of Market Research Reports and Studies
(Findex, E-Econ) 79–443
Publisher: NSA Directories
5161 River Road
Bethesda, Md. 20816

EIU Country Reports (The Economist Intelligence Unit)
Business International
215 Park Avenue South
New York, N.Y. 10003
Tel: (212) 460-0671
Fax: (212) 995-8837

(Chester Burger's) *EuroDirectory*
   (lists 3,000 agencies in nineteen Western countries, information on public
     relations practices, client listings, translation facilities, and other data)
   Publisher: Chester Burger and PIMS International PLC
   171 Madison Avenue
   New York, N.Y. 10016
   Tel: (212) 725-0000
   Fax: (212) 684-4357 $250.00 single subscription

European Advertising, Marketing & Media Data 1989
   (key advertising, marketing, and media information in the sixteen major
     Western European countries with contact names)
   Euromonitor Publications Ltd.
   87–88 Turnmill Street
   London ECIM5QU, U.K.
   Tel: 71-251-8024
Distributed by:
   Gale Research Co.
   835 Penobscot Building
   Detroit, Mich. 48226
   Tel: (313) 961-2242
       (800) 877-4253
   Fax: (313) 961-6083
   Telex: 810-221-7086 $295.00

Europa Year Book (1989)
   Europa Publications Ltd.
   18 Bedford Square
   London WCIB 3JN, U.K.
   Tel: 71-580-8236
   Telex: 21540

Europe's 15,000 Largest Companies, 1989
   ELC International
   Sinclair House
   The Avenue
   London W13 8NT, U.K.
   Tel: 71-706-0919
   Fax: 71-723-6854
   Telex: 25192

The European Directory of Marketing and Information Services
   Euromonitor Publications, Ltd.
   87–88 Turnmill Street
   London ECIM5QU, U.K.
   Tel: 71-251-8024
Distributed by:
   Gale Research Co.
   835 Penobscot Building
   Detroit, Mich. 48226
   Tel: (313) 961-2242

(800) 877-4253
Fax: (313) 961-6083
Telex: 810-221-7086

European Marketing Data & Statistics
(demographics, banking, trade, industry, energy, consumer information, advertising, living standards, and education)
Euromonitor Publications Ltd.
87–88 Turnmill Street
London ECIM5QU, U.K.
Distributed by Gale Research Co.
835 Penobscot Building
Detroit, Mich. 48226
Tel: (313) 961-2242
    (800) 877-4253
Fax: (313) 961-6083
Telex: 810-221-7086

European Affairs (a quarterly publication on Europe's markets)
c/o Elsevier
P.O. Box 470
1000 AL Amsterdam
The Netherlands
Tel: 020-515-91-11
Fax: 020-83-26-17

European Public Affairs Directory
(lists over 3,500 lobbying groups: corporate, professional, media, EC)
Landmarks S.A.
Chaussee de la Nulpe, 185
1170, Brussels
Belgium

Experts in Action: Inside Public Relations, by Bill Cantor (1989)
Publisher:
Longman, Inc.
95 Church Street
White Plains, N.Y. 10601-1501
Tel: (914) 993-5000
Fax: (914) 997-8115

Federal Staff Directory (1989)—Key Word Subject Index Staff Directories
P.O. Box 62
Mt. Vernon, Va. 22121-0062
Tel: (703) 765-3400

Gale's International Directory of Publications, edited by Kay Gill and Darren
L. Smith
Publisher:
Gale Research Co.
835 Penobscot Building
Detroit, Mich. 48226

Tel: (313) 961-2242
(800) 877-4253
Fax: (313) 961-6083
Telex: 810-221-7086

Going International, by Lennie Copeland and Lewis Griggs (1985)
Random House
201 East 50th Street
New York, N.Y. 10022
Tel: (212) 751-2600

Global Competitiveness: Getting the U.S. Back on Track, edited by Martin K.
Starr, 1988
Publisher:
American Assembly Books
Columbia University
New York, N.Y. 10027-6598
Tel: (212) 280-3456

Global Information and World Communications, by Mowlana Hamid (1987)
Publisher:
New Frontier Publishing
4311 Stockton Boulevard
Sacramento, Calif. 95820
or
P.O. Box 246654
Sacramento, Calif. 95824
Tel: (916) 455-5381

Hollis Press and Public Relations Annual
(a guide to worldwide consultancies, services, media, and information sources)
Contact House, Lower Hampton Road
Sunbury-on-Thames, Middlesex TW16 5HG
United Kingdom
Tel: 001-44-0932-784781/782054
Fax: 011-44-0932-787844

International Marketing Strategies, by Erik Wiklund (1987)
Publisher:
McGraw-Hill
1221 Avenue of the Americas
New York, N.Y. 10020
Tel: (212) 512-2000
(212): 391-4570
(800) 262-4729

International Media Guide (IMG)
(gives ad rates and data on print media in over 101 countries, all in English;
in three editions: a) newspapers worldwide; b) business publications [in
four volumes: Asia/Pacific Region, Europe, the Americas, Middle East
and Africa]; c) consumer magazines worldwide)

Publisher: Media Enterprises International Inc.
22 Elizabeth Street
South Norwalk, Conn. 06854
Tel: (203) 853-7880
Fax: (203) 853-7370

International Membership Directory and *Marketing Service Guide*
American Marketing Association
310 Madison Avenue
Suite 1211
New York, N.Y. 10017
Tel: (212) 687-3280

1990 Media Guide, A Critical Review of the Media, edited by Jude Wanniski
Publisher:
Polyconomics, Inc.,
Morristown, N.J. 07961

Managing Across Borders, by Christopher Bartlett and Sumantra Ghoshal (1989)
Harvard Business School Press
Boston, Mass. 02163
Tel: (617) 495-6700

National Trade and Professional Associations of the U.S. (1989)
Columbia Books, Inc.
1350 New York Avenue, N.W., Suite 207
Washington, D.C. 20005

1990 O'Dwyer's Directory of Public Relations Firms
(includes 500 public relations firms in 55 countries)
J.R. O'Dwyer Co.
271 Madison Avenue
New York, N.Y. 10016
Tel: (212) 679-2471
Fax: (212) 683-2750

Political Handbook of the World
(Published by the State University of New York at Binghamton, Center for
    Social Analysis.)
Available from:
McGraw-Hill
1221 Avenue of the Americas
New York, N.Y. 10020
Tel: (212) 512-2000
    (212) 391-4570
    (800) 262-4729

Power Media Selects, 1990
(study of influential European Community media correspondents and orga-
    nizations in the nation's capital)

Broadcast Interview Source
2233 Wisconsin Avenue, N.W., Suite 406
Washington, D.C. 20007
Tel: (202) 333-4904
Fax: (202) 342-5411

Reed's Worldwide Directory of Public Relations Organizations
John M. Reed, Editor
Publisher: Pigafetta Press (May 1990)
P.O. Box 39244
Washington, D.C. 20016
(ISSN 1045-1277)

Reference Book for World Traders
(three volumes of information for export and general business purposes on
    most countries)
Croner Publications, Inc.
Queens Village, New York 11428

Stateman's Yearbook (1989-90)
St. Martin's Press, Inc.
175 Fifth Avenue
New York, New York 10010

Tell It to the World (1982)
Publisher: Halpern, Burton

Trade Directories of the World
(lists over 3500 trade, industry, and technical directories; updated monthly;
    covers 175 countries and over 800 categories)
publ: Croner Publications, Inc.
211–05 Jamaica Avenue
Queens Village, N.Y. 11428
Tel: (718) 464-0866
Fax: (718) 464-5734

Ultimate Overseas Guide for Growing Companies, by Henry Rodkin (1990)
Publisher:
Dow Jones-Irwin
1818 Ridge Road
Homewood, Ill. 60430
Tel: (312) 798-6000
    (800) 634-3966

The World Almanac
Pharos Books
200 Park Avenue
New York, N.Y. 10166
Tel: (212) 692-3830

Washington Journalism Review
  2233 Wisconsin Avenue, N.W.
  Washington, D.C. 20007
  (by the College of Journalism of University of Maryland at College Park)
  Tel: (202) 333-6800
  "Directory of Selected News Sources," lists yearly in its July/August issue
    organizations providing information in various fields:

Advertising/public relations	Finance	News services
Aging	Food/beverage	Pharmaceuticals
Book publishing	Information services	Professional organizations
Broadcasting	Insurance	Real estate/developers
Chemicals	Labor	Science
Communications	Law	Special interest/social issues
Defense/aerospace	Magazines	Textiles
Education	Marketing	Tobacco
Electronics	Medical/health care	Transportation
Energy	Metals	
Environment	Newspapers	

European Markets: A Guide to Company and Industry Sources, April 1990
  (updated every twelve to eighteen months), Walter Seager, ed. $275. Tel:
  (202) 333-3533. (Sources of information on U.S. government, ports and
  harbors, organizations, private sector data bases, published sources, and experts to contact.)
Washington Researchers Publishing
  2612 P Street, N.W.
  Washington, D.C. 20007
  Tel: (202) 333-3533

World Traders *Data Reports*
  (for background information on foreign companies)
  Client Service
  Trade Information Services
  U.S. Department of Commerce
  P.O. Box 14207
  Washington, D.C. 20044
  Tel: (202) 783-3238

Other Periodicals

Business America
Dateline (published by the Overseas Press Club)
International Management
International Marketing Review
Management International Review (Germany)
Management Today (United Kingdom)
Marketing
Marketing News

Modern Language Journal
Personnel Journal
Public Relations Journal
Public Relations Quarterly

Europe—Single Market Information Sources

Organizations

Language-Export (LX) Centers
A national U.K. network. It was started by the DES and the Training Agency. It is a consortium of local colleges, universities, chambers of commerce, and private training agencies that offer assessment of language needs and programs. In addition to language training, they offer translation and interpreting, export advice, and cultural briefings. A list of LX contacts can be obtained from:
Adult Training Promotions Unit, Room 2/2
DES, Elizabeth House
York Road
London SE1 7PH.
United Kingdom

Management Center Europe
(European headquarters of The American Management Association—consultancy, seminars, courses, and publications on business in Europe)
Rue Caroly 15
1040 Brussels, Belgium
Tel: (32 2) 5161911
Telex: 21917
Fax: (32 2) 5137108

Publications

Get Your Business Into Europe
(Institute of Chartered Accountants of England and Wales or contact European Headquarters of The American Management Association, Brussels)

DTI, "A Single Market Checklist for Small Firms"
DTI, "The Single Market: The Facts"
DTI, "Progress on the Commission White Paper"
DTI, "Single Market News" on consultancy services and what specific companies are doing to prepare for 1992 and other booklets on single market standards or industries, contact DTI in Glasgow: Tel: 01-215-5000 (8:30 A.M.–5:30 P.M. their time)

Pressing Ahead to 1992
Eibis International Ltd.,
London
(or contact European Headquarters of the American Management Association, Brussels)

APPENDIX II

Major Communications Media

Below are important media for news dissemination. Those that are American have a wide reach outside the United States. Major media for the countries covered in this book are listed by nation. It should be remembered that some wire services based abroad have a reach as wide or wider than do well-known services such as the Associated Press. Among them would be Agence France Presse (France), Jiji Press and Kyodo (Japan), Reuters (United Kingdom), and Tass (U.S.S.R.). Others, while largely limited to their country of origin, may be the best way to get coverage in a particular area.

Major American Press With Wide Overseas Distribution

Forbes
60 Fifth Avenue
New York, N.Y. 10011
Tel: (212) 620-2200

International Herald Tribune
   (English; owned by *The New York Times)*
181 Avenue Charles de Gaulle
92521 Neuilly, France
Tel: (1) 46-37-93-00

The New York Times
229 West 43rd Street
New York, N.Y. 10036
Tel: (212) 556-1234

Time International
   (circulation 440,000 in Europe)
Time-Life Building
1271 Avenue of the Americas

Rockefeller Center
New York, N.Y. 10020
Tel: (212) 522-1212

U.S. News & World Report
2400 North Street, N.W.
Washington, D.C. 20037-1196
Tel: (202) 955-2111

Worldwide U.S.-Based News Services

Agence France Presse
  (international wire services in French, English, Spanish, Portuguese, German, Arabic, including telephoto services)
1612 K Street, N.W., Suite 400
Washington, D.C. 20006
Tel: (202) 293-9380

Associated Press
  (has bureaus in 141 U.S. cities and 67 foreign countries)
50 Rockefeller Plaza
New York, N.Y. 10020
Tel: (212) 621-1720

Bertelsmann Corporate Communications-News Bureau
  (major media company providing media for information, education, and entertainment in international markets)
Markham-Novell
211 East 43rd Street, Suite 1102
New York, N.Y. 10017
Tel: (212) 687-1765

Bloomberg News Service
499 Park Avenue
New York, N.Y. 10022
Tel: (212) 980-7000
Fax: (212) 980-5892

Congressional Record Clippings Newsvertising
  (Parliamentary Monitoring Services (London and Brussels) and International Press Clipping Bureaus monitoring Capitol Hill and worldwide any subject)
1868 Columbia Road, N.W., Suite 603/402
Washington, D.C. 20009
Tel. (202) 332-2000

Conus Communications
  (satellite newsgathering service)
3415 University Avenue

Minneapolis, Minn. 55414
Tel: (612) 642-4645

Crain News Service
  (*provides Crain stories to editors worldwide by mail or AP High Speed Data
    Feature Wire*)
740 North Rush Street
Chicago, Ill. 60611
Tel: (312) 649-5303

Dow Jones News Service
  (*provides ticker service, Dow Jones International News Service, and others*)
World Financial Center
200 Liberty Street
New York, N.Y. 10281
Tel: (212) 416-2415

Gamma-Liaison Agency
  (*worldwide network of top photojournalists available for assignment as well
    as a large stock file*)
11 East 26th Street
New York, N.Y. 10110
Tel: (212) 447-2534
Fax: (212) 447-2500

Heritage Features Syndicate
  (*markets columns to newspapers nationwide*)
214 Massachusetts Avenue, N.E.
Washington, D.C. 20002
Tel: (202) 543-0440

KRNT News Wire
  (*offers stories to newspapers in North America and abroad*)
790 National Press Building
Washington, D.C. 20045
Tel: (202) 383-6085

King Features Syndicate
  (*markets cartoons and columns to newspapers worldwide*)
235 East 45th Street
New York, N.Y. 10017
Tel: (212) 455-4000

Los Angeles Times Syndicate
  (*distributes syndicated news services and features worldwide*)
Times Mirror Square
Los Angeles, Calif. 90053
Tel: (213) 237-7988

New York Times Syndication Sales Corporation, (the)
   (distributes material from The New York Times *and other news services worldwide)*
130 Fifth Avenue
New York, N.Y. 10011
Tel: (212) 727-4808

Public Relations Newswire
   (transmits releases for major corporations and gives out financial corporate information)
150 East 58th Street
New York, N.Y. 10155
Tel: (212) 832-9400

Reuters America, Inc.
   (distributes information globally)
1700 Broadway
New York, N.Y. 10019
Tel: (212) 603-3587

United Press International
1400 I Street, N.W.
Washington, D.C. 20005
Tel: (202) 898-8254

Worldwide Television News Corporation
   (international television news agency)
1995 Broadway
New York, N.Y. 10023
Tel: (212) 362-4440

ICA (International Communications Agency)
   (operates international wireless file in several languages and feeds into AP and UPI for local use)

Clipping Bureaus

International Press Clipping Bureau, Inc.
5 Beekman Street
New York, N.Y. 10038
Tel: (212) 267-5450

Australia

Newspapers

Canberra Times (daily)
P.O. Box 218

Pirie Street
Fyshwick ACT
Canberra
Telex: 62296 CANADS AA

The Australian (daily)
P.O. Box 4245
2 Holt Street
Surrey Hills, NSW
Sydney
Telex: 123215 TELEAD AA

Australian Financial Review (daily)
P.O. Box 506
235 Jones Street
NSW
Sydney
Telex: 75418

Daily Mirror (daily)
P.O. Box 4245
2 Holt Street
Surrey Hills, NSW
Sydney
Fax: (2) 288 3729
Telex: 123215 TELEAD AA

Daily Telegraph
2 Holt Street
Surrey Hills, NSW
Sydney
Fax: (2) 288 3729
Telex: 123215 TELEAD AA

Sydney Morning Herald
235 Jones Street NSW
Sydney
Telex: 75418

Age (daily)
250 Spencer Street, VIC
Melbourne
Telex: 30449 AGE AA

Herald (daily)
44-74 Flinders Street, VIC
Melbourne
Fax: (3) 6543133
Telex: 30104 HERALD AA

Broadcasting

Radio: Australian Broadcasting Corp.
P.O. Box 9994
Sydney, NSW 2001
Fax: (2) 264 8681
Telex: 26506

TV: Federation of Australian Commercial Television Stations
447 Kent Street
Sydney, NSW 2000
Fax: (2) 2645425
Telex: 121542 FACTS AA

Public Relations Organizations

Public Relations Institute of Australia (PRIA)
26 Alfred Street
Sydney NNSW 2001

Austria

Newspapers

Die Presse
   (circulation about 80,000; national business newspaper (independent); Monday–Saturday mornings)
Parkring 12A
1010 Vienna
Tel: (01)-51-4-14
Telex: 114110

Kurier
   (circulation daily: 417,000; national general interest independent daily, Saturday and Sunday)
Seidengasse 11
A–1072 Vienna
Tel: (01)-96-2-10
Telex: 132631
Fax: (01)-96-78-50

Neue Kronen Zeitung
   (circulation daily: 958,000; national general interest independent daily)
Muthgasse 2
A–1190 Vienna
Tel: (01) 36010
Telex: 114327

Weiner Zeitung (circulation about 50,000—morning; official government paper)
Rennweg 12 A
1037 Vienna
Tel: (01)-78-76-31
Telex: 131805

Neue A–Z (circulation about 100,000—morning, daily and Saturday; a Socialist newspaper)
Viehmarktgasse 4
1030 Vienna
Tel: (01)-72-02-0

Volksstimme (circulation about 40,000—morning daily, with Sunday edition;
a communist newspaper)
Hochstadplatz 3
1206 Vienna
Tel: (01)-33-56-01

Die ganze Woche (circulation about 820,000; general interest weekly news-
paper)
Odoakergusse 34–36
A–1160 Vienna
Tel: (01) 46-26-91
Telex: 134008
Fax: (01) 450-16-81

News Agencies

APA (Austria Presse-Agentur)
Internationales Pressezentrum (IPZ)
Gunoldstr 14
1199 Vienna
Tel: (01)-36-05-0

AFP (Agence France-Presse)
Internationales Pressezentrum (IPZ)
Gunoldstr 14
1199 Vienna
Tel: (01)-36-31-87
Telex: 115833
Fax: (01)-36-92-568

ANSA (Agenzia Nazionale Stampa Associata) (Italy)
Internationales Pressezentrum (IPZ)
Gunoldstr 14
1199 Vienna
Tel: (01)-36-13-00
Telex: 114891

AP (Associated Press) (United States)
Internationales Pressezentrum (IPZ)
Gunoldstr 14
1199 Vienna
Tel: (01)-36-14-58
Telex: 115930

Reuters (United Kingdom)
Borsegasse 11
1010 Vienna 1
Tel: (01)-531-12-0
Telex: 114645
Fax: (01)-531-12-5

Public Relations Organizations

Lintas Werbeagentur GmbH
Prinz Eugen Strasse 8
A–1040 Vienna
Telex: 132614 LINVI A

Publico Public Relations GmbH
Mautner Markhofgasse 45
A–1110 Vienna
Telex: 133572 PUBLP A

Young and Rubicam GmbH
Marc Aurel-Strasse 4
A–1011 Vienna
Telex: 115815

Belgium

Newspapers

De Bond (family interest weekly in Flemish)
Troonstraat 125
B–1050 Brussels

La Lanterne/La Meuse
  (circulation 133,000; independent general interest daily in French)
134, Rue Royale
B–1000 Brussels

Le Soir
  (circulation 213,000; national daily general-interest independent in French)
21, Place de Louvain
B–1000 Brussels

Agence Economique et Financière (AGEFI)
   (business and financial daily)
Quay au Bois à Bruler 5-7
B–1000 Brussels

Informateur Economique et Financièr (daily)
Rue de Boulet
B–1000, Brussels

La Côté Libre (financial daily)
7 Quais au Bois à Bruler
B–1000, Brussels

L'Echo de la Bourse (AGEFI)
   (business and financial daily)
Rue de Birmingham 131
B–1070
Telex: 23396

Public Relations Agencies

Rossel & Cie SA
Rue Royale 112
B–1000, Brussels
Telex: 24298 ROSSEL B

China

Broadcasting

There are about 300 radio stations. CPBS is Central People's Broadcasting Station, the only national network. Newscasts comprise 22.48 percent of the broadcasting time. Radio Beijing is China's international arm. It broadcasts in thirty-eight languages and maintains bureaus in Bangkok and Cairo. Radio is the most effective way of reaching the population.

Newspapers

Beijing Ribao (Beijing Daily News)

Guangming Ribao (Workers' Daily)

News from New China News Agency (Hsinhua News Agency)

Renmin Ribao (People's Daily)

News Agencies

Hsin Hua News Agency—Belongs to the state council and provides a "news pool," distributing to 200 domestic newspapers, radio stations, and television stations.

China News Service—Serves overseas Chinese people in Hong Kong, Macao, and Taiwan.

Public Relations Agencies

There are currently no public relations firms, but Ogilvy & Mather, Dentsu, and Beijing Advertising Corporation have offices and may be helpful.

France

Newspapers

France-Dimanche
6 rue Ancelle
F–92525 Paris
Tel: 1-42-216405
Telex: 211112 FIGAR

France-Soir (circulation 530,000; daily)
Rue de Bercy (or 100 Rue Reaumur)
75112 Paris

Le Monde (circulation 445,000; daily; independent, rightist; intellectual, highly respected; no pictures)
5 rue des Italiens, 9c
75427 Paris Cedex 09
Telex: 650572

Le Figaro (circulation 465,000; right-wing daily)
25 Avenue Matignon
F–75381 Paris Cedex 08
Telex: 211112 FIGAR
Fax: 1-42-216405

Le Quotidien de Paris
2 rue Ancelle
92521 Neuilly-sur-Seine Cedex

Le Parisien Libéré (circulation 421,000)

Libération (Libe) (independent, moderately left, colloquial)

L'Humanité (communist)

Canard Enchaîné (ultraradical, political weekly)

Le Matin

L'Officiel (weekly)

Pariscope (weekly)

International Herald Tribune
181 Avenue Charles de Gaulle
92521 Neuilly, France
Tel: (1) 46-37-93-00

Regional Newspapers

Ouest-France (Rennes)
    (reportedly the largest circulation in France)

Le Progrès (Lyon)

Le Dauphine Libéré (Grenoble)

La Voix de Nord (Lille)
8 Place de General de Gaulle
59800 Lille

Business/Financial Dailies

La Côté Desfosses
42 Rue Notre-Dame des Victoires, 2e
Paris
Telex: 290275 LESECHOS or 680326 CODEFOS

L'Agence Economique et Financière (daily)
2 rue Béranger
F–75003 Paris
Telex: 670092 AGEFI
Fax: 1-42-97-5298

Les Echos (financial and industrial daily)
67 Avenue de Champs Elysées
75381 Paris Cedex 08
Telex: 290275 LESECHOS

La Tribune de l'Economic

La Côté Desfosses

L'Expansion
67 Avenue de Wagram
75017 Paris

News Magazines

L'Express (conservative; circulation 600,000)
Groupe Express S.A.
61 Avenue Hoche
75008 Paris, France
Fax: 42-67-72-93

Le Point (circulation 235,000)
Societe d'Exploitation de l'Hebdomadaire "le Point"
(SEBDO)
140 rue de Rennes
75066 Paris, France

Le Nouvel Observateur (leftist; circulation 450,000)
14 rue Dussoubs
75002 Paris, France

Le Figaro's Sunday color supplement
25 Avenue Matignon
F–75381 Paris Cedex 08
Fax: 1-42-216405
Telex: 211112 FIGAR

Paris-Match (circulation 828,000)
63–65 Champs Elysees
75008 Paris, France
Tel: 42-56-72-72
Telex: 290294

L'Evénement de Jeudi

Valeurs Actuelles (circulation 150,000)
14 rue d'Uzes
75081 Paris Cedex 02, France
Tel: 42-33-21-84

Wire Service

Agence France Presse
11-15 Place de la Bourse
75002 Paris, Cedex 02
Tel: 1-42-33-44-66

Broadcasting

A nine-member council, Conseil Supérieur de l'Audiovisuel (CSA) supervises
all French broadcasting, including allocation of the concessions for private
channels, distribution of cable networks and frequencies, appointment of
heads of state-owned radio and TV companies, monitoring of program standards, and so on. There were an estimated 58 million radios and 25 million
television sets in use in France in 1987.

Radio

Société Nationale de Radiodiffusion (Radio France)
116 Avenue du President Kennedy
75786 Paris Cedex

78, Avenue Raymond Poincaré
F–75116 Paris
Tel: (1) 45-02-18-45

State-owned (Radio France) stations:
France Inter (24 hours a day; specialized and regional programs), France Culture (serious programs on art, culture, thought), France Musique (programming is 96 percent music), and France Sorbonne (educational programs beamed to Paris only)

There are many regional and local radio stations that relay programs from Paris and transmit their own broadcasts.

Many radio stations broadcast from countries outside France but draw large French audiences. These include:
RTL (Luxembourg)
Europe No. 1 (Saarbrucken—includes private capital)
Radio Monte Carlo (Monaco)
Sud Radio

Commercials are permitted.

Television

There are six television channels in France. Two are state-owned and operated:

Société Nationale de Télévision en Couleur (Antenne 2 [A2] is the largest, received by 96.5 percent of the population)
22 Avenue Montaigne
75387 Paris Cedex
French Broadcasting System
1290 Sixth Avenue
New York, N.Y. 10036

Société Nationale de Programmes (France Regions 3 [FR3] is received by 70 percent of the population)
116 Avenue du President Kennedy
75790 Paris Cedex

Four private channels are currently in operation: TF1, Channel 5, Channel 6, and Canal +

Télévision Française 1 (TFI) specializes in U.S. exports such as game shows and movies; 98 percent receive it.
17 Rue de l'Arrivée
75015 Paris Cedex

Télévision Francophone Par Satellite (TV5)
> is run by a trade, commercial, and business organization; programs, mostly foreign light entertainment and programs and films, air in France and Canada, Belgium, and Switzerland with all broadcasts in French.

241 Boulevard Pereire
75017 Paris

M6 (previously TV6)
> is a music and video channel broadcasting general-interest programs.

91 Avenue de Champs Elysées
75008 Paris

Canal +
> is a color channel broadcasting twenty hours a day, mostly films and sports. It carries little advertising.

78 rue Oliview de Serres
75015 Paris

Tele-Luxembourg, Tele-Belge, and Tele Monte-Carlo have large regional audiences; German speakers in the Alsace region can pick up programs generated in Germany. Cable TV is still relatively new, and pan-European satellite broadcasting is being rapidly developed.

Public Relations Organizations

Association Française des Rélations Publiques (AFREP)
8 rue Jean Goujon
F-75008, Paris

Fédération Française des Rélations Publiques
176 Avenue Charles de Gaulle
92522 Neuilly-sur-Seine

Syndicat National de Conseils en R.P. (SNCRP)
9 Avenue Bugeaud
F-75116, Paris

Germany

Newspapers

Frankfurter Allgemeine Zeitung (circulation 355,000; daily; national general; conservative/liberal)
(POB 100808)
Hellerhofstrasse 2-4
D-6000, Frankfurt/Main
Tel: 069-75910
Telex: 4170990 FAZ
Fax: 7591627

Bild (circulation nearly 5 million; published in Hamburg with regional editions)
Godesberger Allee 90
D-5300, Bonn
Telex: 885714
Fax: 373465

Die Welt (circulation 266,000; national general interest; conservative)
Godesberger Allee 90
D-5300, Bonn
Telex: 885714
Fax: 373465
or
Kaiser Wilhelmstrasse 6
Postfach 30 46 30
D-2000, Hamburg 36
Tel: 040-3471

Suddeutsche Zeitung (circulation 367,000; national general interest; liberal)
Senolingerstrasse 80
Postfach 20 22 20
D-8000, Munich
Tel: 089-21830

Frankfurter Rundschau (circulation 205,000; daily; left liberal)
(POB 100660)
Grosse Exchenheimer Strasse 16-18
D-6000, Frankfurt am Main
Fax: 2199521

BZ Berliner Zeitung (circulation 306,400)
Kochstrasse 50
Postfach 11 03 03
D-1000, Berlin 61 (FRG)

Berliner Morgenpost (daily)
Kochstrasse 50
D-1000, Berlin
Telex: 183594
Fax: 25-108 28

Der Tagesspiegel (daily)
Potsdamer Strasse 87
D-1000, Berlin
Telex: 183773
Fax: 30 2693375

General-Anzeiger (daily)
Justus von Liebig-Strasse 15
D-5300, Bonn
Fax: 6688411

Berliner Zeitung
Karl-Liebknecht-Strasse 29
Berlin
X-1020
Telex: 114854 BZV

National Zeitung
Prenzlauer-Allee 36
Berlin
X-1055

Neues Deutschland
Franz Mehring-Platz 1
Berlin
X-1017

Tribune
Am Treptower Park 28
Berlin
X-1193

Other

Bild am Sonntag (liberal)
   Die Zeit (national general interest; liberal)
      Rheinischer Merkur (national general interest; conservative)
Der Spiegel (weekly news)
Bunte
Stern

News Agencies

D.P.A.
Mitterweg 38
2000 Hamburg 13
Germany
Fax: 011-49-40-41-13351

Also:

Deutscher Depechendienst (Bonn)
Evangelischer Pressdienst (EPD)
Katholischer Pressdienst (KNA)
Nachrichtenagentur (Bonn)
Vereinigte Wirtschaftdienste (VWD)

Public Relations Agencies

Advertising and publicity arrangements are handled through the state advertising organization:
Interwerbung GmbH

P.O. Box 230
Hermann Dunker Strasse 89
1157 Berlin
Telex: 112106 INTEG DD

Zentralausschuss der Werbewirtschaft eV (ZAW)
P.O. Box 647
Villichgasse 17
D-5300 Bonn-Bad Godesberg 1
Telex: 885608 ZAWIV D

Gesellschaft Werbeagenturen (GWA) (Association of Advertising Agencies)
Friedensstrasse 11
D-6000 Frankfurt/Main 1
Telex: 413452 GWA D

Broadcasting

There are nine regional radio-television networks in Germany (see list below), which together form the Standing Conference of German Public-Law Broadcasting Corporations (ARD). Together they transmit a national TV program (German Television) called Channel One. They also broadcast "third" television programs, which are local. ARD and ZDF programming includes foreign and domestic news, documentaries, films, and entertainment.

ZDF (Zweites Deutsches Fernsehen, based in Mainz) is Channel Two. It is the sole television station, the only station that is nationwide.

There are two major private television stations. One is RTL Plus in Cologne, and the other is SAT 1 in Mainz. They are received by cable nationally. There are two radio-only federally licensed stations in addition to the stations listed below.

Bayerischer Rundfunk (München, radio and TV)
Hessischer Rundfunk (Frankfurt am Main, radio and TV)
Norddeutscher Rundfunk (Hamburg, radio and TV)
Radio Bremen (Bremen, radio and TV)
Saarländischer Rundfunk (Saarbrücken, radio and TV)
Sender Freies Berlin (Berlin, radio and TV)
Süddeutscher Rundfunk (Stuttgart, radio and TV)
Südwestfunk (Baden-Baden, radio and TV)
Westdeutscher Rundfunk (Köln, radio and TV)

Deutsche Welle (Köln, short and medium wave radio)
Deutschlandfunk (Köln, medium, long wave, and VHF radio)

Zweites Deutsches Fernsehen (Mainz, television)

The first nine listed corporations put out a joint, nationally transmitted television evening program (Channel One or German Television). The Zweites

Deutsches Fernsehen (Channel Two) also transmits its television program nationwide.

Hong Kong

Newspapers

Asian Wall Street Journal (daily in English)
P.O. Box 9825
Hong Kong
Telex: 83828 AWSJ HX

Hong Kong Daily News (daily)
P.O. Box 1586
Hong Kong Industry Building 17F
444 de Voeux Road
Hong Kong
Telex: 83567

Sing Tao Jih Pao (daily in English and Chinese)
Sing Tao Industry Building
830 Laichikok Road
Kowloon, Hong Kong

South China Morning Post (daily in English)
P.O. Box 47
Tong Chong Street
Hong Kong
Telex: 86008 HX

The Star (daily in English and Chinese)
635 Kings Road
Hong Kong
Telex: 74606 ASCO HX

Wah Kiu Yat Po (daily in Chinese)
106-16 Hollywood Road
Hong Kong

Other

Asia Week (weekly)
Federal Building
22 Westlands Road
Hong Kong
Telex: 71758 AWEEK HX

Business Asia (weekly)
P.O. Box 160

406-410 Marine House
Hong Kong

Insight (monthly business)
257 Gloucester Road
Hong Kong

Media (monthly)
Press Foundation of Asia
Hyde Center
223 Gloucester Road
Hong Kong
Telex: 83013 AFNDC HX

Orientations (monthly in English)
257 Gloucester Road
Hong Kong
Telex: 73595 CONHK HX

Broadcasting

Asia Television, Ltd.
81 Broadcast Drive
Kowloon
Telex: 44680 ATV HX

Hong Kong TV Broadcasts, Ltd. (HK-TVB)
77 Broadcast Drive
Kowloon
Telex: 53059 HK TVB HX

Public Relations Agencies

Burson-Marsteller (HK) Ltd.
United Centre 23F
95 Queensway
Hong Kong
Telex: 73995 BURNAR HX

Hill & Knowlton Asia Ltd.
GPO Box 5389
Windsor House
311 Gloucester Road
Hong Kong

Indonesia

Newspapers

Berita Buana (daily)
Jaoan Tanan Abang 33-35
Jakarta
Telex: 46472 BB JKT

Berita Judha (daily)
Jalan Barito 19A
Jakarta
Telex: 47174 YUDHA IA

Bisnis Indonesia (daily)
Kramat V/8
10430 Jakarta
Telex: 45403 BISNIS

Indonesian Observer (English evening daily)
Jalan AM Sangaji 11
Jakarta

The Indonesia Times (English morning daily)
POB 224
31C Jalan Biak
Jakarta
Fax: (21) 37 50 12
Telex: 46968 INATIME IA

The Jakarta Post (English)
Japan Kebahagiaan 6-10
Jakarta
Fax: (21) 54 92 685

Public Relations Agencies

Presko Public Relations Company
AKA Building
Jalan Bangka 11/2, 8F
Keb. Baru, Jakarta

Italy

Newspapers (*internationally known; †important regional)

**La Repubblica*
    (circulation 850,000; major national daily, published Tuesday through Sun-

day; circulation climbs to over one million on Fridays; morning and evening in Italian; leans left)
Societa Editrice "La Repubblica"
Piazza Indipendenza, 11/B
00185 Rome
Tel: 06/49821 or 49881
Telex: 620660

Il Messaggero (circulation 350,000; major national general daily)
Via del Tritone 152
Rome 00187
Tel: 06-6790151
Telex: 624644
   in New York: European Media Representatives
   11-03 46th Avenue
   Long Island City, N.Y. 11101
   Tel: 718-937-4606

* Il Corriere della Sera
   (circulation approximately 900,000; general national daily, morning and evening in Italian, Monday through Sunday; liberal independent leaning)
RCS Ediroiale Quotidiani S.p.A.
Via Solferino 28
20121 Milan
Tel: 02/6339
Telex: 31001

Il Sole/24 Ore
   (circulation 241,000; Tuesday through Sunday, daily morning business paper and comprehensive economic information system; publishes papers, magazines, books, pamphlets, and electronic data bases)
Editrice Il Sole/24 Ore S.p.A.
Via Lomazzo 52
20154 Milan
Tel: 02/31031
Telex: 331325

Il Giornale (circulation 182,400, in Northern Italy)
Europa di Edizioni S.p.A.
Via G. Negri 4
20123 Milan
Tel: 02/85661

Il Giorno
   (circulation 91,300; daily morning business paper)
Societa Editrice Eseda S.p.A.
Via Parigi, 11
00185 Rome
Tel: 06/47490

Avvenire (circulation 91,196; daily Catholic paper)
Via Mauro Macchi 61
20124 Milan

Mondo Economico (economic weekly)
52 Via P. Lomazzo
20154 Milan

MF (financial daily with international outreach; on newsstands; published by
Class Editori)

* *La Stampa* (Turin) and *Stampa Sera*
(daily, morning and evening)
Via Marenco 32
10126 Turin

* *Paese Sera*

Daily American
(circulation 80,000; general daily morning English-language paper)
Via di Porta Pinciana
00187 Rome

International Daily News (morning; English language)
Via Barberini 3
00185 Rome
Tel: 06/4740673
Telex: 614495

* *Milano Finanza*
(financial weekly with in-depth treatment; circulates to Italy, Europe, United
States, Asia, Africa, Australia)
Editori S.p.A.
Corso Italia 22
Milan
Tel: 02/8029250

† *Il Resto del Carlino* (Bologna)
† *La Nazione* (Florence)
† *Il Mattino* (Naples)
† *La Gazzetta de Mezzogiorno* (Bari)
† *Il Giornale de Sicilia* (Palermo)

Illustrated Weeklies

Domenica del Corriere
Epoca
L'Europeo
Oggi

Gente
L'Espresso
Panorama
Il Tempo

Magazines

Capital (monthly; circulation 85,611)
RCS Rizzoli Periodici S.p.A.
Via A Rizzoli 2
201332 Milan
Tel: 02/2588

Espansione "Business Growth"
   (circulation 54,466; monthly; read by business and economic managers in
     Italian industry)
Arnoldo Mondadori S.p.A.
Casella Postale 1833
20090 Segrate (Milan)
Tel: 02/75421

L'Espresso (circulation 369,000; weekly independent; left; illustrated)
Via Po 12
00198 Rome
Tel: 06/84781
Telex: 620629

Gente (circulation 722,000; weekly; illustrated; political; cultural; current events)
Via Vitruvio 43
20124 Milan
Tel: 02/27751

Mondo Economico ("Economic World")
   (weekly; circulation 288,000)
   Societa Editoriale Mondo Economico
Via Paolo Lomazzo 52
20154 Milan

Oggi (circulation 533,878; weekly; topical)
Corso Garibaldi 86
20121 Milan
Tel: 02/665941

Panorama (circulation 440,000; weekly; current affairs)
Arnoldo Mondadori SpN
Via Marconi 27
20090 Milan
Tel: 02/7542

Broadcasting

Radio Televisione Italiana (RAI) transmits in English, French, German, and
Slovenian on FM, medium- and short-waves. It is government regulated and
majority owned. The radio side broadcasts three national stations and additional regional programs. There are many private radio stations as well.
Viale Mazzini 14
00195 Rome
Tel: 02/21621
Telex: 614131 RAIRM I
RAI broadcasts three television channels, but there are also many private television stations. About 80 percent of households receive television transmissions. Hookups are under way with the Economic Community.

Italia 1
Via F. Testi 7
200190 Milan
Tel: 607331

Rete Quattre
Via Marconi 27
20090 Segrate Milan
Tel: 216001

Press Agencies/Wire Services

AGI—Agenzia Giornalistica
Via Nomentana 92
00161 Rome
Tel: 06/84361

ANSA—Agenzia Nazionale Stampa Associata (has a network of several hundred
correspondents with twenty regional branches in Italy and ninety branches
around the world; in Italian, Spanish, French, and English)
Via della Detaria 94
00187 Rome
Tel: 06/6774

IPS—Inter Press Service
Via Panisperna 207
00184 Rome
Tel: 06/485692

Also:

Associated Press
Reuters
United Press International

ICA (International Communications Agency, which operates an international wireless file in several languages and feeds into AP and UPI for local use)

Press Clippings

L'Argo Della Stampa
Via G. Compagnoni 28, Box 12094
20129 Milan

Press Associations

Associazione della Stampa Estera in Italia (Foreign Correspondents Association)
Villa della Mercede 55
00187 Rome
Tel: 06/6786005

Federazione Italiana Editori Giornali (FIEG) (Association newspaper proprietors)
Via Piemonte 64
00187 Rome
Tel: 06/461683

Public Relations Professional Organization and Agencies

Federazione Relazioni Pubbliche Italiana (FERPIS)
Corso Vittorio Emanuele 37B
20122 Milan

Attlio Ruosi
Via Me Mellani
Milan 36 20129
Fax: 71-96-71

Note: Fax is commonly used in Italy instead of the mails.

Japan

Newspapers

Asahi Shimbun
   (major national general daily, morning and evening in Japanese)
8-5 Tsukiji 7-chome
Chuo-ku, Tokyo 104
Telex: 22226

Mainichi Daily News
  (circulation about 8 million, a major national general daily, morning and
    evening in Japanese)
1-1-1 Hitotsubashi
Chiyoda-ku, Tokyo
Tel: 33-211-2509
Telex: 22324

Yomiuri Shimbun
  (major national general daily in Japanese)
1-7-1 Otemachi
Chiyoda-ku, Tokyo 100
Tel: 33-242-1111
Telex: 22201 J

Nihon Keizai Shimbun
  (major national economic/financial daily in Japanese; also publishes the
    prominent English-language weekly *The Japan Economic Journal* circulat-
    ing domestically and abroad)
1-9-5 Ohtemachi
Chiyoda-ku, Tokyo
Tel: 33-270-0251
Telex: J22308
  U.S. office:
1271 Avenue of the Americas
New York, N.Y. 10036
Tel: (212) 391-0937

The Japan Times
  (English-language morning paper)
5-4 Shibaura 4-chome
Minato-ku, Tokyo 108

There are 124 newspaper companies in Japan that are members of the Japan
Newspaper Publishing and Editors Association. The above first four are the
most important dailies that circulate nationwide. All carry general national and
international news and all have smaller English-language editions that are useful but not influential.

The Japan Times does have some importance but rarely if ever breaks any
news. However, it is read by many Japanese English-speaking businesspeople
and is a popular medium for Japanese companies recruiting non-Japanese employees and for American companies recruiting English-speaking Japanese employees.

About 50 million copies of various newspapers are sold every day, making
Japan the country with the highest newspaper readership in the world, topping
even Sweden. Virtually all newspapers are home-delivered. Regional and local
papers proliferate and are read in addition to the nationals, which have both
morning and evening editions. Many households receive both.

Of all media in Japan, newspapers rate highest in credibility; television is highly valued for its educational value. All the above newspapers have an international network and often supply news for their affiliated television stations.

Average newspaper reading time is forty minutes per day, unchanged over about ten years. Each TV network is affiliated with a major newspaper.

Broadcasting

NHK (The National Public Network)
Daini Kyodo Building
7-13 Udagawa-cho
Shibuya-ku, Tokyo 150

There are 104 public television stations (NHK is the public, national network) and 103 commercial stations. The major commercial national networks are Fuji TV, TBS-TV. There is also an English-language cable channel.

Magazines

Diamond Weekly
Diamond, Inc.
1-4-2 Kasumigaseki
Chiyoda-ku, Tokyo
Tel: 33-504-6339

Zaikai (Business World)
Akasaka Tokyo Building
2-chome, Nagata-cho
Chiyoda-ku, Tokyo
Tel: 33-581-6771

Will
Chuo-ku, Tokyo 104
Tel: 33-563-2766
        33-561-5884

Look Japan (in English)
2-2 Kanda Ogawa-machi
Chiyoda-ku, Tokyo 101
Tel: 33-291-8951

President (monthly)
NY office:
1271 Avenue of the Americas
New York, N.Y. 10020

Press Agencies

Jiji Press Ltd.
1-3 Hibiya-koen

Chiyoda-ku, Tokyo
Tel: 33-591-1111
       33-592-0399

Kyodo News Service
2-2-5 Toranomon
Minato-ku, Tokyo
Tel: 33-584-4111

Press Clubs

Keidanren
   (Japan Federation of Economic Organizations)
1-9-4 Otemachi
Chiyoda-ku, Tokyo 100
Tel: 33-279-1411
Telex: J28295

Foreign Press Center/Nippon Press Center
Nippon Press Center Building
2-2-1 Uchisaiwaicho
Chiyoda-ku, Tokyo 100
Tel: 33-501-3401

Foreign Correspondents Club of Japan
Yurakucho Denki Building
1-7-1 Yurakucho, Tokyo
Tel: 33-211-3161

MITI Press Club
   (Ministry of International Trade and Industry)
1-3-1 Kasumigaseki
Chiyoda-ku, Tokyo
Tel: 33-584-4111
Fax: 33-501-1621

Public Relations Organizations

Public Relations Society of Japan
Sanko Building
7-12 Tsukiji 2-chome
Chuo-ku, Tokyo 104

Dentsu Public Relations Center Ltd.
16-7 Ginza 2-chome
Chuo-ku, Tokyo 104

Hakuhodo Incorporated,
International Public Relations Section

Tokyo Building
7-3, 2-chome Marunouchi
Chiyoda-ku, Tokyo
Tel: 33-240-7781
Telex: 2225111 HAKUTO J

International Public Relations Co., Ltd.
Shinbashi Fuji Building
2-1-3 Shinbashi
Minato-ku, Tokyo 105-91
Tel: 33-501-7571
Telex: J24795
Fax: 33-504-0609

Japan Convention Services, Inc.
  (arranges press conferences to be held at the Nippon Press Club)
Nippon Press Center Building
2-1, 2-chome, Uchisaiwai-cho
Chiyoda-ku, Tokyo 100
Tel: 33-508-1211
Telex: (0) 222-9025 JCS-J
Fax: 33-508-1665

Pacific Press Service
  (arranges publicity and press coverage, specializing in photographs)
Tokyo Central Post Office Box 2051
Chiyoda-ku, Tokyo
Telex: J2-6206 PACPRESS

Simul International, Inc.
  (translating and interpreting)
Kowa Building No. 9
1-8-10 Akasaka
Minato-ku, Tokyo 107
Tel: 33-586-30000

Fukuda Editorial Service
  *(writing, translating, public relations and marketing communications, and
    press releases)*
1-22-6-802 Hongo
Bunkyo-ku, Tokyo 113
Tel: 33-818-1231

Korea

Newspapers

Chosun Ilbo (daily)
61 1-ka Taepyung-ro 1

Chung-ku, Seoul
Telex: 23292 CHOL K
Fax: 02-739-8909

Hankook Ilbo (daily)
14 Chunghak-dong
Chongro-ku
Seoul 1
Telex: 23644 HKILBO K
Fax: 02-738-0777

Hyundae Kyungie Ilbo
P.O. Box 960
441 Sunwah-dong
Chung-ku, Seoul
Telex: 23224 JOONOANG K
Fax: 02-756-1652

Korea Herald (daily in English)
P.O. Box 6479
1-12 3-ka Hoeyung-dong
Chung-ku, Seoul
Telex: 22445 HKLBO K
Fax: 02-274-8640

Seoul Shinmun
31 1-ka Taepyung-ro
Chung-du, Seoul
Telex: 24221 SEDAY

Korea Times (daily in English)
P.O. Box 262
14 Chunhak-dong
Vhongro-ku, Seoul
Telex: 22445 HKLBO K
Fax: (02) 738-0777

Maril Kyungje Shinmun (The Daily Economic News)
51 1-Ka Pil-dong
Chung-ku, Seoul
Fax: (02) 274-8640

Professional Organizations

Public Relations Association of Korea
P.O. Box 2147
Seoul

Malaysia

Newspapers

Berita Harian (daily in Malay)
P.O. Box 250
Balai Berita
31 Jalan Riong
Kuala Lumpur

Malay Mail
   (evening daily and Sunday in English)
P.O. Box 250
Balai Berita
31 Jalan Riong
Kuala Lumpur

Malayan Thung-Pau Daily News (Chinese)
P.O. Box 2408
40 Jalan Lima
Kuala Lumpur

New Straits Times and *Sun Times* (English)
P.O. Box 250
31 Jalan Riong
Kuala Lumpur

Kin Kwork Daily News (Chinese)
21 Panglia St.
Ipoh, Perak

Daily Express (English with Malay section)
P.O. Box 139
75 Gaya St.
Kota Kinabalu, Sabah

Kinabalu Sabah Times (English with Malay)
P.O. Box 525
76 Gaya St.
Kota Kinabalu, Sabah

Overseas Chinese Daily News (Chinese)
P.O. Box 525
76 Gaya St.
Kota Kinabalu, Sabah

Philippines

Newspapers

Balita—daily in Pilipino
2249 Pasong Tamo
Makati Rizal

Bulletin Today
Business Day Company
807 EDSA
Quezon City
Telex: 42295 BUSIDAY PM

Manila Evening Post
Oriental Media, Inc.
20th Street and Bonefacio Drive
Port Area, Manila
Telex: 2510 Orient PU

Times Journal
Times Journal Building
Railroad Street
Port Area, Manila

Others

Amcham Journal
   (published by the American Chamber of Commerce of the Philippines, Inc.;
      circulation 5,000)
Corinthian Plaza
Paseo de Roxas
Legaspi, Makati, Manila
or
C.P.O. Box 1572
Makati, Metro Manila 1299

Philippines and You
   (published by the Philippine Industrial and Commercial Bank)
P.O. Box 2958
Manila

Professional Organizations

Association of Philippine Advertising Agencies
Don Santiago Building
Taft Avenue, Room 405
Manila

Public Relations Society of the Philippines
c/o Shell Company of the Philippines
Shell House, Paseo de Roxas Boulevard
Manila

Singapore

Newspapers

Berita Harian (daily in Malay)
Times House
390 Kim Seng Road
Singapore 0923
Tel: 737001
Telex: 50881 TIMEAD RS

Business Times (business and shipping news daily in English)
Times House
390 Kim Seng Road
Singapore 0923
Tel: 7305463

Lianhe Wanbao (Chinese language evening paper)
News Centre
82 Genting Lane
Singapore 1334
Tel: 7438800

Lianhe Zaobao (morning edition of *Lianhe Wanbao*)
News Centre
82 Genting Lane
Singapore 1334
Tel: 7438800

Tamil Murasu (serves Singapore's Tamil minority)
139–141 Lavendar Street
Singapore 1233
Tel: 2923116

Min Pao Daily
62 Bendermeer Road 12
Singapore

The New Nation (evening daily and Sunday in English)
Times House
390 Kim Seng Road
Singapore 0923
Tel: 7370011

Shin Chew Jit Poh (daily in Chinese)
19 Keppel Road 2
Singapore

Shin Min Daily News (popular daily in Chinese)
News Centre
82 Genting Lane
Singapore 1334
Tel: 7438800
Telex: 26170 SMDN RS

Straits Times (circulation about 100,000; morning daily in English) and *Sunday Times* (Sunday in English)
Times House 390 Kim Seng Road
Singapore 0923
Tel: 7305743 and 7370011
Telex: 50881 TIMEAD RS

Broadcasting

Singapore Broadcasting Corporation (SBC)
  (government board with a monopoly on all broadcasting in Singapore; includes Radio Singapore and Television Singapore)
Caldecott Hill
Singapore 1129
Tel: 2560401
Telex: 39265 SBC RS/508 70 SBC RS

Press Agencies

Associated Press
23-02 Standard Chartered Bank Building
6 Battery Road
Singapore 0104

Reuters
17-01 Shell Tower
50 Raffles Place
Singapore 0104

United Press International
23-10 Shaw Towers
100 Beach Road
Singapore 0718

Public Relations Organizations

Contact advertising agencies or independent contractors.

Spain

Newspapers

El País (circulation 361,000; major national general daily; left-leaning; with
   Sunday magazine)
Miguel Yuste 40
Madrid 28037
Telex: 42187 ELPA E

ABC (circulation 300,000; major national general daily; right/conservative)
Serrano 61
Madrid 28006
Tel: (91) 320-1369
   (91) 320-0818
Fax: (91) 320-3620
Telex: 22555 ABCMD E

La Vanguardia (circulation 350,000; national daily with weekend magazine)
Pelayo 28
Barcelona
Tel: (93) 301-5454
Fax: (93) 318-5587
Telex: 54530 VANGU E

El Periódico (circulation 151,000; daily general with Sunday magazine)
Urgell 71-73
Barcelona 08011
Tel: (93) 323-1046
Fax: (93) 45-3232
Telex: 50643

Cinco Días (Five Days) (circulation 50,000; business/economic daily)

Diario 16 (circulation 135,000)
Gran Via 32
Madrid 28013
Tel: (91) 521-0164
Fax: (91) 522-2114

Iberian Daily Sun (English daily)
Zurbano 74
Madrid

Marca (circulation 92,000; daily)
Mateo Inurria 15
Madrid
Telex: 27622 FDICA E

AS (circulation 151,000)
Madrid

El Correo Español and *El Pueble Vasco*
   (circulation 116,000)
Bilbao

YA (circulation 80,000)
Madrid

La Voz de Galicia
(circulation 77,000)
La Coruña

El Diario Vasco (circulation 77,000)
S. Sebastian

Las Provincias (circulation 60,000)
Valencia

Magazines

Interviú
Rocafort, 104
Barcelona 0801J

Cambio 16 (circulation two million; weekly political, economic magazine)
Hermanos Garcia Noblejas 41
Madrid 28037
Tel: (91) 407-2700
    (91) 268-2889

Tiempo (circulation 500,000; weekly news magazine)
O'Donell 12
Madrid 28009
Tel: (91) 522-0072
Fax: (91) 577-7183

Epoca (circulation one million; general weekly)
Alberto Alcocer 32
Madrid 28036
Tel: (91) 458-5152
Fax: (91) 457-6962

Hola (circulation three million; weekly gossip magazine)
Miguel Angel 1
Madrid 28010
Tel: (91) 410-1311
Fax: (91) 410-1012

Panorama

El Independiente

Heraldo de Aragón

Broadcasting

Dirección General de Radiofussión y Televisión Española
Buenos Aires 1-7
Barcelona
Telex: 54181 RTVE E

Radio-Television Española (RTVE) (Channel 1: news, films, entertainment;
   Channel 2: political programs, variety; Channel 3: music and sports)
28023 Prado del Rey
Madrid 11
Tel: (91) 771-8402
Fax: (91) 711-8611
Telex: 23022 MESI E

Antena 3
CTRA, Madrid-Irun
KM-19, 3
Madrid 28700
Tel: (91) 623-0500
Fax: (91) 651-4690

Telecinco
Plaza de Pablo Ruiz Picasso
Madrid 28020
Tel: (91) 396-6100
Fax: (91) 555-0044

On radio, the National Program is general programming, Second Program is
   recreational, and Third Program is educational. There is also the Foreign
   and Overseas Service (Radio Roma). A few thousand private radio stations
   broadcast locally.

Radio

Radio Nacional de España
Paseo de Gracia 1
Barcelona 08007
Tel: (93) 317-1182
Fax: (93) 302-4978

Radio Popular, S.A. (Cope)
Alfonso X1 4
Madrid 28009

Tel: (91) 521-65-76
Fax: (91) 532-20-08

Cadena 13
Diagonal 297
Barcelona 08013

Cadena SER
Gran Via 32
Madrid 28013

News Agencies

Colegio de Periodistas de Cataluna
Rambla de Cataluna 10
Barcelona 08007
Tel: (93) 317-1920

Asociacion de Periodistas Nacional
Juan Bravo 6
Madrid 28006
Tel: (91) 585-0010

Asociacion Empresarial de Agencias de Prensa y Archivos
Paseo de Gracia 55-57
Barcelona 08007
Tel: (93) 215-3508
Fax: (93) 478-1428

Public Relations Organizations

Agrupación Española de Relaciones Públicas (AERP)
(Public Relations Association of Spain)
San Elias 11
Barcelona 6

Nielsen Company
Luchana 23-6
Madrid
Telex: 46278 NIELS E

Compañía Española de Relaciones Públicas (advertising)
Nuñez Balbao 30
Madrid
Telex: 45285 RPMCE

Sweden

Newspapers

Afton Bladet (evening daily)
Vattugatan 12
S-10518 Stockholm
Telex: 17138

Dagens Nyheter (DN)
　(circulation 400,000, national morning daily; broad-based readership; respected independent, morning daily and Sunday, news and features; deadlines: 6 P.M., country edition, 12:00 A.M., last edition.)
Ralambsvagen 17
S-105 15 Stockholm
Tel: 08-7381000
Telex: 10444 ADAGSNYS
　124 West 60th Street
　New York 10023
　(212) 956-3940
　1124 National Press Building
　Washington, D.C. 20045
　(202) 662-7250

Svenska Dagbladets (SVD)
　(circulation 220,000 daily; conservative; upscale readership in finance/economic/business, concentrated in Stockholm, morning daily and Sundays; same deadlines as above)
Ralambsvagen 7-13
105 17 Stockholm
Tel: 08-135000
Telex: 17400 SVEDG S.
　Daily Telegraph Room 833
　50 Rockefeller Plaza
　New York, N.Y. 10020
　Tel: (212) 246-2479
　3701 Connecticut Avenue, N.W., 439
　Washington, D.C. 20008
　(202) 362-8253

Goteborgs-Postens
　(circulation 300,000 daily, morning; liberal; concentrated on the west coast of Sweden; news and features)
Polhemsplatsen 5
S-405 02 Goteborg
Tel: 031-624000
Telex: 2227 GOTPOST

Sydsvenska Dagbladets Snallposten
  (circulation 120,000 daily; liberal; competes with DN and Goteborgsposten;
    strong in southern Sweden; news and features)
P.O. Box 145
Krusegatan 19
S-20121 Malmo
Tel: (040) 281 280
Telex: 32318 SCISREDS
  300 East 75th Street, 27J
  New York, N.Y. 10021
  Tel: (212) 879-8709

Expressen
  (circulation 600,000 daily, evening; liberal but nonsocialistic; sensational;
    Friday edition's nightlife section is popular with young [20s] audience;
    deadline: 4 A.M.)
Gjorwellsgatan 30
S-105 16 Stockholm
Tel: 08-738 3000
Telex: 17480 EXPRESS
  155 East 29th Street, 33D
  New York, N.Y. 10016
  Tel: (212) 797-3931

Magazines

Major Business Magazines

Veckans Affarer (43 issues a year)
Sveavagen 53
10363 Stockholm
Tel: 08-7365600

Affarsvarlden (43 issues a year)
Skeppsbron 22
11182 Stockholm
Tel: 08-7966500

General-Interest Magazines

Manads Journalen (12 issues a year; trendy; for 30- to 50-year-olds)
Ahlen/Akerlunds Forlag Torsgatan 21
10544 Stockholm
Tel: 08-7364000

Clic (6 issues a year; trendy, for 20- to 30-year-old age group)
Jungfrugatan 19
114 44 Stockholm
Tel: 08-200208

Trade Magazines

Aperitif (9 issues a year; for chefs)
Kvarngatan 12
11626 Stockholm
Tel: 08-449755

Tradtoren (11 issues a year; for hotel, restaurant, bar trade)
Tegnergatan 16
113 58 Stockholm
Tel: 08-341909

Svensk Hotell-Revy (12 issues a year; for the hotel/restaurant trade)
Barnhusgatan 20
11181 Stockholm
Tel: 08-2411620

Broadcasting

State-run Swedish Broadcasting Corporation includes National Swedish Radio
and National Swedish Television, which has two channels and broadcasts
nationwide, with local stations in ten cities; it is noncommercial and includes an entertainment section, a magazine program "Magasinet," and news:

National Swedish Television
Oxenstiernsgatan 26-34
10510 Stockholm
Tel: 08-7840000
   Channel 1—News program is "Aktuellt"
   Channel 2—News program is "Rapport"

TV3 (commercial cable-TV based in London, broadcasts in Sweden, Denmark, and Norway. It buys most of its programs from the United States and
the United Kingdom, but also does some of its own. It runs commercials.)

National Swedish Radio (broadcasts nationwide and has ten local stations; state
run, it has three channels; airs news and various interesting programs, such
as: "Metropol," "Efter 3," "Radio Apparaten," and segments according to
the following:
   Channel 1 (P1)—debate programs
   Channel 2 (P2)—classical music
   Channel 3 (P3)—sports, entertainment, lighter talk shows

Newswires

TT (Tidningarnas Telegrambyra)
  (produces news constantly and is nationwide; the only Swedish newswire)
Kungsholmstorg 5
10512 Stockholm
Tel: 08-132600

Public Relations Organizations

Industrial News Source (INS-AB)
  (worldwide press release service)
Sandhamnsgatan 67
Box 27277
10253 Stockholm
Tel: 08-62 1800
Telex: 8106239 INS
Fax: 08-62 1048

Sveriges Public Relations Forening
  (Swedish Public Relations Association)
P.O. Box 12230
S-10226, Stockholm

Taiwan

Newspapers

Central Daily News (daily in Chinese)
83 Chung Hsiao West Road
Taipei

China News (daily in English)
277 Hsin Yi Road
Sec. 2, Taipei

China Post (daily in English)
277 Hsin Yi Road
Sec. 2, Taipei

China Times
132 Da Le Street
Taipei

Economic Daily News (daily in Chinese)
P.O. Box 43060
555 Chung Hsiao East Road
Sec. 4, Taipei

United Daily News (daily in Chinese)
555 Chung Hsiao East Road
Sec. 4, Taipei

News Agencies

Central News Agencies of China (in major cities)
1231 News Building

220 East 42nd Street
New York, New York 10017
Tel: 212-6828583

Public Relations Organizations

Chinese Public Relations Association
1 Lane 3 Lin Yi Street
Taipei

Thailand

Newspapers

Bangkok Post (daily in English)
U Chuliang Building
968 Rama IV Road
Bangkok
Telex: 848 04 BKK POST TH

Ban Muang (daily in Thai)
1 Soi Pluemmanee
Vibhavadi Rangsit
Bangkok

Broadcasting

Operated by: Radio Thailand (RTH)
Vibhawadi Rangsit Road
Bangkok
Telex: 72167 DEPRELA TH

Public Relations Agencies

Presko Public Relations, Ltd.
Bangkok 10500
Telex: 82884 PRESKO TH

Turkey

Newspapers

Ankara Ticaret Gazetesi (commercial daily)
Ruzgarli Sok 2/6
Ankara

Gunaydin
Alaykosku Caddesi
Cagaloglo
Istanbul
Telex: 22246 GUNAY TR

Hurriyet
  (circulation 7,000; general daily morning paper centered in Istanbul but with
    national distribution)
Hurriyet Gazeteillik ve Matbaacilik
A.S. Babiali Cad.
15-17 Cagalouglu
Istanbul
Tel: (1) 526-31-81
Telex: 22249 HUR TR
Fax: 512-0016

Turkish Daily News (daily in English)
Tunus Caddesi 49/7
Ankara

Turkiye Iktisat Gazetesi (commercial daily)
Karanfil Sokak 56
Bakanlikar

Hurriyet Pazar
  (circulation 8,000; Sunday weekly magazine address same as above)

Milliyet
  (circulation 200,000 daily, 250,000 Sunday; morning general paper centered
    in Istanbul but with national distribution)

Daily News
  (circulation 700 distributed nationally daily except Sunday; English lan-
    guage, conservative leaning)
Ankara
Tel: 282-956
Telex: 42340

Aksam
  (circulation 95,000 daily, 10,000 Sunday; general morning daily based in
    Istanbul, circulated nationally; strong on politics, conservative)

Istanbul Ticaret
  (circulation 17,000, weekly business paper in Turkish)
Istanbul Chamber of Commerce
P.O. Box 377
Istanbul

Turkish Daily News (daily in English)
Tunus Caddesi 49/7
Ankara

Turkiye Iktisat Gazetisi commercial daily
Karanfil Sokak 56
Bakanlikar
Ankara

There are also many industry and trade publications.

Broadcasting

Turkiye Radyo Telvizyon Kurumu (TRT)
Nevat Tandogan Caddesi 2
Kavaklidere
Ankara

Press Agencies

Mine Hekimoglu
Sok 2515 Kadikoy
Istanbul
Tel: 1-337-5507
Telex: 29400 ADBETR

The Bosphorus Institute
Mete Caddest No. 44
12 Taksim, Istanbul
Tel: 11-45275
Telex: 25879

Monch Turkey Media, Ltd.
Ahmet Mithat Efendi Sok
No. 2012, 06550 Cankaya
Ankara
Tel: 41-39-19-37/39 5889
Fax: 41-39-57-24

Faik Sanag
Spor Yazarlarl Sitesi 39/3
Akatiar-Istanbul
Tel: 90-1-168-16-88
Telex: 26869 SSGX TR

Tarkars Yavaz
Kocamansur Sokak 11/75
Altun Apt. SIsli-Istanbul
Tel: (90) 1-147-47-34
Telex: 26015 netx tr

Tit Ajans Dis Tanitum AS.
4 Gazeteciler Sitesi A1/2
1 Levent Istanbul
Tel: 1-170-00-35-170-00036
Telex: 26-538-TIT TR

Trans Ocean Company
1436 Sokak No. 8/6
TR-ALsancak Ixmir
Telex: 52683

Public Relations Agencies

Talk to advertising agencies. Public relations and market research are usually
   handled by advertising agencies. The Izmir Trade Fair is a valuable opportunity for exposure.

United Kingdom

Main Newspapers (*national papers)

News of the World
   (circulation 5 million; Sunday; sensationalist)
200 Grey's Inn Road
London WC1

The Sun
   (circulation 4 million; sensationalist)
London

Daily Mirror
   (circulation 3 million; pro-Labour)
Northcliffe House, Carmelite St.
London EC4

Sunday Mirror
   (circulation 3 million; pro-Labour)
Holburn Circus
London EC1

The Sunday People
   (circulation 2.9 million; independent)
Holburn Circus
London EC1

Daily Express
   (circulation 1.8 million; independent daily)

121–128 Fleet Street
London EC4P 4JT

Sunday Express
  (circulation 2.2 million; independent)
121-128 Fleet Street, EC4
London

*Daily Mail
  (circulation 1.8 million; independent)
Northcliffe House
Tudor Street
London EC44 OJA

The Mail on Sunday
  (circulation 1.7 million)
Northcliffe House, Carmelite Street
London EC4

*The Star
  (circulation 1.4 million)
121 Fleet Street
London EC4

*Daily Telegraph
  (circulation 1.2 million; quality conservative; daily)
135 Fleet Street
London EC4P 4BL

Sunday Telegraph
  (720,900; conservative)
181 Marsh Wall
London E14

The Observer
  (circulation 773,000; Sunday; independent)
8 St. Andrew's Hill
London EC4

London Standard
  (circulation 522,100; conservative)
118 Fleet Street
London EC4

*The Guardian
  (circulation 493,600; quality daily; independent)
London and Manchester
119 Farringdon Road
London EC1

* Financial Times
  (circulation 306,857; quality daily circulated nationally and abroad)
Bracken House
10 Cannon St.
London EC4P 4BY

* The Times of London
  (circulation 447,279; quality daily; moderate conservative)
Virginia Street
London E1

The Sunday Times and *Sunday Times Magazine*
  (circulation 1.2 million; independent)
Virginia Street
London E1

Economist
  (weekly news magazines)
25 St. James Place
London SW1A 1NT

Today
  (circulation 307,300; independent)

The Independent
  (circulation 292,700)

Birmingham Evening Mail
  (circulation 275,000; independent)

Liverpool Daily Post
  (circulation 72,000; independent)

The Journal
  (circulation 66,000; independent)

Wales: *South Wales Echo*

Scotland: *Sunday Post, Daily Record, Scottish Daily Express, Evening Times, Courier and Advertiser, Evening News, Glasgow Herald, The Press and Journal, The Scotsman*

News Wires

Reuters-worldwide
Associated Press
Exchange Telegraph Company, Ltd.
Press Association, Ltd.
United Press International

Broadcasting

British Broadcasting Corporation (BBC) is state owned and financed by license fees and accepts no commercials. It operates two color channels, BBC-1 and BBC-2, and four domestic radio services. BBC does not give publicity to any company or organized interest group except when it is inherent in the informational content of a program.

Independent Television News (ITV) is controlled by IBA and Channel 4 is owned by Independent Broadcasting Agency (IBA). Programs are produced by independent companies and by Channel 4 television company, a subsidiary. There are fourteen program companies that have contracted to produce IBA programs. They derive most of their revenue from commercials, which are limited to seven minutes in an hour of broadcasting, or nine minutes on independent local stations. IBA prohibits advertisments for cigarettes, gambling, politics, or religion.

BBC programming includes a wide variety of general interest subjects, although BBC-1 tends toward entertainment, sports, and current affairs while BBC-2 is heavy on minority interests and documentaries and travel films.

BBC carries no advertising on radio. There is no independent radio service, although IBA has permission to build such a service. There are thirty-two local BBC radio stations and forty-four independent local radio stations. The local stations do accept advertising. Programming follows the following format:

Radio 1: rock and pop music
Radio 2: light entertainment and sports
Radio 3: classical music and drama
Radio 4: news and current affairs

Cable television restrictions have been loosened to allow development of a wide range of services and facilities. The national cable authority issues licenses and promotes development. At this writing, about twenty cable systems have been granted licenses.

Satellite transmission is under development in conjunction with Economic Community members. It is projected that by the end of the century advertisers will be able to reach 125 million families in the twelve EC countries through Direct Broadcasting Satellites.

Public Relations Agencies

Institute of Public Relations
Gate House
St. John's Square
London EC1M 4DH

Public Relations Consultants Association
10 Belgrave Square
London SW1X 8PH

APPENDIX III

Fact Sheets on Selected Nations

Australia, Belgium, the Chinese People's Republic and the Republic of China, France, Germany, Hong Kong, Indonesia, Italy, Japan, Korea, Malaysia, Philippines, Singapore, Spain, Sweden, Thailand, Turkey, the United Kingdom, and Vietnam were selected for coverage in this appendix for several reasons. They give a good cross-sectional view of possible target markets and they all seem to be areas that capture the interest of many Americans. Some are rich and highly developed; others are the opposite, adding to the value of the composite group. None have been included with any idea of recommending them as target markets to any reader. The information about them may, however, be helpful background to businesspeople interested in their potential. Changes in Eastern Europe, which opened those countries to new capital investment and trade, had to be recognized. Therefore, brief information has been included for them as well.

Country's Formal Name: Commonwealth of Australia

Size: 2,966,151 square miles

Geographical Location: Bounded on the north by the Timor and Arafura seas; on the east by the Coral Sea, the Pacific Ocean and the Tasman Sea; and on the south and west by the Indian Ocean.

Capital: Canberra; the largest city is Sydney.

Currency: Australian dollar

Population: 16.5 million, 85 percent in urban areas; multicultural

Education: 99 percent literacy rate; schooling is compulsory between the ages of 6 and 15.

Language: English

Religion: Protestant, Roman Catholic, and others about evenly divided

Minority Groups: Ethnic Maoris, Chinese, Vietnamese, Korean, Japanese

Major Industries: Foodstuffs, minerals, wool, coal; opportunities grow in development and tourism

Exports: Iron and steel (it's the world's biggest coal exporter); wool, wheat, beef, minerals. 1989: $45 million

Imports: 1989: $52 million

Major Corporations: Petrocorp (oil), Air New Zealand, Elders IXL

Gross National Product: 1989: $U.S. 283 million

Average Income/Standard of Living: Real gross domestic product is $11,929 per capita; average real GDP over the past five years is 4.6 percent.

Form of Government: Democratic republic

Political Environment: Stable

Top Government Titles: Monarch of the United Kingdom and Australia represented by the governor-general. Prime minister is head of the government. The government body is the Federal Parliament consisting of a Senate and House of Representatives. It's a national federation of six states: New South Wales, Queensland, South Australia, Tasmania, Victoria, West Australia, and two federal territories: Australian Capital Territory and Northern Territory.

Business Environment: Low GDP growth, a relaxed work ethic, and a large number of workdays lost to strikes (third in Asia after the Philippines and South Korea); high unemployment (7 percent in 1989). Labor costs are higher than elsewhere in Asia; the labor market needs to be deregulated. There's a need for privatization in the public sector. Interest rates are high (about 18 percent). Business hours: Monday to Friday 9:00 A.M.–5:00 P.M. and Saturday 9:00 A.M.– 12:00 N.

Holidays: January 1, Australia Day (last Monday in January), Commonwealth Day, Good Friday, Easter Sunday, Easter Monday

Transportation and Communications: On a par with other developed nations. Overseas private telecommunications is provided by communications satellites, submarine cables, and shortwave radio. Satellites carry more than 60 percent of Australia's telecommunications. Telecom Australia is gradually providing equipment and service to many parts of Asia.
Telephone country code-61; Adelaide-8; Brisbane-7; Melbourne-3; Newcastle-49; Perth-9; Sydney-2
Time: EST plus fifteen hours

Press: Print media includes a national Sunday paper and two national dailies as well as four dozen morning or afternoon dailies and general magazines. There are a large number of special-interest and trade periodicals as well.

Broadcasting: Radio and TV are under the government by the Australian Broadcasting Commission and communications satellites. There are over 130 radio stations and over 50 television stations. Commercial airtime is available.

Information Sources:
Australian News and Information Bureau
630 Fifth Avenue
New York, N.Y. 10111
Tel: 212-245-4000
Fax: 212-265-4917
    Branches are also in Chicago, Houston, Los Angeles, Miami, and San Francisco.

Country's Formal Name: Austria (Österreich)

Size: 32,376 square miles

Geographical Location: Landlocked in Europe. Bounded on the west by Germany and Switzerland, the south by Italy and Yugoslavia, the east by Hungary, and the north by Czechoslovakia.

Capital: Vienna (Wein)

Currency: Schilling = 100 groschen

Population: 7.6 million

Education: 99 percent literacy

Language: German

Religion: Mostly Roman Catholic (89 percent), with some Lutheran, others

Major Industries: agriculture, livestock, production of natural resources such as gas, petroleum, zinc, lead, iron ore, lignite, magnesite, sand, and gravel. Manufacturing and tourism are also major.

Exports: 1989: $50.1 million; machinery, metal products, paper, shoes, textiles, wood, wood products, prepared foods

Imports: 1989: $49.9 million (vehicles, machinery, clothes)

Gross National Product: $126 million

Defense: Austria has been neutral since 1955. Military service is compulsory for six months followed by fifteen years of active reserve duty.

Form of Government: Federal republic divided into nine states, each with its own government. The federal president is elected for six years.

Business Environment: Conservative, prior appointments necessary. Vacations generally taken during July and August. Business hours: Monday to Friday 8:30 A.M.–4:30 P.M.

Holidays: January 1, 6; Easter Monday; May 1, 20; Whit Monday; Corpus Christi; August 15; October 26; November 1; December 8, 25, 26.

Transportation and Communications: Both are convenient and efficient—on a par with other industrialized countries. A main river running through Austria, Germany, and Czechoslovakia is used for trade and passengers.
Telephone country code-43; Graz-316; Innsbruck-5222; Linz/Donau-732; Salzburg-662; Vienna-1

Time: EST plus six hours

Press: Free press, no censorship. There are several dozen daily papers and hundreds of regional, trade, and special-interest publications. Newspapers and television rate about equal in popularity as media for advertisers. Radio ranks next.

Broadcasting: Austria Broadcasting Company oversees radio and television but there is no government interference in programming.

Trade Fairs:
Fachmessen Salzburg
P.O. Box 285
A-5021 Salzburg
Tel: 43-662-375510
Telex: 633131

Wiener Messe AG
P.O. Box 124
Messeplatz 1
A-1071, Vienna 7
Tel: 43-222-315511
Telex: 133491

Information Sources:
Austrian Trade Commission Office
500 North Michigan Avenue, Suite 544
Chicago, Ill. 60611
Tel: 312-644-5556
or
150 East 52nd Street
New York, N.Y. 10020
Tel: (212) 421-5250
Fax: (212) 751-4675

Country's Formal Name: Belgium

Geographical Location: Bounded on the west by the North Sea, on the north by the Netherlands, on the east by Luxembourg and Germany, and on the south by France.

Capital: Brussels

Currency: Belgian franc = 100 centimes

Population: 9.9 million (Flemings 58 percent; Walloons 42 percent) A low birthrate translates into stable population size, with somewhat higher growth in the north. High population density.

Education: 99 percent literacy; dual educational system of state secular and private denominational schools. School is compulsory between ages 6 and 18.

Language: Flemish in the north, French in the south (Walloon region)

Religion: Roman Catholic (90 percent), with Protestant and Muslim minorities

Major Industries: Few natural resources; most raw materials are imported

Exports: 1989: $110 million

Imports: 1989: $108.5 million, mostly raw materials

Gross National Product: $170 million

Form of Government: Hereditary constitutional monarchy with a democratic bicameral parliamentary system of government

Political Environment: Nine provinces; the seat of NATO and European Community headquarters

Social Environment: There is tension between the Flemings in the north, who speak a form of Dutch, and the French-speaking Walloons in the south. The social welfare programs are well developed and available to almost all the population.

Business Environment: Wage costs are now competitive with Europe; the environment is conservative; vacations taken in July and August. The Belgian economy is service-based, with light and heavy industries and international trade. The north has grown better than the south. Belgium is heavily reliant on international trade. Working hours: Monday to Friday 9:00 A.M.–12:00 N. and 2:00–5:30 P.M., Saturday 9:00 A.M.–12:00 N.

Holidays: January 1, Easter Monday, May 1, Ascension Day, Whit Monday, National Independence Day, Assumption Day, Armistice Day, December 25.

Transportation and Communications: Belgium has the densest railroad network in the world as well as extensive inland waterways and roads. Modern phone, fax, and other facilities are readily available.
Telephone country code-32; Antwerp-3; Brussels-2; Charleroi-71; Ghent-91; La Louviere-64; Liege-41
Time: EST plus 6 hours

Press: There is no censorship. The print media is largely family-owned. There are over 34 dailies in French, Flemish, and English, with many trade magazines. Newspapers are the best advertising medium; total circulation of all newspapers is over two million.

Broadcast Media: No commercials over the national broadcasting system, but advertisers use Radio Luxembourg.

Trade Fairs: Foire Internacionale de Bruxelles
Parc des Expositions
B-1020 Brussels
Tel: (32) (2)478–4830
Telex: 23643
Fax: 32-2-478-8023

Information Sources:
Belgian-American Chamber of Commerce in the U.S. Inc.
350 Fifth Avenue, Suite 703
New York, N.Y. 10118
Tel: 212-967-9898
Fax: 212-629-0349

Belgian Industrial Development Section
c/o Consul General of Belgium
50 Rockefeller Plaza
New York, N.Y. 10020
Tel: 212-586-5110

Belgian National Tourist Office
745 Fifth Avenue
New York, N.Y. 10151
Tel: 212-758-8130

Country's Formal Name: People's Republic of China (Chung-Kuo)

Capital: Beijing (Peking)

Geographical Location: Bounded on the north by the U.S.S.R. and Mongolia; on the east by Korea, the Yellow Sea, and the South China Sea; on the south by Nepal, Bhutan, India, Myannmai (Burma), Laos, Vietnam; and on the west by India, Pakistan, and Afghanistan.

Size: 3,696,100 square miles

Currency: Renminbi (yuan = 100 fen)

Population: 1.1 billion, with 40 percent in urban areas

Education: 70-85 percent are literate; six-year primary school attendance is compulsory.

Language: Mandarin is the official language; many dialects of Chinese are spoken across the country.

Religion: Officially atheist, but Buddhism, Confucianism, and Taoism are tolerated as are Christianity, Islam, Lamaism, and others.

Exports: About $39.5 billion. Water to Hong Kong as well as meat and vegetables, textiles, metals, oil, mineral fuel, and foodstuffs.

Imports: About $43.4 billion. Grain, equipment; a net importer of food, fertilizers, raw materials, machinery, textiles, grains, iron, and steel.

Average Income/Standard of Living: Low; real gross national product is $299 per person; average real GNP over the last five years is 11.2 percent.

Form of Government: Communist republic. Six-member Politburo Standing Committee is elected by the Chinese Communist Party's (CCP) Central Committee. According to the constitution, the highest government body is the National People's Congress (NPC), which is elected.

Political Environment: Not very stable in view of signs that many Chinese people are restless with the existing strict Communist regime of Deng. Power depends on personal connections. Corruption is reportedly rampant. Leadership is entrenched. There is a strong need to establish an impartial legal and political system.

Business Environment: The government-owned, centrally managed economy shows signs of change. Agriculture and forestry still use most of the labor force. Rice is the largest crop. Fishing and livestock are major. China is rich in natural resources, especially fossil fuels, ores, and minerals. National banking is state controlled; some foreign banks are allowed to operate. Foreign trade is conducted through foreign trade agencies representing various industries and overseen by the Ministry of Foreign Trade. The best way to enter the Chinese market may be through a joint venture. The bureaucracy is frustrating. Business hours are: Monday through Sunday from 8:00 A.M.–6:00 P.M. Sunday is a holiday for banks and government.

Holidays: January 1; February 9, 10; May 1; October 1, 2, 3.

Transportation and Communications: Ministry of Railways controls all railroads. Inland waterways carry more than one-third of all internal freight and are linked to the nine main ports. 30 percent of roads are paved.
Telephone country code-86; Beijing-1; Fuzhou-591; Ghuangzhou (Canton)-20 Shanghai-21
Time: EST plus thirteen hours.

Press: Strictly controlled by government and used for political purposes. *Renmin Ribao* (People's Daily) is the official paper of CCP's Central Committee.

Other: Billboard displays are used as well as radio and television. Advertisers in China must register first with MOFERT, whether using print or broadcast media. Radio is very influential.

Information Sources:
National Council for U.S.-China Trade
1050 17th Street, N.W.
Washington, D.C. 20036
Tel: (202) 429-0340
Telex: 64517 NC USCTUW

American Chamber of Commerce of the PRC
International Club
Telex: 22402 ALTNA CN

National Council for U.S. Trade
Beijing Hotel, Room 1136

Beijing Hotel, Room 1136
Beijing
Telex: 22637 NCPEK CN

PUBLICATIONS:
The following are available from:
The U.S.-China Business Council
1818 N Street, N.W., Suite 500
Washington, D.C. 20036
Tel: (202) 429-0340
     (202) 775-2476

China Business Review (bimonthly)
Guide to China's Trade and Investment Organizations
US-China Business Services Directory

Other publications include:

Beijing Review (weekly)
China International Book Trading Corp.
P.O. Box 399
Beijing, P.R.C.

Business China (fortnightly)
Business International Asia/Pacific, Ltd.
Asia House
One Hennessey Road
Hong Kong

Far East Economic Review (weekly)—Published in the United States by Review
   Publishing Company, Ltd.

China Media Book—Published by Anglo Publications, Ltd., 1989. Discusses
   media, regulations, and developments in China.

Advertising and Selling to the PRC, Tom Gorman and Jeffrey S. Muir, editors.
Available from:
China Consultants International (Hong Kong), Ltd.
Suite 905, Guardian House
320 Kwan Road
Happy Valley, Hong Kong

The Chinese Official Yearbook 1986/87

Country's Formal Name: Republic of France (République Française)
Capital: Paris, which is also the largest city (2.2 million population)

Geographical Location: Near the geographical center of western Europe; bounded on the north by the English Channel, Belgium, and Luxembourg; by the Bay of Biscay on the west; on the east by Germany; on the south by the Mediterranean Sea and Spain. Corsica and several other territories are also part of France. Over 1,875 miles of coastline. Shares common frontiers with Andorra, Belgium, Germany, Italy, Luxembourg, Spain, and Switzerland.

Currency: French franc = 100 centimes

Size: 213,000 square miles, in Europe second in size only to the U.S.S.R.

Population: 55.7 million (as of January 1987); lowest rate of density in Europe; 20 percent of the population is in Paris. The average age is 36.7 years; 13.6 percent are over 65; 58.2 percent are between 20 and 64 years, and a little over a fourth (28.2 percent) are under 20 years of age.

Education: Free compulsory education from 6 to 16 years old. By district: primary school until age 11, then four years of (collèges) first cycle *enseignement secondaire*, then second cycle (lycée) at about age 15 for two years of technical training leading to "brevet d'études professionnelles" (commercial, administrative, industrial options) or three years of general education leading to a baccalaureate. Following the baccalaureate students are qualified for university courses. Public and private schools coexist. Literacy rate is 99 percent. About 17.7 percent of the national budget is spent on education.

Language: French

Religion: Primarily Christian, 90 percent of those Roman Catholic. Church and state are separate and other religions co-exist, Muslim being the largest minority.

Minority Groups: 160,000 political refugees from Eastern Europe, Asia, Latin America, and Africa. Muslims (from Algeria, Morocco, Tunisia) form an important minority group. Others come from Italy, Portugal, and Spain.

Major Industries: Europe's leading agricultural nation; farming occupied about 7 percent of population in 1985, and food and agricultural products form an important industry group. Manufacturing is important: intermediate goods, steel, motor vehicles, aircraft; mechanical, industrial, household, and electrical goods; textiles, chemicals, bauxite, natural gas, hydroelectric power; and high-tech industries: aerospace, telecommunications, software. The fastest-growing sector is services: advertising, computer services, management consulting, tourism.

Exports: Cereals, sugar, dairy products, wine, livestock; manufactured as well as agricultural products. 1989: $223 billion.

Imports: Energy (mostly oil) and other energy products and mineral raw materials (bauxite is the only native natural resource), consumer goods, and metal products. 1989: $221 billion.

Major Corporations: Phone-Poulenc, Essilor, many others

Major American Multinationals: General Foods France, American Express

Gross National Product: 1989: $948 billion

Average Income/Standard of Living: Fighting to strengthen its economy, France has been able to keep salary increases in line with price-rise levels. Unemployment is high.

Form of Government: Republic. President and prime minister, with a bicameral parliament: Senate with 319 members and National Assembly with 577. Senators are elected for nine-year terms by an electoral college from the National Assembly; the assembly is elected by universal suffrage for five-year terms. President is elected directly by popular vote for a seven-year term; he or she appoints prime minister and approves prime minister's selection of other ministers.

Political Environment: Generally very stable. France still has four overseas departments: French Guiana, Guadeloupe, Martinique, Réunion; three collective territorials: Mayotte, St. Pierre, and Mignelon; and four overseas territories: French Polynesia, French Southern and Antarctic Territories, New Caledonia, Wallis and Futura Islands.

Social Environment: Social security compulsory for all wage earners and self-employed. Contributions from both employers and employees provide: sick care, unemployment, maternity, disability, family allowances. Socialized medicine. There is a minimum wage.

Defense: Compulsory service for twelve to eighteen months for men aged 18 to 35; active armed forces number about 547,000 plus 390,000 reserves. 1987 defense budget was FF178,000 (about 19 percent of total budget). Some 475,000 women are in the armed forces.

Business Environment: After strong trends toward socialization, a five-year program was introduced in 1986 to privatize 65 state-operated enterprises. A free-market system exists with foreign investment actively promoted by the government through investment incentives, favorable conditions, free trade zones, and export incentives. Forty percent of the labor force is women, mostly in clerical, sales, and human services positions. Business hours: Monday to Friday 9:00 A.M.–12:00 N and 2:00 P.M.–6:00 P.M. Vacations are usually July through September, and especially in August.

Holidays: January 1; Good Friday; Easter Monday; Labor Day; Ascension Thursday; Whit Monday; July 14; August 15; November 1, 11; December 25.

Press: Free, but with some restrictions such as on official secrets, libel, false information, and on children's literature. Almost 3,000 newspapers and periodicals published, including 11 daily newspapers with national circulation (total circulation 2.7 million), 80 provincial dailies (total circulation 7.5 million), and 1,500 specialized publications. Some provincial papers pool advertising. There are two major news magazines. Papers are independently owned and nonpolitical except for the Communist party organ, *l'Humanité*. Major metropolitan papers are: *Le Monde* (445,000), *Le Figaro* (465,000), *France-Soir* (530,000), *Le Parisien Liberé* (421,000), and *International Herald Tribune* (in English, 168,908). Others are: *Le Ma-*

tin, Le Quotidien de Paris, and *Libération*. Newspapers are a popular advertising medium.

Press Agencies: Agence France-Presse, Agence Parisienne de Presse, Agence République d'Information (politics, domestic and foreign), and Press Services. Associated Press and other foreign agencies have bureaus in Paris.

Broadcast Media: About 58 million radios and 25 million television sets. The communications commission supervises all French broadcasting. There are six TV channels, of which two are government-owned and-run, three are private, and one is pay cable. EC cable stations are received in Paris and other major cities. Most channels accept advertising.

Transportation and Communications: Nationalized and generally excellent, with high-tech, computer/telephone work stations available to every home provided by the government, an excellent train and bus system, the world's fastest long-distance trains (TGV), and a fine, extensive subway system in Paris.

Telephone country code-33; Bordeaux-56; Lyon-7; Marseille-91; Nice-93; Paris-1; Toulouse-61

Time: EST plus six hours

Other: Soccer, bicycling, and rugby are the most popular sports, with tennis enjoying a boom and swimming, golf, fishing, boating, sailing, camping, mountain climbing, and various winter sports also popular. Extensive literary, artistic, and musical productions are available, both traditional and modern.

Trade Fair Organizers:

Comité des Expositions de Paris
55 Quai Alphonse de Gallo
POB 317
92107 Boulogne Billancourt Cedex
Tel: 33-01-49-09-60-00
Telex: 632580
Fax: 01-49-09-60-03

Promosalons
17 Rue Daru 8 ME
F 75008 Paris
Telex: 842650100

Information Sources:

ORGANIZATIONS:

French-American Chamber of Commerce in United States
509 Madison Avenue, Suite 190
New York, N.Y. 10022
Tel: 212-371-4466

    Chambre de Commerce Franco-Américaine aux Etats-Unis
    7 Rue Jean Goujon
    75008 Paris
    Tel: (1) 43-59-63-35

American Chamber of Commerce in France
21 Avenue George V

75008 Paris
Tel: (1) 47-23-80-26

Paris Chamber of Commerce & Industry
(Chambre de Commerce et d'Industrie de Paris, Direction des Relations
   Internationales)
2 Rue Viarmes
75001 Paris
Tel: (1) 45-08-36-00

Union of French Chambers of Commerce Abroad
(Union des Chambres de Commerce Française à l'Etranger
2 Rue de Viarmes
75001 Paris
Tel: (1) 45-08-39-10

Statistical and Economic Studies
Centre de Recherches pour L'Expansion de l'Économie (Rexeco)
141 Boulevard Haussmann
75008 Paris
Tel: (1) 43-59-04-56

GOVERNMENT GROUPS:
French Industrial Development Agency
610 Fifth Avenue
New York, N.Y. 10020
Tel: (212) 757-9340
   (Also in Chicago, Los Angeles, and Houston)

French Industrial Development Agency
Délégation à l'Amenagement du Territoire et l'Action Regionale
DATAR
1 Avenue Charles Floquet
75007 Paris
Tel: (1) 47-83-61-20

Ministry of Research & Technology
1 Rue Descartes
75231 Paris Cedex 05
Tel: (1) 46-34-35-35

Ministry of Industry, Telecommunications & Tourism
101 Rue de Grenelle
75700 Paris
Tel: (1) 45-56-36-36

National Bureau of Statistics and Economic Studies
Institut National de la Statistique et des Etudes Economiques
I.N.S.E.E.
12 Rue Boulitte
75675 Paris Cedex 14
Tel: (1) 49-44-10-10

Research Financing and Commercialization
Agence Nationale de Valorisation de la Recherche
43 Rue Caumartin

65436 Paris Cedex 09
Tel: (1) 40 17 83 100

Fundamental Research
Centre National de la Recherche Scientifique (CNRS)
15 Quai Anatole-France
75700 Paris
Tel: (1) 45-55-92-25

Health and Medical Research
Institut National de la Santé et de la Recherche Médicale
(INSERM)
101 Rue de Tolbiac
75654 Paris Cedex 13
Tel: (1) 45-84-14-41

TRADE FEDERATIONS:
Agribusiness:
Association National des Industries Agro-Alimentaires
A.N.I.A.
52 Rue du Fauborg-Saint-Honoré
75008 Paris
Tel: (1) 42-66-40-14

Chemicals:
Union des Industries Chimiques
64 Avenue Marceau
75008 Oarus
Tel: (1) 47-20-56-03

Plastics:
Franplast
65 Rue de Prony
75854 Paris Cedex 17
Tel: (1) 47-63-12-59

Country's Formal Name: Federal Republic of Germany (Bundesrepublik
Deutschland)

Size: 137,705 square miles (248,700 square kilometers)

Geographical Location: Bounded on the west by The Netherlands, Belgium,
and Luxembourg; on the north by the North Sea, the Baltic Sea, and
Denmark; on the east by Czechoslovakia and Poland; and on the south by
Switzerland and Austria.

Capital: Bonn

Currency: Deutsche mark = 100 pfennig

Population: 78.25 million

Education: 99 percent literacy

Language: High German in the south and center; Low German in the north. Standardized High German is used in schools, businesses, and in the media.

Religion: Roman Catholic 26 percent; Protestant 45 percent, and others 29 percent

Form of Government: Parliamentary democracy headed by a federal chancellor; head of state is the federal president; legislature has two houses: Bundestag and Bundesrat.

Major Industries: Agriculture, manufacturing

Exports (before unification of the two Germanys): 1989 for then-West Germany: $413.7 billion in machinery, vehicles, electrical equipment, and steel products; and for then-East Germany: $28 billion (1987) in machinery, transportation equipment, electrical equipment, chemicals

Imports (before unification): Then-West Germany, 1989: $338 billion in petroleum and petroleum products, foods, and clothing; then-East Germany, 1989: $27 billion in petroleum and petroleum products, machinery, and foods

Gross National Product: Then-West Germany, 1989: $1.2 trillion; then-East Germany, 1986: $187.5 billion

Business Environment: Conservative; holidays taken in July and August; always use surnames unless asked to do otherwise.
Business hours: Monday to Friday, 8:30 A.M.–5:00 P.M.

Holidays: January 1, Good Friday, Easter Monday, May 1, Ascension Day, Whit Monday, Corpus Christi, October 3 (German National Day), November 1, Repentance Day, December 25, 26

Transportation and Communications: One of the most extensive railroads in the world; excellent highways; river and canal systems connect with ports; government owns the post, telegraph, and telephone
Telephone country codes (these may be changed in the future):
GFR-49; W. Berlin-30; Bonn-228; Frankfurt-69; Hamburg-40; Munich-89
GDR-37; E. Berlin-2; Dresden-51; Karl-Marx Stadt-71; Leipzig-41; Magedeburg-91
Time: EST plus six hours

Press: About 350 daily newspapers just in what was formerly West Germany. *Bild Zeitung* is biggest. There is no government censorship; newspaper publishing is shrinking, but Germany is known as a major publisher of books. *Junge Welt* and *Deutschland* are the largest newspapers in what was formerly East Germany.

Broadcasting: There is nearly 100 percent proliferation of television all over Germany. There are three major channels owned by public corporations and strictly controlled by the government in what was West Germany. There are few commercials. Former East Germany has two radio stations and one television station.

Trade Fairs:

Germany is known for its trade fairs. The German Council of Trade Fairs and Exhibitions publishes a yearly calendar of fairs and exhibitions of national or international significance (see below).

Austellungs-und Messe Ausschuss der Deutschen Wirtschaft eV, Lindendenstrasse 8
D-5000 Cologne 1
Fax: (2) (21) 20907-12
Telex: 8881507 AUMA

Hannover Fair is the largest trade fair in the world. It takes place every spring with nearly 6,000 exhibitors of capital and consumer durables. Other major trade fairs take place in Berlin, Cologne, Dusseldorf, Essen, Frankfurt am Main, Hamburg, Munich, Nuremburg, and Stuttgart. Some are listed below. The spring and autumn consumer goods fairs in Frankfurt am Main and the Frankfurt Book Fair are particularly well known.

Austellungs-und Messe Ausschuss der
Deutschen Wirtschaft eV
Lindenstrasse 8
D-5000 Cologne
Fax: (2) (21) 20907-12
Telex: 8881507 AUMA

Hannover Fairs
103 Carnegie Center
Suite 207
Princeton, New Jersey 08540
Tel: (609) 987-1202
Fax: (609) 987-0092

AMK GmbH Kongress
22 Messendamm
D-1000 Berlin 19 OFR
Tel: (49) (30) 3 03 80
Telex: 0182908

Messe-und Ausstellungs GmbH
P.O. Box 970126
D-6000 Frankfurt 97
Tel: (069) 75 75 0
Telex: 411558

Leipzig Fair (Leipziger Messeamt)
P.O. Box 720
Markt 11/15
X-7010 Leipzig
Telex: 0512294

Internazionales Handelszentrum (an international trade center for exhibitions, conferences, and seminars
Friedrichstrasse
X-1086 Berlin
Telex: 114381 1HZB DD

Information Sources:

Federation of German Chambers of Commerce
P.O. Box 1446
Bonn 5300
Telex: 886805 DIHT D

American Chamber of Commerce in Germany (Industrie und Handels-
kammer)
P.O. Box 3229
Boersen Platz
D-6000 Frankfurt/Main
Telex: 411255 1HKF D

German-American Chamber of Commerce, Inc.
666 Fifth Avenue
New York, N.Y. 10103
Tel: (212) 974-8830
Fax: (212) 974-8867

German Information Center
950 Third Avenue, 24F
New York, N.Y. 10022
Tel: (212) 888-9840
Telex: (212) 752-6691

German Consular Office
Economic Division
460 Park Avenue
New York, N.Y. 10103
Tel: (212) 308-8700

International Trade Center
Friedrichstrasse
X-1086
Telex: 114381 1HZB DD

Country's Formal Name: Hong Kong (British Crown Colony)

Geographical Location: On the southern coast of China in the South China
Sea, east of the Pearl River Estuary. Consists of the island of Victoria,
with Kowloon and the new territories.

Capital: Victoria

Size: 410 square miles

Currency: British pound

Population: 5.6 million, with 90 percent in the city; about 98 percent Chinese

Education: 88 percent literacy; free compulsory education in China; English is taught as a second language.

Language: Primarily Cantonese and English; both are used in business. Mandarin sometimes used.

Religion: Buddhism, Taoism, ancestor worship, and others including Christian denominations, especially Anglican

Minor Groups: Other Asian and Western communities make up about 2 percent.

Major Industries: Foreign currency trading, financial futures dealing, banking, shipbuilding, machinery fabrication, textile and clothing production, light manufacturing, fishing. It is a major financial center, with excellent communications.

Exports: Heavy reliance on exports such as clothing, electronic goods. 1989: $74.6 million.

Imports: Basically everything: fruit, vegetables, meat, water (mostly from mainland China) and natural resources, tourism; raw materials for manufacturing. Total in 1989: $75.1 million.

Major Corporations: Hongkong & Shanghai Banking Corp., Cheung Kong (controls Hutchison Whampoa trading conglomerate), Bank of East Asia; every major bank of the world is represented in Hong Kong.

Gross National Product: 1989: $63.4 million

Average Income/Standard of Living: Real gross domestic product is $8,158 per capita; average real GDP over the past five years was 8.4 percent. Average factory wage is $595.

Form of Government: Colony with a British governor and Executive Council; a legislative Council enacts laws and approves the budget. In 1997 ownership will revert to China, which will make Hong Kong a Special Administrative Region.

Political Environment: There is uncertainty in Hong Kong about how the Chinese will treat the colony once they take over. The flight of capital and people is under way. A flat income tax of 17 percent creates an incentive to work hard.

Social Environment: Crowded and stratified; sharp division between rich and poor, but British apply generous social welfare aid.

Major Social Problems: Continuing problem with overcrowding caused by refugees; concern for the future and applications for passports or other documents to allow residents to leave.

Business Environment: Low tax rate, high interest rates, no tariffs (free port status), excellent entrepreneurial atmosphere at present. A market economy based on light industry and international trade.
Business hours: Monday to Friday 9:00 A.M.–1:00 P.M. and 2:00–5:00 P.M.; Saturday 9:00 A.M.–1:00 P.M.

Holidays: January 1; Chinese New Year; Good Friday; Easter Monday; April 5, 21; Queen's Birthday; Tuen Ng Festival; Half Year holiday; September 28; Chung Yeung Festival; December 25, 26

Press: Free; most unrestricted in Asia outside of Japan; both English and Chinese

Press Agencies: All major agencies are represented.

Broadcast Media: Primarily in Chinese but with several English stations. Broadcasting is carefully regulated with at least eight hours of educational programming per weekday by TV stations. Radio and television are covered by two companies. HKTVB broadcasts on two channels in English and Chinese. There is also commercial cable Rediffusion.

Transportation and Communications: Excellent; Telephone country code-852; Castle Peak-0; Hong Kong-5; Kowloon-3; Sha Tin-0; Tai Po-0.
Time: EST plus thirteen hours

General Tax Structure: See above

Information Sources:

Office of Commissioner of Commercial Affairs Hong Kong
680 Fifth Avenue, 22F
New York, N.Y. 10019
Tel: (212) 265-8888
Fax: (212) 974-3209

Hong Kong Trade Development Council
673 Fifth Avenue, 4F
New York, N.Y. 10022
Tel: (212) 838-8688
Fax: (212) 838-8941

Hong Kong Economics and Trade Office
680 Fifth Avenue
New York, New York 10022
Tel: (212) 265-8888

Country's Formal Name: Republic of Indonesia (Republik Indonesia)

Size: 741,098 square miles

Geographical Location: More than 13,500 islands covering over 3,000 miles of ocean. On the north is the Andaman Sea and the Indian Ocean; on the west, the Pacific Ocean; on the east is Papua New Guinea; on the south is the Arafura Sea. There are seven geographical divisions: Sumatra, Java, Indonesian Borneo, Salawesi, the lesser Sunda Islands, the Moluccas, and Irian Jaya.

Capital: Jakarta

Currency: Rupiah = 100 sen

Population: 187.7 million; 25 percent in urban areas

Education: About 72 percent literacy rate; school is required for children 8 to 14.

Language: Bahasa Indonesia, although many other languages and dialects are spoken.

Religion: Islam (85 percent), Christianity, Animism, Hinduism, Buddhism

Minority Groups: With over 3,000 inhabited islands, the population is diverse.

Major Industries: Huge oil reserves (9 billion barrels) and rich industrial mineral resources

Exports: Oil, liquified natural gas, minerals, forestry products, rubber, coffee, tin, palm products, fish, copper, tea

Imports: Tourism

Major Corporations: Astra Group, Indonesian Aircraft Industry (state owned)

Average Income/Standard of Living: Gross domestic product is $338 per capita; average growth in real GDP over the past five years is 4.2 percent. Average factory wage is $60.

Form of Government: Constitutional republic headed by a president

Business Environment: Looking for investment technology and professionalism. There's an abundance of red tape.

Hours: Monday to Friday 8:00 A.M.–4:00 P.M.; Saturday 8:00 A.M.–1:00 P.M.

Holidays: January 1, Good Friday, Ascension Day, August 17, December 25. Other religious holidays based on the lunar calendar, which is 352 days.

Political Environment: Stable now, but President Suharto, who has been in office for twenty-five years, expected to make his current term his last. The large national debt is a problem, although Indonesia has an excellent credit record. There are three major parties.

Names of Ministries: The national legislature consists of a single chamber, the House of People's Representatives (Dewan Perwakilan Rakyat). Its 364 members are elected for five-year terms by universal suffrage. Another 96 House members are appointed by the government. There is also a People's Consultative Assembly that meets once every five years.

Social Environment: Shortage of medical personnel; malnutrition is prevalent.

Transportation and Communications: Railroad and shipping systems are good, but coordination between them is not. Telephone country code-62; Bandung-22; Jakarta-21; Palembang-711; Semarang-24.
Time: EST plus twelve hours.

Press: Over ninety dailies and several weeklies; radio and TV are government controlled, although there is some local independent broadcasting. Telecommunications facilities effectively link all the communications systems in the nation.

Information Sources:
American Indonesian Chamber of Commerce Inc.
711 Third Avenue, 17F
New York, N.Y. 10022
Fax: (212) 867-9882

Trade Promotion Office
5 East 68th Street

New York, N.Y. 10021
Tel: (212) 879-0600

Country's Formal Name: Repubblica Italiana (Republic of Italy)

Geographical Location: In central/southern Europe, Italy is a 750-mile long peninsula plus two large islands, Sicily and Sardinia, and several small islands. The Alps form the northern border to France, Switzerland, Austria, and Yugoslavia.

Capital: Rome

Size: 116,000 square miles

Currency: Lira = 100 centesimi

Population: Almost 60 million. Rome is the largest city with nearly 3 million, followed by Milan, Naples, Turin, Genoa, Palermo, Bologna, Florence, Catania, Bari, and Venice. Population has been moving north to industrial centers in recent years.

Education: Universal, free education, compulsory until age 14. One-third of children complete elementary school. Literacy is 98 percent.

Religion: Roman Catholic Apostolic is state-supported. Other religions are tolerated if they are consistent with principles of public order and morality. Appointment of archbishops and bishops must be approved by the government. Catholicism is taught in all the schools; only Catholic marriages are entered automatically into the civil register.

Minority Groups: German, French, Slovenes, and Albanians form minority groups.

Major Industries: Services make up over half the GNP and some 60 percent of the work force, followed by manufacturing, construction, agriculture, and energy resources. Nearly 90 percent of Italy's land space is given to agriculture. Italy is also well known for its fashion and design, and consumer goods.

Exports: Machinery is the largest export, followed by clothing/leather goods, miscellaneous, motor vehicles, metallurgy, chemicals, foodstuffs, and fuel. Germany is the biggest buyer, followed by France and the United States. 1989: $165.7 million.

Imports: Machinery is also the biggest import, followed by foodstuffs, fuel, chemicals, metallurgy, motor vehicles, miscellaneous, and cloth/leather goods. Raw materials and over 80 percent of energy are imported. There is a serious trade deficit. 1989: $171.4 million.

Average Income/Standard of Living: About $14,000 (1988). Standard of living for professionals and upper and middle management is comparable to that in other developed countries. Skilled workers received high wages and generous benefits. Housing is tight.

Gross National Product: 1989: $899.1 million.

Form of Government: A "democratic republic founded on work" and headed by a president with parliament, executive, and judiciary branches. Major parties are Christian Democrats, Socialists, Social Democrats, Liberals, Republicans, Communists, and the Italian Social Movement.

Political Environment: Since World War II there have been forty governments in Italy.

Social Environment: High unemployment caused by high labor costs. There are four main labor unions, which leads to a rigid job market and protective legislation. Skilled labor is scarce, and that available is well paid.

Major Social Problems: Burdensome social security contributions that are paid by employers, amounting to nearly 49 percent of gross wages; a worsening deficit; widespread tax evasion; crime; mafia; drugs.

Defense: Italy holds a strategic position on the Mediterranean and was a founding member of NATO.

Business Environment: About half the business enterprises are owned or managed by the government, which carries with it the burdens of bureaucracy. The private sector focuses on service industry. The government tried to stimulate growth by holding down inflation, by deregulating, and by promoting exports. The Milan-Genoa-Turin triangle covers the manufacturing area in the industrial north. Tourism is a big industry and with remittances from Italian workers abroad helps the foreign trade deficit. The GNP has risen every year since 1983. Atmosphere is conservative. July and August are vacation times. Office hours: Monday-Friday 8:30 A.M.–12:45 P.M. and 2:00–6:30 P.M.; Saturday 8:30 A.M.–1:30 P.M.

Holidays: January 1, 6; Easter Monday; April 25; May 1; June 9; August 15; November 1; December 8, 25, 26.

Regulatory Environment (industry): Regulations proliferate, taxes are high; dividends to nonresident companies or individuals are subject to a 32.4 percent withholding tax.

Legal Environment (industry): Labor unions are strong.

Press: Free press; broadcast media (radio and television) are state-controlled and supported.

Press Agencies: Over seventy daily newspapers with a combined circulation of 6.71 million copies. Fourteen are published in Rome and seven in Milan. Daily papers are also published in English, German, and Slovene.

Broadcast Media: Supported and owned by the state: RAI (Radiotelevisione Italiana—public broadcasting) broadcasts three national and other regional radio networks, with transmissions in English, French, German, and Slovenian as well as Italian. RAI is government-regulated. The state owns a majority interest.

Communications: About 80 percent of Italian households have television. Advertising is an extremely important communications tool, with magazines particularly important because there are few real national newspapers and newspapers in general are considered to be slanted toward men. Radio and television combined account for 22 percent of advertising expenses. Telephone country code-39; Bologna-51; Florence-55; Genoa-10; Milan-2; Naples-81; Rome-6.

Time: EST plus six hours.

Trade Fairs:

Mostra Internazional dell'Artigianato
Fortezza da Basso
I-50129 Florence
Telex: 50129

Fiera de Milano
P.O. Box 1270
20145 Milano
Tel: 02 4 99 71
Telex: 331360

Information Sources:

ORGANIZATIONS:

Italian-American Chamber of Commerce, Inc.
350 Fifth Avenue, Suite 3015
New York, N.Y. 10118
Tel: (212) 909-5454

Italian Information Service (for cultural, language, and general information)
686 Park Avenue
New York, N.Y. 10021
Tel: (212) 249-6264

Italian Trade Commission
499 Park Avenue
New York, N.Y. 10022
Tel: (212) 980-1500

Italian Embassy
1601 Fuller Street, N.W.
Washington, D.C. 20009
    (Commercial Office at same address)

Italian Government Tourist Office
630 Fifth Avenue
New York, N.Y. 10111
Tel: (212) 245-4822

U.S. Embassy
Via Veneto 119/A
00187 A, Rome
Tel: (06) 46-742

U.S. Consulate
Piazza della Republica 32
Milan
    Banca d'America e d'Italia

Piazza Portello 6
Genoa
    38 Lungarno Amerigo Vespucci 38
    Florence

U.S. International Marketing Center
Via Gattamelata 5
20149 Milan

U.S. Trade Center
Via Gattamelata
Milan

American Chamber of Commerce
(Camera de Commercio Americana)
Via Agnello 12
Milan
    Via Abruzzi 25
    Rome
        Division of International Commerce
        230 Park Avenue
        New York, N.Y. 10169
        Tel: (212) 309-0513

Embassy of the United States of America
Via Vittorio Veneto 199A
00187 Rome
Tel: (06) 4674

Italian Information Office of the European Commission
Corso Magenta 61
I-20123 Milano
Tel: 801-56-78

Italian Information Office of the European Parliament
Via Poli 29
I-00186 Rome
Tel: 678-97-22

Instituto Nazionale per il commerico Estero (ICE)
(National Institute for Foreign Trade)
EUR-Via Liszt, 21
00100 Rome
Tel: (06) 59921

Rome Secretarial Bureau (supplies bilingual clerical help)
Via Torino 40
Rome

U.S. Department of Commerce
Office of Service Industries, Room 1128
14th and Constitution Avenue, N.W.
Washington, D.C. 20230
Tel: (202) 377–3575

PUBLICATIONS:

Guide to Italy (cultural information)
Intercultural Press
P.O. Box 768
Yarmouth, Maine 04096
Tel: (207) 846-5168

Italian American Business Directory
American Chamber of Commerce in Italy
Via Cantu 1
20123 Milan

Italian Trends
Banco Nazionale del Lavoro
Via Veneto 199
Rome

Italy—Background Notes, U.S. Department of State, April 1987.

Doing Business in Italy, Price Waterhouse, 1988

Country's Formal Name: Japan (Nippon or Nihon)

Capital City: Tokyo

Geographical Location: An island nation off the eastern coast of the Asian continent and the Korean peninsula and consisting of four main islands: Hokkaido, Honshu, Kyushu, Shikoku, and many smaller ones. Bounded on the north by the Sea of Okhotsk, on the east by the Pacific Ocean, on the south by the Philippine Sea, and on the west by the Sea of Japan and the Korean Strait.

Size: 145,875 square miles including the Soviet-occupied northern territories of Kunashiri, Etorofu, Shikotan, and Habomai.

Population: 123.2 million, 77 percent in urban areas

Education: 99 percent literacy; six years of elementary school, three years lower secondary are compulsory; nine-tenths of lower secondary graduates go to upper secondary for three years. College follows.

Language: Japanese

Currency: Yen

Religion: Buddhism and Shintoism; there is freedom of religion. Some Christians.

Minority Groups: Burakumin (the "untouchables"), Koreans and other Asians, and the Ainu, who are ethnic peoples centered around Hokkaido.

Major Industries: Electronic equipment manufacturing, high fashion clothing, transportation equipment, foodstuffs, iron and steel, general machinery and machine tools, chemicals, fishing

Exports: Passenger cars, ships and boats, electronic equipment

Imports: Natural resources, minerals, metals, oil and other fuels, foods, paper goods, lumber

Major Corporations: Toyota Motor, Mitsui, Mitsubishi, Sumitomo, Matsushita, Seibu, Dentsu, Morinaga Milk Industry Co., Nomura Securities, Industrial Bank of Japan

Average Income/Standard of Living: Gross domestic product is $22,772 per capita; average real GDP over the last five years is 4.5 percent; average household income exceeds that of the United States.

Form of Government: Constitutional empire headed by an emperor, who is the "symbol of the State and of the unity of the people." The Diet is very stable.

Political Environment: Stable and largely predictable

Social Environment: Japan has a social welfare, unemployment, and federal pension system.

Major Social Problems: The aging of society, the heavy child-rearing responsibilities of women and their lack of opportunity in the workplace, and the severe educational demands placed on children

Defense: Self-defense force only, no army

Business Environment: About 30 percent of workers are union members but labor often participates in management. Promotion is still mainly by seniority. *Nemawashi,* or informal interpersonal interaction, is key to Japanese management. Consensus is the argument/decision that results. Business hours: Monday-Friday 9:00 A.M.–5:00 P.M.; Saturday 9:00 A.M.–12:00 N for many offices, or these hours on alternate weekends.

Transportation and Communications: Modern, prompt, clean public transportation in all major cities with excellent rail connections to outlying areas. Japanese high-speed trains *(Shinkansen)* are comparable with the French and run now to major cities. Subways in Tokyo are excellent; trains run every two to four minutes to every part of the city.
Telephone country code-81; Kobe-78; Kyoto-75; Nagoya-52; Osaka-6; Sapporo-11; Tokyo-3; Yokohama-45
Time: EST plus fourteen hours

Press: No censorship; Japanese are avid readers. News dissemination within the industry relies heavily on press "clubs" that reporters belong to. More information is provided in the text.

Information Sources:
ORGANIZATIONS:
   Associated Japan-America Societies has branches in many cities throughout the United States as well as a sister organization in Japan. They offer classes, seminars, and cultural and library resources. The New York Society is the largest of the group.

Associated Japan-America Society headquarters and the Japan Society, Inc.
333 East 47th Street
New York, N.Y. 10017
Tel: (212) 832-1155
Fax: (212) 755-6752 (there are branches in most main cities)

United States-Japan Foundation
145 East 32nd Street
New York, N.Y. 10016
Tel: (212) 481-8753
Fax: (212) 481-8762

Japan Information Services
299 Park Avenue
New York, N.Y. 10017
Tel: (212) 371-8222

Japanese Chamber of Commerce of New York
145 West 57th Street
New York, N.Y. 10019
Tel: (212) 246-9774

Keizai Koho Center (Japan Institute for Social and Economic Affairs)
Otemachi Building
6-1 Otemachi 1-chome
Chiyoda-ku, Tokyo 100
Tel: 33-201-1414
Telex: 03-222-3188 KDRTOK J

JETRO (Japan External Trade Organization)
2-5 Toranomon 2-chome
Minato-ku, Tokyo
Tel: 33-582-5511
    1221 Avenue of the Americas
    New York, N.Y. 10020
    Tel: (212) 997-0400

American Chamber of Commerce in Japan
Fukide Building No. 2
1-21 Toranomon 4-chome
Minato-ku, Tokyo 105
Telex: 23736 KYLETYO J

Japan Chamber of Commerce and Industry *(Nippon Shoko Kaigisho)*
  (publishes weekly trade news and tries to answer individual inquiries)
Tosho Building
2-2 Marunouchi 3-chome
Chiyoda-ku, Tokyo 100
Telex: 222-4920 JONCCI J

PUBLICATIONS:
  American Chamber of Commerce in Japan Directory (a listing of members
    published yearly)
  ACCJ
  Fukide No. 2 Bldg., 7F

1-21, Toranomon 4-chome
Minato-ku, Tokyo, 105

Business Tokyo (monthly magazine that aims to give coverage of Japan's
    domestic markets in English)
104 Fifth Avenue
New York, N.Y. 10011
Tel: (212) 633-1880
Fax: (212) 633-1883

Intersect (monthly publication by a Matsushita subsidiary that carries gen-
    eral-interest stories about Japan)
PHP Institute, Inc.
3-10 Sanbancho
Chiyoda-ku, Tokyo 102
Tel: 33-239-6238
Telex: PIT J29551
Fax: 33-222-0424
PHP Institute of America, Inc.
400 Madison Avenue, Suite 305
New York, N.Y. 10017
Tel: (212) 688-3110

The Japan Economic Journal (weekly business and economic news of Japan)
Nihon Keizai Shimbun, Inc.
9-5 Otemachi 1-chome
Chiyoda-ku, Tokyo 100-66
c/o OCS America, Inc.
5 East 44th Street
New York, N.Y. 10017
Attn: JEJ Subscription Department
or
Nihon Keizai Shimbun America, Inc.
1271 Avenue of the Americas
New York, N.Y. 10020
Tel: (212) 391-0937

Country's Formal Name: Taehan Min'guk or Republic of (South) Korea

Capital City: Seoul

Geographical Location: Peninsula extending south from the border with North
    Korea, between the Yellow Sea and the Sea of Japan

Size: 38,031 square miles

Currency: Won = 100 cheun

Population: 45 million, 75 percent in urban areas

Language: Korean; English spoken by many businesspeople

Education: 92 percent literacy rate; six years primary education is compulsory and free.

Religion: Confucian tradition with Buddhist and Christian minorities

Major Industries: The market economy is based on services and light and heavy industries.

Exports: The world's least expensive steel, personal computers, video recorders, cars, memory chips, ships, airplane parts

Imports: Manufactured goods, machinery, and transportation equipment

Major Corporations: *Chaebol*, the giant conglomerates, retain major power. The four largest: Samsung (textiles, paper, pharmaceuticals, watches, home appliances, semiconductors), Hyundai (cars, semiconductors), Daewoo (home appliances, real estate, cars, heavy industry equipment), and Lucky-Goldstar (electronics) have revenues totaling more than 40 percent of the country's gross national product. Another *chaebol*: Ssangyong Group (cement, oil refining, hotel construction, automobile manufacturing), TriGem Computer

Major American Multinationals: Samsung Corning, General Electric, AT&T, Caterpillar, General Motors

Average Income/Standard of Living: Real gross domestic product is $3,436 per capita, with an average growth rate over the past five years of 11.4 percent. Average manufacturing wage is over $650 a month, close to that of Taiwan and Singapore.

Form of Government: Democratic republic with centralized presidential system. Executive power is vested in the president, who is elected for one seven-year term. The State Council is appointed and includes the prime minister and heads of ministries.

Political Environment: Stable at the moment, with a still-delicate balance between Communist-run North Korea, which invaded in 1950, causing the Korean War. The traditionally strained relationship with Japan, Korea's neighbor to the east, was not helped by the Japanese occupation of Korea from 1910 to 1945 and has not improved much since. Since mid-1987 the government has been more democratic.

Business Environment: Koreans are hardworking, ambitious, and in 1989 recorded a $14 billion trade surplus. However, labor strikes can be a problem. Business hours: Monday to Friday 9:00 A.M.–12:00 N. and 1:00 P.M.–5:00 P.M.; Saturday 9:00 A.M.–1:00 P.M.

Holidays: January 1, 2, 3; March 1, 10; April 5; May 5; June 6; July 17; August 15; October 1, 3, 7, 9; December 25

Social Environment: Health conditions are inadequate and poor sanitation is a problem.

Press: Newspapers are privately owned but closely supervised by the government. Korean Broadcasting Service is state owned and controls all broadcasting.

Transportation and Communications:
Telephone country code-82; Inchon-32; Kwangju-62; Pusan-51; Seoul-2; Taegu-53
Time: EST plus fourteen hours

Information Sources:
Korean-American Chamber of Commerce
5941 North Lincoln Avenue
Chicago, Ill. 60659
Tel: (312) 728-3040

Korea National Tourist Corporation
460 Park Avenue, Suite 400
New York, N.Y. 10022
Tel: (212) 688-7543
Fax: (212) 371-1086

Country's Formal Name: Federation of Malaysia

Geographical Location: The southernmost part of the mainland of southeast Asia, with territory both on the Malay Peninsula and the northern part of the island of Borneo.

Capital: Kuala Lumpur

Size: 127,316 square miles of territory. The Malay Peninsula extends from the Isthmus of Kra in southern Thailand to the Johor Strait, which separates Malaysia from Singapore. Malaysia is bounded on the east by the Sulu Sea and Celibes Sea; on the south by Indonesia and Johor Strait; on the west by the Strait of Malacca and the Andaman Sea; on the north by Thailand, the South China Sea, and Brunei.

Currency: Malaysian ringgit (M$) = 100 sen (cents)

Population: 16.9 million, about 34 percent in urban areas; about 80 percent on the peninsula

Education: 80 percent literacy rate; free education (in Malay) between ages of 6 and 19

Language: Behasa Malay, English for business, Chinese, Tamil

Religion: Islam, Confucianism, Buddhism, and Hindu

Minority Groups: Chinese (33 percent), Indian (9 percent) and indigenous tribes

Major Industries: Semiconductors, commodities, rubber, palm oil, tin, pineapple and other fruits, hardwoods

Exports: Semiconductors, petroleum, palm oil, rubber, tin, timber, cocoa

Imports: Silicon wafers and other key ingredients in semiconductors

Major Corporations: Petronas, Innoprise Corporation, Antah Holdings

Average Income/Standard of Living: Real gross domestic product is $2,018 per capita; average real GDP grew by 4.2 percent during the last five years. Average monthly factory wage is $270.

Form of Government: Constitutional monarchy headed by a Paramount Ruler (Yang di-Pertuan Agong) elected for a five-year term by the heads of the thirteen states from among nine hereditary royal rulers. It has an elected house of representatives (Dewan Raayat) and a prime minister.

Political Environment: Relatively stable but with very substantial political infighting and subpar foreign reserves

Social Environment: The nation is a mix of many different people; each enjoys minority status.

Major Social Problems: Tension is noticeable between the Malays and Chinese.

Business Environment: Low inflation (about 1.6 percent over five years); the high-tech sector is growing rapidly. Much of the work force speaks English. Malaysia has good roads, harbors, and abundant electric power. High per capita income. Malays predominate in agriculture; Chinese and Indians predominate in business. Privatization is under way. Foreigners can own 100 percent of a business's equity if 80 percent of its produce is for export. The country has diversified into manufacturing. Business hours: Monday-Friday 8:00 A.M.–4:30 P.M.; during Ramadan 8:00 A.M.–2:00 P.M.; Saturday 8:00 A.M.–12:45 P.M.

Holidays: January 1, 18; February 5; March 12; May 30; June 7; July 31; August 31; November 4; December 25 as well as other religious and local holidays.

Transportation and Communications: Modern roads, instant telecommunications
Telephone country code-60; Ipoh-5; Johor Bahru-7; Kajang-3; Kuala Lumpur-3
Time: EST plus thirteen hours

Press: Privately owned but legally restricted from carrying information harmful to the country's security, order, or morality. Newspapers in Malay, English, Chinese, Indian, Punjabi.

Broadcast: Broadcast media are privately owned.

Information Sources:
Commercial Counsellor
Embassy of Malaysia Trade Office
630 Third Avenue, 11F
New York, N.Y. 10017
Tel: (212) 682-0231

Malaysian International Chamber of Commerce and Industry
Box 192
Kuala Lumpur
Telex: 32120 MA

Country's Formal Name: Republic of the Philippines

Geographical Location: In the Pacific Ocean; to the north is the Philippine Sea and Taiwan, Indonesia is to the south, and the South China Sea is to the west.

Size: The archipelago consists of over 7,000 islands totaling 116,000 square miles. Eleven of the largest make up 95 percent of the nation.

Capital: Formally, Quezon City is capital; in actuality, Manila.

Currency: Peso = 100 centavos

Population: 61.9 million; 50 percent in urban areas

Language: Pilipino (a variation of Tagalog) and English. Some Spanish is spoken. There are many native dialects.

Education: 88 percent are literate; education is compulsory from seven to twelve years of age.

Religion: Some 95 percent are Christians, Roman Catholic predominating.

Average Income/Standard of Living: Real gross domestic product is $527 per capita; average real GDP over past five years is .5 percent.

Government: Constitutional government headed by a president, vice-president, and bicameral congress (Senate and House of Representatives)

Major Industries: Agriculture, forestry, fishing, mining (especially chromite, copper, gold, and nickel), and manufacturing (cement, chemicals, clothing, electronic equipment, foods)

Exports: $5.6 billion (1988)

Imports: $7.1 billion (1988)

Political Environment: The current government is struggling to eliminate the corruption that has traditionally plagued the Philippines while strengthening and stabilizing a democratic government. A history of nepotism and graft combined with a nation made up of thousands of islands in varying stages of development and speaking different dialects make this a formidable task. There is still doubt about both political and economic stability.

Business Environment: Foreign investment is enthusiastically encouraged and English is widely spoken. The economy is picking up. However, there is a high rate of workdays lost to strikes and the Communist threat suggests growing instability. Business hours: Monday-Friday: 8:00 A.M.–12:00 N. and 2:00–5:00 P.M. Saturday 8:00 a.m.–12:00 N.

Holidays: January 1; Holy Thursday; Good Friday; May 1; June 12; July 4; September 21; November 30; December 25, 30, 31. In some provinces, Muslim holidays are also observed.

Transportation and Communications: One of the best transportation systems in Asia, with buses, jeepneys, and railroads (Luzon). Manila has a rapid transit system.
Telephone country code-63; Bacolod-34; Cebu City-32; Davao-35; Lloilo City-33; Manila-2; Tarlac City-47
Time: EST plus thirteen hours

Press: Twenty daily newspapers in English, Pilipino, Chinese. *Bulletin Today* and *The Times Journal* are biggest.

Broadcast: There is one television set for every fifteen people and several TV stations: ABS-CBN Philippine Broadcasting Service, Bohol Avenue, Quezon City (Telex: 42220); Radio Philippine Network, Inc., Broadcast City Complex, Capitol Hills Ditiman, Quezon City (Telex: 63886).

Information Sources:
Philippine-American Chamber of Commerce
711 Third Avenue
New York, N.Y. 10017
Tel: (212) 972-9326

Foreign Trade Promo
556 Fifth Avenue
New York, N.Y. 10036
Tel: (212) 575–7925

Philippine Tourist Office
556 Fifth Avenue
New York, N.Y. 10036
Tel: (212) 575-7915

Country's Formal Name: Republic of Singapore

Capital: Singapore

Geographical Location: Island nation south of Malaysia and roughly north of Indonesia consisting of one large island (Singapore) and over fifty smaller islands. Joined to Malaysia by three-quarter-mile long causeway with a road and railroad. Singapore is a major transportation hub of Southeast Asia.

Size: 240 square miles

Currency: Singapore dollar

Population: 2.7 million, mostly Chinese; Singapore is all urban; its population is the smallest in Southeast Asia.

Education: Literacy 87 percent

Language: Mandarin Chinese (official), Malay (national), Tamil, and English (commercial)

Religion: Islam, Buddhism, Christianity

Ethnic Groups: Chinese, Malay, Indian, and Western nationalities

Major Industries: Oil refining and manufacturing, high-tech items, foreign currency trading, financial futures dealing, chemicals, electronic equipment, lumber, machinery, metals, paper

Exports: 1989: $59.7 million—electronic parts, financial services, palm oil, petroleum and petroleum products, rubber, textiles, tin

Imports: 1989: $57 million

Gross National Product: 1989: $27 million

Average Income/Standard of Living: One of the highest living standards in Asia. Real gross domestic product is $8,819 per capita; average growth rate over the past five years is 5.6 percent. Average annual wage is $4,800 (Singaporeans spend 44 percent of their income on imported goods). Average monthly factory wage is $500.

Form of Government: Democratic republic headed by a prime minister and cabinet, one-house parliament; president serves as head of state but actually has little power.

Political Environment: Stable. Chinese tend to dominate the political and business communities.

Top Government Titles and People Holding Them: Former Prime Minister Lee Kuan Yew, who had been in power for thirty years, stepped down November 28, 1990. Goh Chok Bong is now prime minister.

Defense: Men over 18 are required to serve 2 to 2½ years in the armed forces.

Business Environment: Free port, built around its harbor. Major manufacturing center, major financial center. Low unemployment but also few resources; a free-enterprise economy
Business hours: Monday-Friday 8:00 A.M.–5:30 P.M.; Saturday 8:30 A.M.– 12:30 P.M.

Holidays: January 1; Chinese New Year; Good Friday; May 1, 30; Hari Raya Haji; August 9; Deepavali; December 25, 26. The holidays of Buddhist Chinese, Muslim Malays, Hindi Indians, and Christians are observed.

Transportation and Communications: Modern; a good network with buses, rapid transit rail lines, and railroads
Telephone country code-65
Time: EST plus thirteen hours

Press: Ten daily newspapers with at least one in each of the four major languages. Largest is the English-language *Straits Times*. There is no real competition for news, so from a public relations standpoint, it is important to formulate news releases in such a way that they conform with government objectives. TV coverage is possible for major events. Radio is popular during rush hours.

Broadcast: Both radio and television broadcast in all four languages and both radio and television sets proliferate. The government oversees broadcasts and keeps an eye on the press.

Trade Fairs: Singapore has an international reputation as an exhibition center and is a popular destination for Southeast Asian businesspeople. Media coverage is ample. A full list of exhibition schedules can be obtained from:
The Singapore Convention Bureau in the U.S.A.
% The Singapore Tourist Promotion Board
590 Fifth Avenue
New York, New York 10036

    Other services are:

Singapore Exhibition Services (Pte.), Ltd.
11 Dhoby Ghaut
Cathay Building
Singapore
Telex: 23597 SINGEX RS

Interfama Exhibitions, (Pte.), Ltd.
One Marine Parade Road
Singapore 1544
Telex: 24980 INFAMA

Other: Newspaper and magazine special supplements are other fruitful means of publicizing a client company. Minimum is usually one page. With magazines, a reprint for later use (as in direct mail) is an added advantage.

Public Relations Agencies:
Asia Media House (Pte.), Ltd.
605A MacPherson Road
Citimac Industrial Complex
Singapore
Fax: 284-7161
Telex: 43394 ACMGTS RS

Information Sources:
Singapore Economic Development Board
55 East 59th Street
New York, N.Y. 10022 (and other U.S. cities)
Tel: (212) 421-2200
Fax: (212) 421-2206
American Business Council
10-12 Shaw House
356 Orchard Road
Singapore 0923
Fax: 732-5917
Telex: 50296 ABC RS
Singapore Trade Office
745 Fifth Avenue, Suite 1601
New York, N.Y. 10022
Tel: (212) 421-2207
Fax: (212) 888-2897
Singapore Tourist Promotion Board/Convention Bureau
590 Fifth Avenue
New York, New York 10036
Tel: (212) 302-4861

Country's Formal Name: Spain (España or Estado Español)

Capital: Madrid

Geographical Location: Southern Europe; bounded on the north by France, on the west by Portugal and the Atlantic Ocean, on the south by Gibraltar and the Mediterranean Sea, and on the east by the Mediterranean Sea. It includes the Balearic Islands and the Canary Islands, which are provinces.

Size: 195,988 square miles

Currency: Peseta = 1000 centimos

Population: 39.7 million

Education: 93 percent literacy with schooling required between the ages of 6 and 13. Primary school runs for eight years, secondary school for three, and university follows.

Language: Castilian Spanish is the official language. Catalan, Basque, Galician, and Valencian are official in their respective areas.

Religion: 99 percent Roman Catholic, but it is not an official religion

Major Industries: There are few natural resources. Among them are iron, copper, lead, mercury, potash, pyrite, salt, titanium, uranium, and zinc. Spain is a leading producer of cars, cement, chemical products, electrical appliances, machinery, iron and steel, plastics, rubber goods, ships, shoes, clothing, textiles. Tourism and fishing are important.

Exports: $44.4 billion (1989): fruits, vehicles, iron, steel, footwear, textiles.

Imports: $71.5 billion (1989): fuels, machinery, chemicals, foodstuffs, vehicles.

Gross National Product: $399.9 billion (1989)

Average Income/Standard of Living: Still behind most EC countries but catching up rapidly

Form of Government: Constitutional monarchy headed by a king, a prime minister, and an elected, bicameral parliament (*Las Cortes Españolas*). Spain has fifty provinces, each headed by a governor. The two largest political parties are the left wing Socialist Workers' party and the right wing Popular Alliance.

Social Environment: Very regionally divided because of natural barriers. Both economic and social disparity in the standard of living is felt. Ongoing separatist movements are active in the Basque region, Catalonia, and Galicia. *Tertulias,* or informal social clubs where friends and neighbors meet, are an important part of the social fabric.

Major Social Problems: Terrorism and separatist nationalism

Defense: Army, navy, air force. Men twenty-one to thirty-five may be drafted to serve one year.

Business Environment: Not much work gets done two weeks before and after Christmas and the week before and after Easter. July and August are the vacation months. About half the labor force are in service industries. Labor costs and taxes are both still low. The United States is Spain's major trading partner. Spain joined the EC in 1986.
Business hours: Monday-Friday: 9:00 A.M. – 12:00 N. and 4:30 P.M. – 7:00 P.M.

Holidays: January 1, 6; March 19; Holy Thursday; Good Friday; May 1; Corpus Christi; May 25; June 24; July 8, 25; August 15; October 12; November 1; December 8, 25

Press: There are over 100 daily newspapers and over 5,500 magazines and weekly periodicals. Most newspapers were privatized in May 1984; now seven major news companies own many newspapers: Prisa owns *El País*; Godo has three newspapers; Prensa Española had two; Editorial Católica Edica, four; Ibarra, two; "Grupo 16," one; and Javier Moll, six. Local area newspapers are still important, as are those printed in Catalan and Basque languages.

Broadcast: RTVE, state-owned, is the broadcast network and consists of Radio Nacional de España, Radio Cadena Española and Televisión Española. Regional television is controlled by another state-owned system. Despite television having the largest overall audience breadth, radio is the main source of information. Nationally, the most important companies are: Sociedad Española de Radiodiffusión (SER), which has seventy-three stations and almost seven million listeners. Cadena de Oudas Populares des España (COPE) has forty-seven radio stations and over three million listeners. Radio Nacional de España is the official station and has about three million listeners with thirty-two broadcasting stations, three programs, and twenty medium-wave stations as well as a foreign service. Antena 3 was set up as a limited company and has seventy-three stations and about a million and a half listeners.

Press Agencies: EFE, Agencia Editorial Prensa 21, S.A., Agencia Interinsular de Noticias, Colpisa, Europa Press Group, and others.

Transportation and Communications: Public transportation networks and roads are extremely overburdened. Ambitious plans are under way to improve commuter train, bus, and underground train services. Government operates post and telegraph services as well as television and radio broadcasting.
Telephone country code-34; Barcelona-3; Bilbao-4; Madrid-1; Malaga-42; Seville-54; Valencia-6
Time: EST plus six hours

Trade Fairs:
Feria de Barcelona
Avda. Maria Christine
E-08004 Barcelona 4
Tel: 4-23-31-01
Telex: 53117

Information Sources:
Spain-U.S. Chamber of Commerce, Inc.
350 Fifth Avenue, Suite 3514
New York, N.Y. 10118
Tel: (212) 967-2170
Fax: same as telephone

Commercial Office of Spain
405 Lexington Avenue
New York, N.Y. 10017
Tel: 212-661-4959

Country's Formal Name: Sweden (Sverige)

Capital: Stockholm

Geographical Location: Between Norway and Finland; east coast faces the Baltic Sea and the Gulf of Bothnia; it is a northerly, Scandinavian country, far from the equator.

Size: 179,000 square miles; fourth largest country in Europe; heavily forested (half the area)

Currency: Krona (or Kroner or Kroner or Sek) = 100 Oere

Population: 8.5 million; 85 percent live in the south of the country.

Education: From the age of seven, nine years of compulsory education; 90 percent complete two years of upper secondary school. The state operates over thirty schools of free higher education. Literacy rate is 99 percent.

Language: Swedish. English widely understood in business.

Religion: Ninety-five percent of the people belong to the Lutheran State Church.

Minority Groups: Sami (Lapps) are indigenous, ethnic, linguistic minority; they are usually reindeer herders.

Major Industries: Car manufacturing, pharmaceutical, paper and pulp companies. Steel and textiles are encountering trouble.

Exports: Engineering products account for over 50 percent. Forest products including papers comprise about 11 percent. Major market is western Europe, especially Germany (12 percent), United Kingdom (11 percent). United States is third (10 percent). 1989: $61.6 million.

Imports: Engineering products (43 percent), oil and other petroleum products. Germany supplies almost one-fourth of Sweden's imports. The United Kingdom and United States are also big suppliers. 1989: $60.5 million.

Gross National Product: 1989: $189.3 million.

Average Income/Standard of Living: Over 70 percent of married women work; unemployment is very low; retirement age is 65. Normal work week is forty hours with five paid vacation weeks per year. Forty percent of the average income goes for taxes. Average gross income for an industrial worker is 18,750 SEK at an exchange rate of $1 = 6.4 SEK.

Form of Government: Constitutional monarchy with King Carl XVI Gustaf as titular head of state. The parliament (Riksdagen) has one chamber with directly elected members who hold three-year terms. The Social Democratic party is most frequently in power. There are thirteen ministries.

Political Environment: The Swedish Trade Union Confederation (LO) lists 90 percent of blue-collar workers as members and strongly influences politics. Sweden tries to maintain a basically neutral stance and is a member of the UN, OECD, EFTA, and the council of Europe; it has a free-trade agreement with the EC on industrial products.

Top Government Titles: Foreign Trade Minister, Tel: 08-7633168 and Deputy, 08-7633165 (in Sweden)

Social Environment: Voting age is eighteen; suffrage is universal. All residents are covered by national health insurance and if ill get a taxable daily allowance amounting to 90 percent of lost income. Parents get a total of twelve months' paid leave from work when they have a child, and receive tax-free child allowances until the child reaches sixteen. Most workers receive unemployment insurance through their union. Low-income families and pensioners can get housing allowances.

Major Social Problems: AIDS, drug and alcohol abuse; lack of sufficient day-care for working parents; high cost of buying apartments and houses and lack of available rentals.

Defense: Sweden has general male conscription requiring 7.5-10 months of basic training; Sweden's neutrality policy is seen to demand a strong defense system; the defense budget totals about 3 percent of the GDP.

Business Environment: Similar to the 90 percent of blue-collar workers belonging to LO, about 75 percent of white-collar workers belong to a union. Private corporations account for 80 to 90 percent of Swedish industry, with public enterprises and cooperatives sharing the rest. Cooperatives have 20 percent of retail domestic sales. National railway, telecommunications, and post office are state owned. Business hours: Monday-Friday 9:00 A.M.– 5:00 P.M.

Holidays: January 1; Good Friday; Easter Monday; April 30; May 1; Ascension Day; Whit Monday; Mid-Summer Eve (last Saturday before June 27); November 1; December 24, 25, 26, 31.

Regulatory Environment (industry): Private corporations account for 80 to 90 percent of industry. Environmental regulations governing air and safety are enforced, with help from an ombudsman *(skyddsombud)* at each place of work.

Press: The press is free and includes access to public documents. Sweden has among the largest newspaper readerships in proportion to population. There are thousands of magazines and daily and weekly newspapers. Major cities have press clubs. There are eleven national dailies and many regional morning papers as well as special-interest periodicals. No advertising is permitted on radio and television. Newspapers and direct mail are the most popular advertising media.

Press Agencies: TT is the Swedish news agency.

Broadcast Media: Swedish Broadcasting Corporation (SBC) operates under a state concession that is monopolistic. Shareholders in SBC are private industry, 20 percent; press, 20 percent; and national popular movements, 60 percent. SBC operates four program radio and television companies. No commercials are allowed. Cable television is supervised by the National Cable TV Board. Advertising of alcoholic drinks is prohibited.

Transportation and Communications: State owned. See above. Telephone country code-46; Goteborg-31; Malmo-40; Stockholm-8; Uppsala-18; Vasteras-21

Time: EST plus six hours

General Tax Structure: See above

Public Relations Agencies:

Advertising or help with public relations, direct mail, and marketing can be had from:

Svenska Reklambyra Forbundet (SRF)

(Swedish Federation of Advertising Agencies)

P.O. Box 3160

Luntmakargatan 66

S-103 63 Stockholm

Information Sources:

Swedish-American Chamber of Commerce, Inc.

825 Third Avenue

New York, N.Y. 10022

Tel: (212) 838-5530

The Swedish Consulate

825 Third Avenue

New York, N.Y. 10022

Foreign Trade Ministry (Utrikeshandels)

Riksdagen

10012 Stockholm

Tel: 08-7633168

Swedish Information Service

825 Third Avenue

New York, N.Y. 10022

Tel: (212) 751-5900

Country's Formal Name: Republic of China (Taiwan)

Capital: Taipei

Geographical Location: An island about 90 miles off the southeastern coast of mainland China. Taiwan, which includes fourteen other islands, is northeast of Hong Kong and west of Okinawa. It is divided into two special municipalities: Taipei and Kaohsiung, and five municipalities: Taichung, Keelung, Tainan, Chiayi, and Hsinchu.

Size: Total area is 13,969 square miles.

Currency: New Taiwan dollar = 100 cents

Population: 19.8 million

Education: 90 percent literate. Free compulsory education for grades six through fifteen.

Language: Mandarin, with English understood by many, especially in business; Fukien and other dialects also widely used.

Religion: Buddhists predominate (3.11 million), followed by Taoists (1.98 million). Christians total fewer than one million.

Minority Groups: About 325,000 aborigines; small numbers of foreigners led by Japanese and Americans

Major Industries: Steel bars, pig iron, shipbuilding, sugar, cement, fertilizers, paper, and cotton fabrics. Stock exchange with volumes on a par with New York and Tokyo. Resources include coal, gold, copper, sulphur, and natural gas. Agricultural products are rice, tea, bananas, pineapples, sugarcane, sweet potatoes, wheat, soybeans, peanuts.

Exports: 1989: $67.1 million in textiles, electronic and agricultural products, metal goods, plastic products

Imports: 1989: $54.4 million in oil, chemicals, machinery, electronic products

Major Corporations: Acer (computer products), Chinese Petroleum

Gross National Product: Real GNP is $4,837 per capita with average real growth rate in GNP over five years ending late 1988 of 9.3 percent. 1989: $139.4 million.

Average Income/Standard of Living: Among the highest in Asia. Telephones, television sets, and other major appliances proliferate in the countryside as well as the cities.

Form of Government: Taiwan's government has evolved from the Nationalist Government, ruled by the Kuomintang. There are three political parties: the Kuomintang, Young China party, and China Democratic Socialist party and a National Assembly with 964 delegates. Five councils are Executive, Legislative, Judicial, Examination, and Control Yuan. The prime minister heads the Executive Yuan, the highest administrative body.

Political Environment: Stable, but with relations between giant neighbor China testy. After the U.S. established diplomatic ties with the People's Republic of China, diplomatic relations with the U.S. were terminated but Congress approved legislation maintaining commercial, cultural, and other relations between Taiwan and the U.S. A trade group called the Coordination Council for North American Affairs serves as the unofficial embassy and has diplomatic status.

Top Government Titles: President, prime minister, vice premier, foreign minister, and ministers of Defense, Interior, Finance, Education, Justice, Economic Affairs, and Communications.

Social Environment: Family-oriented. The Republic of China was founded by Dr. Sun Yat-Sen, who believed in putting power in the hands of the people. The nation's press, religious, and other freedoms are guaranteed. Confucianism is still the basis of education of the young.

Major Social Goals: Eliminating illiteracy

Defense: Army, navy, and air force are outfitted with U.S. vessels and aircraft. Conscription system for two years plus reserve liability.

Business Environment: Taiwan has a series of development plans. Banking is regulated by the Central Bank of China. The Bank of Taiwan is the largest commercial bank. Foreign trade is handled by the China External Trade Development Council. Avoid visiting two weeks before and after Chinese New Year. Business hours: Monday-Friday: 9:00 A.M.–12:00 N. and 1:00–5:00 P.M.; Saturday 8:00 A.M.–12:00 N.

Holidays: January 1, 2; Chinese New Year (late January or early February); March 29; April 4; September 28; October 10, 25; November 12; December 25

Transportation and Communications: Two airports have regular outbound flights and serve about sixteen international airlines. The island is also served by ship. Railroad networks and buslines serve all parts of the island. Telephone, telex, telefax, and cable are all readily available as are satellite hookups for international communications. Domestically, telephone and telegraph connections are modern and convenient.
Telephone country code-886; Kaosuing-7; Tainan-6; Taipei-2
Time: EST plus thirteen hours

Press: Free press; newspaper readership high. About sixty-seven national dailies plus regionals and magazines. Most advertising is in newspapers, on television, in direct mail, and then in magazines.

Broadcast Media: There are three television networks and 34 stations, and 178 radio stations, including relay stations.

Information Sources:
Coordination Council for North American Affairs
801 Second Avenue, 6F
New York, N.Y. 10017 (and other major U.S. cities)
Tel: (212) 697-1250

China External Trade Development Council (CETDC)
41 Madison Avenue, 14F
New York, N.Y. 10010 (and other major U.S. cities)
Tel: (212) 532-7055

Coordination Council for North America Information Division
1230 Avenue of the Americas
New York, N.Y. 10020 (and other major U.S. cities)
Tel: (212) 376-1800
Fax: (212) 373-1866

Central News Agency of China
1231 News Building
220 East 42nd Street
New York, N.Y. 10017
Tel: (212) 682-8583

American Chamber of Commerce in the Republic of China
Chia Hsin Building 11, Room N-1012
96 Chung Shan North Road
Sec. 2, Taipei
Tel: 551-2515
Telex: 27841 AM CHAM

Investment and Trade Office (of Taiwan)
126 East 56th Street
New York, N.Y. 10022
Tel: (212) 752-2340
Fax: (212) 826-3615

Country's Formal Name: Kingdom of Thailand (Prathet Thai), (Muang Thai)

Geographical Location: Southeast Asia on the Gulf of Thailand and the Andaman Sea, bounded on the north and west by Burma, in the east and
northeast by Laos, on the southeast by Kampuchea (Cambodia), and on
the south by Malaysia.

Capital: Bangkok

Size: 198,115 square miles

Currency: Baht = 100 satang

Population: 55 million, 17 percent in urban areas

Education: 89 percent literacy rate, school compulsory for ages 7 through 14

Language: Thai; English has become popular to study for government and
commerce; Chinese.

Religion: Buddhism, Islam

Minority Groups: Chinese (14 percent), Malays (4 percent), Mon, Khmer, and
other hill people

Major Industries: Rice, cassava, corn, canned tuna products, petrochemicals,
natural gas, plastics, foodstuffs, machine parts

Exports: Textiles, footwear, rice, fish, foodstuffs

Imports: Raw materials and semiprocessed raw materials, capital goods

Major Corporations: Unicord of Thailand (bought Bumble Bee Seafoods);
Mantrust (Indonesian owned, bought Van Camp Seafood and ships Chicken
of the Sea tuna), Siam Cement Group, Bangkok Bank

Average Income/Standard of Living: Real gross domestic product is $930 per capita; average real GDP grew by 7.2 percent during the last five years. Factory wages start at about $117 a month.

Form of Government: Constitutional monarchy

Political Environment: Remarkably stable, considering the neighborhood

Top Government Titles and People Holding Them: King Bhumibol Adulyadej reigns, with Queen Sirikit. Prime minister leads with his cabinet and a bicameral legislature (National Assembly).

Defense: Military is influential in political affairs. The top military officer often takes the top political post or backs the candidate that wins. There are periodic military coups.

Business Environment: New investment from abroad has been growing faster than anywhere else in Southeast Asia, but there are basic weaknesses in the economy. Business hours: Monday-Friday: 8:30 A.M.–12:00 N. and 2:00 P.M.–4:30 P.M.

Holidays: January 1; Chinese New Year; April 6, 13; May 14, 29; July 28, 29; August 12; October 23; December 5, 10, 25, 31; and religious holidays based on the lunar calendar

Transportation and Communications: Available and reasonably modern, but traffic is continually snarled; telephones, electricity, roads, and ports are scarce and require patience. The canal system is still important to commerce. Telephone country code-66; Bangkok-2; Lampang-54; Nakhon Sawan-56; Nong Khai-42
Time: EST plus twelve hours

Press: Four national dailies in English and four in Chinese. There are many regional dailies and general magazines.

Broadcast: Over one hundred radio and nine television stations carry commercials.

Information Sources:
American Chamber of Commerce in Thailand
Kiang Gwan Building
140 Wireless Road
Bangkok 10500

Thai Chamber of Commerce
150 Rajabophit Road
Bangkok 10200
Telex: 72093 TCC TH

Thailand Consulate General
351 East 52nd Street
New York, N.Y. 10022
Tel: (212) 754-1770

Thai Trade Office
5 World Trade Office
New York, N.Y. 10038
Tel: (212) 466-1777

Country's Formal Name: Republic of Turkey

Geographical Location: In Eastern Europe; bounded by the Black Sea to the north; U.S.S.R. to the east; Iran, Iraq, and the Mediterranean Sea to the south; and the Mediterranean Sea, Greece, and Bulgaria to the west

Capital: Ankara

Size: About 301,000 square miles, or slightly less than twice the size of California

Currency: Turkish lira = 100 kurus

Population: 54 million

Education: 70 percent literacy rate by some estimates, to 99 percent by others

Language: Turkish. English, French, and German are often understood; so are Kurdish and Arabic.

Religion: 98 percent Muslim (mostly Sunni), 2 percent all other

Minority Groups: 12 percent Kurd, 3 percent "other" out of total population

Major Industries: Textiles, food processing, mining (of coal, chromite, copper, and boron minerals), steel, petroleum, construction, lumber, paper

Gross National Product: $81 million

Exports: $8 billion (1986) includes cotton, tobacco, fruits, nuts, metals, livestock products, textiles and clothing, cement, leather, glass, ceramics. 1989: $18,854,000

Imports: $11 billion (1986) including crude oil, machinery, transport equipment, metals, pharmaceuticals, dyes, plastics, rubber, mineral fuels, fertilizers, chemicals. 1989: $21,446,000.

Average Income/Standard of Living: Over half the population is in farming.

Form of Government: Republican parliamentary democracy with a constitution and a president who is empowered to call elections and promulgate laws; a unicameral legislature (450-member Grand National Assembly)

Political Environment: Major parties are the ANAP (Motherland Party), SHP (Social Democratic Populist Party, TPP (True Path Party). The military has considerable political influence. Turkey is an associate member of the European Community and is headed for full membership. Tensions historically exist with Greece over Cyprus.

Major Social Problems: Turkey, being a Muslim country, is viewed with uncertainty by EC countries that question whether it will fit in with Western Christian-Judeo tradition.

Defense: Turkey is a NATO member; it has one of the biggest armies in the world, as well as navy, air force, and gendarmerie. Males 15 to 49 are subject to draft; the military gets 20 percent of the central government budget.

Business Environment: Free enterprise. There is high unemployment (15.5 percent in 1986) and a conservative climate; appointments are needed. July and August are vacation times. Business hours: Monday-Friday 9:00 A.M.–12:00 N. and 1:30 P.M.–5:00 P.M., Saturday 9:00 A.M.–1:00 P.M.

Holidays: January 1; April 22, 23; May 1, 19, 26, 27; August 30; October 28, 29, 30; December 31 and other religious holidays based on the lunar calendar

Transportation and Communications: Telephone country code-90; Adana-711; Ankara-41; Bursa-241; Istanbul-1; Eskisehir-221; Izmir-51
Time: EST plus seven hours

Press: (see Appendix II) Press is the most popular advertising medium. There are six national dailies and a dozen or so weeklies.

Broadcast: There are eleven commercial radio stations and one commercial television station. Dissemination includes most households. Cinemas are a popular advertising alternative, as are outdoor posters.

Information Sources:
Central Bank of Turkey/Representative Office
Turkish Center
821 UN Plaza 7F
New York, N.Y. 10017
Tel: (213) 682-8717
Fax: (212) 867-1958

Turkish Consulate General Office of the Economic and Commercial
  Counselor
821 U.N. Plaza, 4F
New York, N.Y. 10017
Tel: (212) 687-1530
Fax: (212) 687-2078

Turkish Government Tourism and Information Office
821 U.N. Plaza
New York, N.Y. 10017
Tel: (212) 687-2194

Country's Formal Name: United Kingdom of Great Britain and Northern Ireland (U.K.)

Capital: London

Geographical Location: Island group between the Atlantic Ocean and the North Sea, with the English Channel separating it from Europe. United Kingdom comprises Great Britain and Northern Ireland; Great Britain includes England, Wales, and Scotland.

Size: About 94,250 square miles including England and Wales, Scotland, and Northern Ireland; slightly smaller than Oregon, with 7,800 miles of coastland.

Currency: Pound sterling = 100 pence

Population: 57 million

Language: English

Education: 99 percent literacy; principal language is English.

Religion: Two established churches, the Church of England (Episcopal) and the Church of Scotland (Presbyterian), but there is no limit on religious freedom.

Minority Groups: Scottish, Irish, Welsh, Ulster, West Indian, Indian, Pakistani, and others

Major Industries: Manufacturing and service industries including transport, commerce, and finance. Resources are coal, crude oil, natural gas, tin, limestone, iron ore, salt, clay, chalk, gypsum, lead, silica.

Gross National Product: $842.9 million in 1989

Exports: Machinery and transport equipment, basic manufactures, chemicals, and mineral fuels, plus foodstuffs. $201.7 million in 1989.

Imports: Machinery, basic manufactures, and agricultural products. $233 million in 1989.

Form of Government: Constitutional monarchy; the Parliament consists of the House of Commons, elected by universal adult suffrage, which is the main legislative and financial authority, and the House of Lords, which retains power to review, amend, or delay legislation. Commons has 635 members elected for five years, and the Speaker, elected from the majority party, wields considerable power. Lords has 1,200 members who have no real power.

Political Environment: There are three main parties: Conservative, Labour, and Social and Liberal Democrats. Overall, the political climate has been very stable.

Top Government Titles: After the royal family headed by Queen Elizabeth, the prime minister, deputy leader, leader of the House of Commons (Speaker), leader of the House of Lords, secretaries of state, and foreign minister

Secretaries of State: Defense, Education and Science, Employment, Energy, Environment, Foreign and Commonwealth Affairs, Home Department, Northern Ireland, Scotland, Social Services, Trade and Industry, Transport, Wales

Business Hours: Monday-Friday: 9:00 A.M.–5:30 P.M.

Press Agencies: Reuters is British-based and the world's oldest agency; Associated Press, Exchange Telegraph Co., Ltd., The Press Association, Ltd., United Press International, are others.

Press: Free press, but responsible treatment of news is expected; libel laws are strict. National daily newspapers circulate about fifteen million copies.

Broadcast Media: British Broadcasting Corporation (BBC) is semiofficial; Independent Broadcasting Authority (BA) is a public corporation.

Transportation and Communications: Subways, railroads, busses, and taxis are well run and reasonably priced; communications facilities are modern and available.

Telephone country code-44; Belfast-232; Birmingham-21; Edinborough-1; Glasgow-41; Liverpool-51; Manchester-61; Sheffield-742; London-071 (central) and 081 (periphery)

Time: EST plus five hours; the same as Greenwich Mean Time (GMT)

Information Sources:

British-American Chamber of Commerce
275 Madison Avenue, Suite 1714
New York, N.Y. 10016 (and other major U.S. cities)
Tel: (212) 889-0680

American Chamber of Commerce (U.K.)
75 Brook Street
London W1Y 2EB
Telex: 23675 G

British Information Services
845 Third Avenue
New York, N.Y. 10022
Tel: (212) 752-5747

British Government Offices
845 Third Avenue
New York, N.Y. 10022
Tel: (212) 752-8400

Country's Formal Name: Socialist Republic of Vietnam

Capital: Hanoi

Population: 66.7 million with 19 percent in urban areas

Education: 94 percent literacy rate

Language: Vietnamese; French and English are commonly used for business.

Religion: Buddhist and Roman Catholic

Average Income/Standard of Living: Very low; real gross domestic product is $34 per capita; average GDP over the past five years is 3.4 percent.

Form of Government: Communism. Previously, the north formed a capitalistic entity, and the south a socialist/communist government. With unification, the nation becomes a democratic republic. Many specifics are subject to change as the new nation is defined.

Political Environment: Tightly regulated, with a recent attempt to modify with *doi moi*, the Vietnamese version of *perestroika*: Farmers can keep half their crops. Still, the current regime is repressive but has managed to dramatically raise the rate of literacy and is encouraging foreign investment.

Social Environment: Few civil rights and little welfare

Major Social Problems: Joblessness

Business Environment: Per capita GDP is lowest in the Pacific Rim and inflation is the highest (over 300 percent in 1988).

Legal Environment: Americans are barred by U.S. law from investing in or trading with Vietnam.

Country's Formal Name: Republic of Yemen (North and South Yemen were unified on May 22, 1990.)

Geographical Location: Between Saudi Arabia and the Gulf of Aden

Capital: Sana'a (political capital) and Aden (economic capital)

Size: approximately 150,000 square miles

Population: 10 million (combined)

Language: Arabic

Education: Literacy rate is 10 percent.

Religion: Very traditional, devout Muslim (see Political Environment)

Major Industries: Oil of high quality, which was just discovered in 1987

Exports: Mocha coffee

Average Income/Standard of Living: Poor, compared to its neighbors on the peninsula; it receives aid from other countries and also counts remittances from the approximately one million Yemenites working abroad as a major source of income. GNP per capita was U.S. $510 in 1987. Eighty percent of the inhabitants still live in rural areas.

Form of Government: Republic, headed by a president who is elected by a people's constituent assembly. The president is the chairman of the Presidential Council. Five men form the Presidential Council, which is elected by a house of representatives. The Council of Ministers forms a second governing body.

Political Environment: Officially a republic but traditionally a highly tribal society. Two main sects conflict: Shiites of the Zaydis sect (59 percent of population) who are concentrated in the capital Sana'a and in the north, center, and eastern part of the country. They are considered descendants of Mohammed and are the political leaders. The Sunnites of the Shafii sect (39 percent of the population) are merchants. They live in the southern and southeastern area and control the ports and commerce.

Major Social Problems: Tension between the Shiites and the Sunnites

Business Environment: Although oil is promising, unstable oil prices make the future uncertain. Government puts priorities on development of the infrastructure, industry, and human and mineral resources. It wants to be self-sufficient in food processing, clothing, and construction. Existing industries include three cement plants, plastic industry, chemical and metal working, and textile.

Regulatory Environment (industry): Import licenses are issued in accordance with government's plan (see Business Environment above).

Legal Environment (industry): There are three major merchant families who traditionally run most of the trade and industry in the country. The practice is to form joint ventures with these families. According to Yemenite law, the local partner has to own at least 51 percent. Your business partner has to be influential in government for your business to succeed; through him you can be introduced to the people that count.

Press: Media is government controlled; because of the high illiteracy rate, the press does not have much impact. The national major daily is published in Sana'a.

Press Agencies: One national news agency (Saba News Agency)

Broadcast Media: One national radio station in Sana'a; regional ones in Hodeida and Taiz. There is one government-run TV station, financed through advertising.

Other: International Bank of Yemen is one of the four local banks in Yemen. All are headquartered in Sana'a. Their relationships with government and merchant families can help foreign companies find local partners and establish contacts. Through your local partner you can contact the Department of Trade, the Department of Development, and the Department of Finance and Economy. Also, the Yemen Chamber of Commerce in Sana'a is helpful, as is the Yemen Embassy in Washington.

Information Sources:

Embassy of Yemen
600 New Hampshire Avenue, N.W.
Washington, D.C. 20037
Tel: (202) 965-4760

Yemen Repulic to the U.N. Mission
866 U.N. Plaza
New York, N.Y. 10017
Tel: (212) 355-1730

APPENDIX IV

Facts on
Eastern Europe

In the rapidly changing environment of Eastern Europe, where the Communist governments have either surrendered power or partly relinquished it, the centralized economies are being dismantled and slowly being replaced by market-oriented systems. The eventual business potential is great, but the investment is medium-to-long term, as suggested earlier in the text (see Chapter 2, the section on technology and communications abroad for more information on communications and transportation). Money is in short supply, as are equipment and facilities.

There is no legal framework to deal with foreign ownership of companies. Negotiations with the state can take years, and the state still owns 95 percent of industry. Substandard materials and supply problems make the environment additionally challenging.

Direct investment in terms of equity investment, skill, and technology transfer is the only practical route to take at this time.[1] The financial marketplace will take years to develop. Bond and stock markets hardly exist, and even the Budapest Stock Exchange sees minimal action.

Under the current situation, public relations means setting up meetings or fairs to show products, introducing American businesspeople to officials in the area and vice versa, overseeing activities of visitors, and otherwise trying to make life easier for Americans visiting the region. The other side is to assist Eastern European officials who hope to learn from U.S. business. These Eastern European officials can offer products for export or low-cost manufacturing facilities in their countries.

1. Simon Brady, "Financing the Great Leap Forward," *Euromoney Supplement* to August 1990 issue, pp. 70–78.

Bulgaria

Capital: Sofia

Lev = 100 stotinkit
Reforms here are slowed by internal strife between Turkish Muslims (1.5 million) and the majority group. Private enterprises are legal. Foreign joint ventures are permitted, but Bulgarian ownership must make up at least 50 percent. Hard currency profit transfer is allowed. However, the economy is not in good shape.

Czechoslovakia

Capital: Prague
Koruna = 100 haleru
As its neighbors are doing, Czechoslovakia is restructuring to a market economy, although privatization is not a priority. Foreign joint ventures are allowed, and Western imports are in demand.

RAPID, the largest and most modern national advertising and marketing agency, handles advertising, public relations, direct mail services for foreign companies. All media are controlled by the government. Industry-directed marketing communications is a popular form of advertising. Trade fairs are also popular. Contact:

Brno Trade Fairs and Exhibitions
VYstavista 1
CSSR-60200 Brno
Telex: 06294, 06295, 06239

RAPID
Rijna 13
Prague
Telex: 121142 REAG
Fax: (2) 232 7520

Czech Commercial Representatives:
Association of Firms for Foreign Agencies
14060 Prague 4

Czechoslovak Travel Bureau—CEDOK
10 East 40th Street

New York, N.Y. 10017
Tel: (212) 689-9720

Hungary

Capital: Budapest
Forint = 100 filler

Free market reforms were introduced here earlier than in other Eastern bloc countries, resulting in greater stability. Still, the economy is in difficulty. Among other things, there is a shortage of fuel and mineral resources. Legally any enterprise can be privatized. Foreign companies can buy and sell real estate. Tax penalties on foreign-owned business have been abolished; 100 percent foreign ownership is allowed.

International Fairs and Exhibitions:
HUNGEXPO
P.O. Box 44
H-1441
Budapest

Hungarian Embassy
3910 Shoemaker Street, N.W.
Washington, D.C. 20008
Tel: (202) 362-6730

Commercial Counselor's Office
150 East 50th Street
New York, N.Y. 10022 (also in Washington and Chicago)
Tel: (212) 752-3060

Hungarian Consulate General
8 East 75th Street
New York, N.Y. 10021
Tel: (212) 879-4125

Poland

Capital: Warsaw
Zloty = 100 groszy

The economy, a traditional centralized, socialist setup, is quite unstable. State enterprises and cooperatives account for about 75 percent of GDP and the private sector is mainly agricultural. The government is moving forward with privatization of industry. It's aiming at producing manufactured goods to Western standards of quality and efficiency.

Commercial Counselors:
820 Second Avenue, 17F
New York, N.Y. 10017 (and in Chicago)
Tel: (212) 370-5300

Polish National Tourist Office
333 North Michigan Avenue
Chicago, Ill. 60601

Romania

Capital: Bucharest
Leu = 100 bani
The economy here is unstable and so is the political situation. The *per capita* GDP is about $1,000. No real liberalization has occurred and the country is one of the most backward in Europe.

Offices of the Economic Counselor
537-577 Third Avenue
New York, N.Y. 10016
Tel: (212) 682-9120

Romanian National Tourist Office
573 Third Avenue
New York, N.Y. 10016
Tel: (212) 697-6971

U.S.S.R.

Capital: Moscow
Ruble = 100 kopecks

Sovero is a state-owned and -operated agency. It handles public relations and advertising, and has a database of 60,000 Soviet enterprises by industries, trades, and sectors for use in direct mail promotions; offers printing service, symposia arrangements, advertising in trade, government, scientific, technical, and industrial publications. Sovero's INOREKLAMA division advises on all types of promotional services, including broadcast.
c/o Amtorg (Soviet Foreign Trade Office)
1755 Broadway, 7F
New York, N.Y. 10019
Tel: (212) 956-3010

State (Public Relations and) Advertising Bureau
V/O Vneshtorgreklama, Korp., 2,
31 UI Kakhovla
Moscow 113461
Telex: 411265

Trade Fairs:
V/O Expocentr
1-A Sokolnichesky VAL
Moscow 107232

U.S.-U.S.S.R. Trade and Economic Council
805 Third Avenue
New York, N.Y. 10017
Tel: (212) 644-4550

Newspapers and Magazines

Argumenty i Fakty—progressive

Moscow News—popular, irreverent weekly of free thinkers

The Week—magazine

Pravda—hardline, state-run daily newspaper

Zhurnalist—"trade" paper

Index

[Italic page numbers refer to figures and tables.]

DATE DUE			

Wouters   231943